The Hope in Hope Street

Hope Congregational Church

and

Bethel Evangelical Free Church

200 Years in Hanley

Pastor Gervase N. Charmley

Foreword by Hon. Tristram Hunt, M.P.

Bethel Evangelical Free Church, Hanley
2012

Fig. 1. Bethel Evangelical Free Church in 2010

This book is published by Bethel Evangelical Free Church
Newhall Street, Hanley, Stoke on Trent ST 1 5 HQ
The copyright is vested in Bethel Evangelical Free Church
All royalties from the sale of this book will go to the Church

Foreword by the Hon. Tristram Hunt, M.P.

The history of Stoke-on-Trent is also the history of Protestant Nonconformity. It was amidst the Meeting Houses and Chapels of the Six Towns that Methodism, Congregationalism and Unitarianism found some of its most ardent adherents. And for two hundred years, the Hope Street Church has been an essential part of that story - playing its role in the development of The Potteries, educating the poor, ministering to a changing congregation, and contributing to the doctrinal development of modern Nonconformity.

In today's increasingly secular age, we are all too often at risk of losing sight of the profound contribution which the Nonconformist movement has made to British history and culture. The post-war years witnessed a sustained loss of connection to our Nonconformist heritage and its modern legacies. All of which is why I am delighted to welcome the Reverend Gervase Charmley's scholarly yet accessible history of Hope Street. As Charmley rightly says, "The beauty of our story is that it is the story of a typical chapel in the Industrial Midlands; a story of a part of England that has largely been forgotten, but which should be remembered."

But it is also so much more: a gripping account of the Church's theological development and organisational struggles, against the backdrop of the changing nature of Stoke-on-Trent and the Nonconformist movement. This is an important, persuasive and compelling book, proving once again the powerful bond between Protestant Dissent and The Potteries.

— *The Hon. Tristram Hunt, M.P. For Stoke-on-Trent Central*

Acknowledgements

This book is the result of many months of research and hard work, and many people gave valuable assistance in this work. It is impossible to refer to all of them, but my thanks must be recorded to several people and institutions in particular.

The first place must be given to the late Mr. Richard Rowland, who was associated with Bethel for many years and gave much valuable service as a Deacon and Church administrator. He was responsible for retaining so many of the documents that have been used in telling the story of the Church since 1953. Richard was aware of this project in its very earliest stages, but sadly did not live to see its completion.

Mr. Geoff Green of Liverpool supplied copies of pages from the *Bethel Messenger* magazine from his own collection. Professor Liz Farmer, of Australia, supplied a great deal of information about her ancestor Rev. William Farmer, who was the second pastor at Hope. Mrs. Helen Sharpe supplied information about Rev. Mark Bairstow, her great-grandfather. Mr. Alan Cunnington of Leicester supplied some information concerning Pastor Desmond Evans. Mr. David Mead, son of pastor A.W. Mead, supplied biographical information about his father.

Thanks are also due to the Doctor Williams Centre for Dissenting Studies, who assisted in various ways with research into the history of the Congregational period of the Church; the Staffordshire Record Office, who hold the records of the Staffordshire Congregational Union; the Stoke on Trent City Archives for their collection of old newspapers; the John Rylands Library of the University of Manchester, who allowed access to some of their holdings.

Most of all, I wish to express my thanks to the Church assembling at Bethel in Newhall Street, Hanley, who have been so helpful and supportive of their pastor.

Gervase N. Charmley, Hanley, 2012

Contents

Foreword by Hon. Tristram Hunt, M.P.	P. 3
Acknowledgements	P. 5
Introduction	P. 9
Chapter 1: Background	P. 12
Chapter 2: Hope Church is Founded	P. 23
Chapter 3: Rev. William Farmer	P. 34
Chapter 4: The First Missionaries	P. 47
Chapter 5: 1824-1845	P. 59
Chapter 6: 1845-1864	P. 73
Chapter 7: Rev. David Horne	P. 92
Chapter 8: Rev. William Lansdell	P. 105
Chapter 9: The Edwardians	P. 127
Chapter 10: War and Decline	P. 135
Chapter 11: Trials and Revival	P. 146
Chapter 12: Under New Management	P. 164
Chapter 13: Pastor A.W. Mead	P. 180
Chapter 14: Pastor Desmond Evans	P. 193
Chapter 15: Seeking a Successor	P. 205
Chapter 16: Paul Brown: Early Years	P. 209
Chapter 17: Urban Regeneration	P. 218

Chapter 18: Tesco:	P. 225
Chapter 19: Paul Brown: Later Years	P. 238
Chapter 20: The Sunday School	P. 246
Chapter 21: Public Worship	P. 254
Chapter 22: The Church Since 1994	P. 265
Epilogue:	P. 268
Illustrative Bibliography	P. 270

Introduction

In October 1812 a new Congregational chapel opened its doors in the thriving industrial town of Hanley, at the heart of the North Staffordshire Potteries. In 2012, while practically every other Church in central Hanley has closed, along with the industry, somehow that same Church is still there on the same street corner two centuries later, though the old chapel has been replaced by a neat modern 1970s building.

There have been great changes in the Church and the town in the intervening years, yet what we do and teach on that corner would still be recognised by the men and women who built the old chapel all those years ago as essentially what they did then. That is not to say that things have not changed at all; of course they have. We have electric lighting, the singing is accompanied by an organ, and the congregation sit in comfortable chairs and pay nothing for the privilege, to name just a few changes. But the message of the Church has not changed; it is still the same Christ who has been proclaimed through those two hundred years.

This is the story of the 200-year history of a local church which, under the name of Hope Congregational Church, then Bethel Temple, and finally Bethel Evangelical Free Church, has occupied this site since October 1812. While the history is largely taken up with the story of the various men who have been pastors, it must be emphasised that the church *is* the people and that the families who have worshipped here during those two hundred years are the people to whom this history really belongs.

Bethel began its long and varied life as a Congregational Church. Once a common sight, Congregational Churches are now comparatively rare. The majority of the Congregational churches in England became a part of the United Reformed Church in 1972, and this, coupled with the general collapse of Nonconformity, can make it hard for us to realise just how important the Congregationalists were in 19th century England. Rev. Charles Silvester Horne, whose uncle Rev. David Horne was pastor at our Church for twenty years between 1865 and 1885, wrote a book on *Nonconformity in the XIXth Century* that gave pride of place to the Nonconformist contribution to the political changes of the century[1], though not without conceding that they were first of all Churches, not a political pressure group. In many ways Congregationalists were at the heart of Protestant Nonconformity, second only to the Methodists in numerical size, and second to none in political influence through the Liberal Party. Their main strength was, like that of most Nonconformist denominations, in the growing and thriving industrial cities of England; the story of a typical urban Congregational Church is therefore the history of a great part of the English urban population.

In the Congregational period the Hope Street Church typifies the progress and eventual decline of the Congregational body as a whole. Trouble before World War I is followed by massive losses and decline after the war. Historians have debated whether or not World War I was the cause of the rapid decline of Congregational and other Nonconformist churches in the period that followed, but what is clear from the record of Hope Chapel is that history would have taken a different course had it not been for the war.

The period after World War I in England is marked by the rise of Pentecostal and Evangelical churches separate from the historic denominations, and the Bethel in Hanley finds its place squarely in that development through the decision taken by the troubled Congregational Church to move into the moderate semi- Pentecostalism represented by Edward Jeffreys. Following the Second World War, the church moved to the non-denominational evangelical tradition of the FIEC, via the Brethren-influenced former Bethel pastor Archie Mead. The Reformed Recovery of the 1960s reached us through Paul Brown, a student of Ernest Kevan at the London Bible College. Though we cannot claim to have been at the centre of any of the major currents of Protestant Nonconformity over the last 200 years, we have been in many of them. The beauty of our story is that it is the story of a typical chapel in the Industrial Midlands; a story of a part of England that has largely been forgotten, but which should be remembered. It is my hope that this book will help that process of remembering.

---

[1] Charles Silvester Horne, *Nonconformity in the XIXth Century* (London, 1905)

Although we are no longer called a Congregational Church, we have been committed to Congregational principles for most of our history, and remain so today. To the Congregationalist the Church is not merely a human association or club, it is the body of Christ, and the local church is itself the manifestation of the universal Church. Holding this high view of the Church, we insist that a local Church is never unimportant, and the very least church has a story that is worth telling to the glory of God. But this is not only a divine story; it is a human story as well, with all the weaknesses that we are compassed with as humans. There are things in the story that will cause us to rejoice, and others that will cause sorrow. The church is indeed, as the hymn-writer says,

> *With schisms torn asunder,*
> *With heresies distressed,*

And that is true of the local church as well as the church universal.

> *Till with the vision glorious*
> *Her watching eyes are blessed,*
> *And the great Church victorious*
> *Becomes the Church at rest.*

Chapter 1: The Background

Hanley

Ours is an industrial city.[2] Before the Industrial Revolution there was no Stoke on Trent as we know it today, just a number of scattered settlements in an upland area of the Midlands. The Parish of Stoke on Trent was rural, with a central church located close to the present-day site of Stoke Minister. This ancient church was established in the 7th century by missionaries associated with St. Chad who probably took over a pagan holy site by the river Trent and set up a small church, perhaps bringing Christianity to the area for the very first time. Today its site and the remains of a Medieval church can be seen in the churchyard of the Minster. The other major ecclesiastical establishment in the district, the Cistercian abbey of Hulton, was established by Henry de Audley in around 1220, as a daughter house of Combermere Abbey in Cheshire, in the sort of isolation that attracted the Cistercians. The monks from the Abbey also established a church dedicated to St. John the Baptist in the small township of Burslem. This was originally a timber structure, but a stone tower was later added, probably shortly before the dissolution of the monasteries. This tower still survives, now attached to a later church, and is the oldest surviving structure in the Potteries.

What is now the town of Hanley began as two small communities in the forest that once covered the area. The name Hanley, originally spelled 'Hanlih' means either a high wood or a clearing in a high wood, and first appears in the records in 1227. The land is poor agriculturally; what attracted people to North Staffordshire was primarily industrial, initially small-scale coal mining in Shelton. In the 17th century pottery manufacture began in earnest in North Staffordshire, and the industry began to grow. At this time Hanley was two settlements, about a mile apart. These were called respectively Hanley Upper Green and

---

[2] Without a doubt one of the best (and most beautiful) books on our city is Matthew Rice, *The Lost City of Stoke on Trent* (London, 2010)

Hanley Lower Green. Once the two had grown together the name Hanley Green remained in use until the middle of the 19th century, though it was becoming increasingly inappropriate as industrialisation took place and smoking bottle-ovens took the place of trees.

Hanley only gained a church of its own in 1738, when a small red-brick building with a tower was constructed on a site on what is now Town Road, but was then called the High Street. This was a plain building with three windows on each side, a gallery around three sides of the interior, and a small chancel. It originally seated 400, and the town's rapidly increasing population forced its enlargement in 1764. Coal-mining, seeking more fuel for the pottery kilns, undermined the building, so in 1788 it was replaced by the innovative iron-framed Church of St. John the Evangelist, built to seat 1200, which survives today, although it was closed as a place of worship in 1985, and at the time of writing is being renovated for use as a restaurant after a long period of disuse and dereliction.

North Staffordshire has had a chequered religious history. At the Reformation many of the local landowners remained attached to the Roman Catholic Church and did not support the Church of England; the relative isolation of the district meant that even when religious affiliation could be a test of loyalty, it was unlikely that secret masses in the homes of lords and gentry would be disturbed by the authorities so long as those same lords and gentry did not rebel against the crown. During the religious ferment of the 17th century Presbyterian and Quaker meetings were established in the area by those who were more radical in their beliefs. Quaint old Quaker Meeting-Houses still survive at Leek and Cheddleton, though the Cheddleton building is now in agricultural use. As for the Presbyterians, Trinity Church in Leek is built on the site of a Presbyterian Chapel of about 1700, and the Unitarian Meeting-House at Newcastle was built in 1717 to replace a Presbyterian chapel of 1694 that had been destroyed in a riot in 1715. Many Quakers became prominent businessmen, and while the Presbyterians drifted into Unitarianism, they produced many leading citizens, not least the great Josiah Wedgwood. The Quakers did not have a Meeting in Stoke until 1831, and the Presbyterians (later Unitarians), had a congregation at Burslem in 1715 that, however, disappeared at some point during the 18th century. Apart from this, until the revival of the 18th century the Potteries were the sole preserve of the Church of England.

In the Potteries, as in much of England, it was the tireless John Wesley who brought the revival's message. Mounted on horseback, the diminutive Anglican clergyman was possessed by a burning desire to tell the nation of the love of God in Christ Jesus. John Wesley came to north Staffordshire in March 1760, when he preached at Burslem and Biddulph. He describes Burslem at the time as, "A scattered town on the top of a hill, inhabited almost entirely by potters, a multitude of whom assembled at five in the evening. Deep attention sat on every face, though as yet accompanied with deep ignorance."[3] The people of the Potteries received Wesley and heard him gladly, and a Methodist society was formed at Burslem. In 1781 he wrote of Burslem, "How is the whole face of this country changed in about twenty years! Since the potteries were introduced, inhabitants have continually flowed in from every side. Hence the wilderness is literally become a fruitful field. Houses, villages, towns have sprung up. And the country is not more improved than the people. The word of God has free course among them. Sinners are daily awakened and converted to God, and believers grow in the knowledge of Christ."[4]

John Wesley regarded himself as a faithful Anglican all his life, and regarded his Methodist Societies as religious societies within the Church of England. In practice, however, unless there was a sympathetic parish clergyman, Methodist Societies were actually Nonconformist congregations. They held their own meetings, had their own leaders and preachers, and were independent of the Parish clergy. Wesley was all too aware of how hostile many of his brethren among the Anglican clergy were towards him and his work, but he still gathered his converts into societies; this he regarded as imperative for their spiritual growth. During his lifetime, through his influence and that of his brother Charles, the Methodists remained in a strange semi-detached position as regarded the Church of England; though they had their own services in their own buildings, the Methodists were expected to go to the local Parish Church for communion, often from a clergyman who was hostile to them. It is no

---

[3] Nehemiah Curnock (ed.) *John Wesley's Journal* (London, no date) Vol. iv, P. 370
[4] *John Wesley's Journal* Vol..vi, Pp. 309-10

surprise that there were some Methodists who decided to go one step further than Wesley and join Nonconformist churches, or sometimes organise their own.

John Wesley did not visit Hanley until March of 1784, but in the meantime the preachers from Burslem brought Methodism there, so that when Wesley came to Hanley he found a large congregation ready to hear him. "I preached in the new preaching-house at Hanley Green, but this was far too small to hold the congregation. Indeed, this whole country is all on fire, and the flame is still spreading from village to village," Wesley records.[5] The revival was not confined to the Wesleyan Methodists; there were now Congregationalists active in the Potteries.

Congregationalism

Although most histories will refer to Congregationalists as their heirs of the Puritans, it must be borne in mind that Congregationalism in England is in fact the product of two distinct periods of our religious history; the Puritan era and the Evangelical Revival of the 18th century. Historically the name Congregational was used interchangeably with 'Independent', and referred to those churches that practised infant baptism and held each local congregation to be autonomous, independent of any central church government and governed by the church-meeting of members rather than a series of courts of elders and ministers. The Congregationalist recognises only two uses of the word 'Church' as valid; the universal Church and the local Church. Historically Baptists and Congregationalists have agreed in their understanding of the Church, differing only in their views on baptism, so that some have spoken of one Congregational movement with two wings.

The history of English Congregationalism can be traced back to the 16th century and Robert Browne, a graduate of Corpus Christi College, Cambridge. A Puritan, Browne took the Puritan call for further reformation of the Church of England further than any before him, challenging both episcopacy and the Parish system. In company with a friend, Robert Harrison, Browne founded a Congregational Church in the city of Norwich.[6] Owing to persecution, these 'separatists' as they were

---
[5] *John Wesley's Journal* Vol. vi, P. 491
[6] R. Tudur Jones, *Congregationalism in England, 1662-1962* (London, 1962) P. 15

known, fled to Holland, where there was far more religious freedom for them. While in-fighting ultimately led to the end of Browne's experiment and his final return to the Church of England, others followed in the path that he and his associates had laid out, and a number of Congregational Churches were formed in various parts of England. At the time it was illegal for a subject of the English crown to belong to any church other than the Church of England, and so these Congregational pioneers suffered persecution and in some cases death for their dissent. Many left these islands entirely, some followed the example of Browne and his Church and settled in Holland, from where some travelled to North America, but others remained in Britain despite persecution that led to several prominent Congregationalists dying in prison.

During the 17th century a number of leaders among what are generally known as the Puritans were Independents or Congregationalists, among the most noted of whom were Thomas Goodwin, member of the Westminster Assembly and President of Magdalen College, Oxford; John Owen, 'The Atlas of Independency', Vice-Chancellor of Oxford and author of many great books; and Oliver Cromwell himself, Lord Protector of England, Scotland, Wales and Ireland. While the Presbyterians had initially wanted the reform of the state Church to conform to their views, Cromwell created a state Church which embraced diversity and supported Presbyterian, Independent and even Baptist congregations. The wide freedom given to religious groups in the Commonwealth under Oliver Cromwell allowed the Independent Churches to thrive, and their numbers increased enormously.

Following the Restoration of King Charles II in 1660, and the restoration of the episcopal system that followed, all ministers in the national Church who would not submit to the Book of Common Prayer and the restored episcopacy were ejected from their churches and parishes. Around 2000 ministers were ejected, among them some of the most learned and able pastors in the kingdom. The people did not all abandon them; many of the ejected ministers gathered churches which met in secret. These nonconformists, so called because they would not 'conform' to the Church of England, suffered various degrees of legal persecution until the Glorious Revolution of 1688, when King William III gave them legal freedom to worship, though nonconformists continued to suffer from a variety of legal restrictions until the second half of the 19th century.

The period that followed 1688 was marked by a decline from the high standards set by the Puritans. Worn out by persecution and debarred from various high offices, nonconformists suffered from a series of doctrinal disputes, including the decline of some congregations, principally Presbyterian and General Baptist[7], into Unitarianism, the denial of the Trinity. In general the Independents remained orthodox in their faith, while a majority of the English Presbyterians declined into Unitarianism. Independents furnished some of the better-known names among 18th century Nonconformity; the hymn-writers Philip Doddridge and Isaac Watts were both Independent pastors, and Doddridge was also the principal of an academy that trained young men for the ministry. These men formed the bridge between the Puritan era and the Evangelical revival.

While the great revival of the 18th century is usually identified with Methodism, there were in fact a number of distinct and different groups and preachers operating in England, not to mention Scotland and Wales, where conditions were rather different. The word 'Methodism' was initially used as a term of abuse, and came to mean almost what the word 'Fundamentalist' means today. It originally referred to those in the Church of England who we would call 'evangelical'. Methodism itself was divided into two strains, the Wesleyan and the Calvinistic. John Wesley's talent for organisation kept the Wesleyan branch of the revival together for the most part, apart from a small group of his converts led by Dan Taylor, a Wesleyan local preacher who embraced Baptist sentiments and formed the New Connexion of General Baptists. The Calvinistic wing was, outside of Wales, divided into several branches associated with a number of more or less local leaders[8]. These leaders had varied ecclesiastical connections; while most were within the Church of England, others found it desirable or necessary to separate from the Establishment. Most of these either identified with Congregationalism

---

[7] English Baptists are historically classified as either Particular or General depending on whether they teach a Particular Redemption (Calvinism) or a General Atonement (Arminianism)

[8] For example, in the area of Chester an Anglican minister without charge, Rev. Philip Oliver, had a small group of chapels under his oversight. These later joined the Welsh Calvinistic Methodists as English-speaking churches.

themselves, or founded Churches which over the course of time became Independent congregations[9]; this is what happened in North Staffordshire.

Congregationalism in North Staffordshire was entirely the result of the Evangelical Revival; before the revival there were no Congregational Churches at all in the area, and the men who introduced Congregationalism into the district were themselves converts of the Revival. There was little in the way of a surviving Puritan tradition; what Nonconformity there had been was Presbyterian. The two pioneers of Staffordshire Congregationalism were Captain Jonathan Scott and the Rev. George Burder, both converts of the Revival rather than representatives of the older Congregationalism.

Captain Jonathan Scott was born in Shrewsbury in 1735, into a good family. He joined the army at the age of 17 and saw active service in Europe during the war of 1759 with France. Scott was a respectable and outwardly religious man who read his Bible daily, but who was seeking to be saved by his own good works. He continued in this sort of religion until, around 1765, while hunting near Ote Hall, near Brighton, he was forced to take shelter from the rain in the cottage of a local farm worker. Inside the locals were talking about religion, and the upper-class officer was amazed at how intelligently they talked about the subject. Asking them where they had learned this, he was told that it had been at meetings held in the Hall by Lady Huntingdon, where Mr. William Romaine, an evangelical London clergyman, was preaching. Scott decided to attend one of the meetings, and found that Romaine's preaching was extremely helpful.[10]

Although he found Romaine initially rather reserved towards him, the anxious Scott persevered with the clergyman, and he was converted through Romaine's ministry. Following his conversion, Scott sought to share the Gospel with everyone he could, and even began to preach in the open-air wherever his military duties led him. This irregular conduct, as it was seen, soon drew the disapproval of his

---

[9] For example, the two Tabernacles founded by George Whitefield in London both became Independent, Congregational churches.

[10] Tim Shenton: *An Iron Pillar: the Life and Times of William Romaine* (Darlington, 2004) Pp. 215-16

superiors, who told him that if he wanted to continue preaching he would have to leave the army. Faced with this choice, he chose to leave the army, and resigned his commission in 1769, though he continued to be known as Captain Scott, and often preached in uniform to deter troublemakers. He retired to Shropshire and there his preaching gathered an Independent church.

Although he had been converted within Anglicanism, there was no place in the Church of England for a lay-preacher, and the church authorities would not as a rule ordain 'Methodists', whether Calvinistic or not. Because he held to Calvinistic theology, Scott could not become one of Wesley's preachers, and therefore the only option that seemed open to him was to join the Congregationalists. Warmed by the revival, they welcomed him, and in 1776 he was ordained as a 'Presbyter at large', in other words, a travelling evangelist; the Congregational equivalent of a Methodist circuit-preacher, at Lancaster. The Congregationalists recognised that a man like Scott could be very useful among them if they did not circumscribe his activities.

Following his ordination, Scott came to Staffordshire, preaching at Newcastle-under-Lyme where he founded a Congregational Church that still exists today. In Leek his converts joined the Presbyterian Church, which was in the process of becoming Unitarian, eventually bringing the whole Church into Congregationalism.[11] He was also instrumental in founding Congregational churches at Stone and Uttoxeter.

John Wesley did not like the fact that Scott and his associates were at work in the Potteries; since Wesley felt he had "Broken the ground", he felt that the Congregationalists were moving in on his territory and poaching his converts, "We cannot commend them for breaking in upon our labours after we have borne the burden and heat of the day"[12] he complained in his journal. The reasons that the Congregationalists worked in the same areas as the Wesleyans were twofold; first of all, the industrial cities were growing faster than the Church of England was able to cope with; even where new Churches

---

[11] For details see Henry Woodhouse: *The Story of a Leek Church* (Leek, 1988)
[12] *Wesley's Journal* March 26th 1781

were built, that did not mean that people would automatically come in. Secondly, the Congregationalists disagreed with Wesley theologically; he was an Arminian, while they were Calvinists. Each thought that the other was in error, and there were occasional pamphlet-wars in which one side would accuse the other of heresy and the other replied in kind. In an age of weak relativism we often find their language uncomfortable, but surely their conviction was better than our indifference to the very idea of truth. While both Arminians and Calvinists agreed that the other side were true Christians, they nevertheless wanted people to hear the pure truth and not truth mixed with error.

With the rapid growth of industrial towns, there were plenty of people to go around, and the competition between Calvinist and Arminian may even have been a spur to evangelism. It also led in due course to architectural competition, and to some of the most distinguished buildings in our cities, not least the vast Bethesda Chapel in Hanley.

The Rev. George Burder, Scott's main associate, was born in London in 1852. He was brought to faith under the preaching of the Wesleys and Whitefield, and it was the saintly French Swiss aristocrat turned Anglican minister, Rev. John Fletcher, vicar of Madeley in Shropshire, who first encouraged Burder to preach. He preached his first sermon in Newport, Shropshire, in a house belonging to his father, and the fact that several people were converted or helped by that sermon led him to seek to become an itinerant preacher. Like Scott, he was a convinced Calvinist, and that led him down the same road as the former army captain. He joined Scott as a Congregational evangelist, and it was he who began the preaching at Hanley, taking his stand in the open air. In later life Burder helped found both the London Missionary Society and the Religious Tract Society.

Burder and Scott's preaching at Hanley led to many conversions, and a society was gathered. In order to provide a meeting-place for these converts, a red-brick building called the Tabernacle was built in Town Road in 1784. Some older residents of the Potteries may recall its successor, the handsome red-brick 'Nonconformist Cathedral' of 1883 with its tower and spire that stood in Town Road until it was demolished to make way for the Potteries Link Road in the 1970s. The original Tabernacle stood on the other side of the road; after functioning as a school and then an Anglican mission-hall, was used as a roller-skating rink before it too was demolished.

From its foundation in the 1780s until the opening of the Congregational Church at Clayton in 1952,[13] the Tabernacle was at the centre of Congregationalism in Hanley and the Potteries. Its first pastor was Rev. James Boden, a native of Chester and a graduate of Homerton Academy. He served from 1785 until 1794, when he was succeeded by Rev. Robert Little. These men were stalwarts of the Evangelical cause, and continued to reach out with the Gospel. Later noted pastors of the Tabernacle include Rev. Joseph Fletcher, Robert McAll, founder of the McAll Mission in France, and Dugald MacFadyen. The Tabernacle congregation planted churches in Cheadle and Stafford, and perhaps the most ambitious foreign missions project of the church was in 1839, when the pastor, William Newland, led a party from the Church in a migration to Australia where they formed a Church and founded a new community, complete with a new Tabernacle Church.

Other Congregational Churches followed in the Potteries; Milton in 1808, Hope in 1812, Longton in 1820, Burslem in 1821, and Tunstall in 1853. A Congregational Church was formed in Stoke in 1823, but it was short-lived, and by 1834 the chapel had been sold to the Quakers. A new Church in Stoke was formed in 1851. A Church was formed in Dresden in 1868, and the Churches at the Tabernacle in Hanley and at Burslem maintained mission halls, respectively called the Tabernacle Town Mission, built in 1879, and Wycliffe Hall, Burslem, built 1885. Park Church, Shelton, was formed in 1901, and Wolstanton Congregational Church was formed in 1902, though its present building only dates from 1922. The last Congregational Church to be formed in the Potteries was that at Clayton, Newcastle-Under-Lyme, which was formed in 1952. Money from the sale of the buildings at Milton and

---

[13] The opening of the Clayton church spelled the end for the Tabernacle. Rev. Arthur Oates, the pastor at the Tabernacle, became the first pastor at Clayton. Membership at the Tabernacle had declined from 451 in 1900 to 177 in 1952. Following Oates' departure the congregation declined precipitously, and by 1960 there were only 77 members in a building that seated over a thousand. In 1964 the chapel was closed and the church merged with Trinity Presbyterian Church.

Copeland Street, Stoke-on-Trent, was used to pay for the Clayton building. Today the only Congregational Church in the area is that in Newcastle-Under-Lyme; the others entered the United Reformed Church when the majority of English Congregational churches united with the English Presbyterians in 1972.[14]

---

[14] The story is told from the United Reformed Church side in Kenneth Slack, *The United Reformed Church* (Exeter, 1978) and from the perspective of those Congregationalists who did not join the union in R.W. Cleaves, *Congregationalism 1960-1976* (Swansea, 1977).

Chapter 2: Hope Chapel is Founded

Even the best churches occasionally suffer from internal troubles, and the Tabernacle was no exception to this. It is impossible for us to know, at this remove in time, exactly what happened and who was in the wrong. A. G. Matthews writes, "One of the deacons was unduly given to strong liquors, and... outraged public opinion by falling off his horse the worse for drink in the streets of Hanley."[15] The man was admonished, but the admonishments had no effect, and he was accordingly suspended from his post as a deacon and from his membership in the Church. He was a popular man with some, and some of his friends declared that he was penitent and should be readmitted to membership. The church did so, but the matter did not end there; those who advocated his restoration are said to have gone about the business in "a violent manner" which led to their being investigated by a special committee of the Church for the disturbance they had caused in the Church meeting. They refused to submit to this investigation, which they regarded as unlawful, and left the Tabernacle.

The seceders from the Tabernacle worshipped in temporary accommodation for some years while they raised funds for a building of their own.[16] During this time they considered uniting with the Baptists, but their convictions about baptism were too strong, and the scheme came to nothing.[17] The fund-raising efforts were successful, and they were soon in a position to acquire a plot of land and begin the construction of a chapel.

The site that was acquired for the new building was a part of the Shelton New Hall estate. The New Hall itself, also known as Shelton Hall, occupied part of the site now occupied by Go Outdoors (formerly Tesco). Fronting onto what is now Newhall Street, it had been an elegant country house, but the growth of Hanley and increasing levels of smoke

---

[15] A.G. Matthews, *The Congregational Churches of Staffordshire* (London, 1924) P. 175
[16] Matthews, P. 175
[17] Matthews, P. 176

23

from the potteries meant that it was no longer a desirable residence, and in 1773 the New Hall was sold to one Humphrey Palmer, who converted the house and outbuildings into a pottery factory. After his death his daughter let the estate to a group of seven potters who had formed a partnership, and on her death in 1805 the estate was sold to the partnership. The sale was finally completed in 1810. The old mansion was called the New Hall Pottery; under a succession of owners, the works continued in operation until the 1960s.

The purchase of the estate involved considerable capital outlay, and as the factory had no use for most of the New Hall estate, it was divided up and sold off in parcels to recoup some of the costs of purchase. Some of the portions were sold for industrial use, others for commercial and residential. A portion of what was called the Hall Meadow, a prominent site close to the hall and fronting onto the road that passed in front of the mansion, was secured by the new Congregational Church for a chapel and burial-ground. The sale of parts of the state did not begin until 1811, and one of the earliest buildings put up on it was Hope Chapel; so in October 1812 we must picture the chapel as standing in a largely empty street on the edge of the town, next to the old mansion, and with only empty ground to the other side of it. On the other side of the road there would have been some cottages and, where Bar 360 now stands, the Crown and Anchor Inn. It was not until 1814 that a new road was cut through the Shelton Hall estate beside Hope chapel's burial ground; the street was named Hope Street after Hope Chapel.[18]

As the name of the old mansion that stood beside it suggests, when the chapel was built, Hope was in Shelton; boundaries have since moved. In 1812 Shelton was a district of Hanley Parish; it was created as a separate Parish in the 1830s, and St. Mark's built 1831-4. When Shelton Parish was itself divided in 1845, the new Parish that covered much of central Hanley was at first called Hope Parish, after the Congregational chapel; surely one of very few cases in which a Nonconformist place of worship has given its name to an Anglican parish. The Parish Church was Holy Trinity, a Romanesque building located on Trinity Street in Hanley; this was demolished in the 1950s, but the old church hall still survives in Lower Foundry Street, and after a

---

[18] Audrey M. Dudson, *Dudson: A Family of Potters Since 1800* (Stoke on Trent, 1985) Pp. 29-31

period of commercial use is now used by Breathe City Church of Abbey Hulton. After its formation, Hope Parish was regarded as a part of Hanley, and thus Hope Chapel in Shelton became Hope Chapel, Hanley. The confusion over the location of the chapel led in one case to a writer in the *Congregational Yearbook* for 1881 describing the chapel's location as "Shelton Hanley" in the obituary of a former pastor.

Hope Chapel opened for worship on 7th October 1812. It was a handsome building in the common style of the day, built of red brick with a slate roof, the common materials of the period employed in the potbanks and the homes of their owners. It had round-headed windows and a symmetrical façade with twin doors with fanlights and columned surrounds. The façade was architecturally accomplished, with a string-course of stone below the gallery windows, and coping-stones above the windows. The central three bays, topped with a pediment, projected slightly, and a cornice ran above the windows and under the pediment. The architecture is typical of chapels of the period including the Grosvenor Street chapel in Manchester, opened in 1807. Such five-bay façades, with and without pediments, are found all over the country.

Fig. 2: A pen drawing of the original chapel by Mrs. Valerie Shenton, daughter of Pastor A.W. Mead, made in the 1960s.

Internally, Hope Chapel resembled other town chapels of the period; a high pulpit on the end wall would have dominated the sanctuary, there would have been a small area in front of the pulpit for the communion table, and a gallery ran around three sides of the chapel, with the gallery facing the pulpit deeper than those along the other two sides. Seating for those who could afford to pay a pew-rent would have been in high box pews of oak, while at the back there would have been simpler benches, free seats for those who could not afford to rent a family pew. The system of pew-rents was a major source of income for churches, and gave the church a fixed and steady income. The description of a similar chapel in the city of Norwich gives some idea of what Hope would have looked like in the early years, "Straight-backed pews, lined with worn and faded baize. Behind them were wooden benches for the free seats, fenced off by a breast-high partition... under the pulpit... there were two square pews, well screened by green curtains. There were similar family pews at the back of the Church, and in the corners of the galleries... The aisles were of brick."[19] The building seated 600, about half the capacity of the Parish Church.

The opening services of the chapel would have been a major event, intended as much as publicity for the Church as anything else. Invitations were sent to many of the leading Congregationalist leaders in the area, and many of them were present on the day of the opening. The right preacher was essential, and the man in the pulpit that day was Rev. William Roby of Grosvenor Street Chapel, Manchester.[20] One of the great leaders of the denomination, and *the* great leader of Congregationalism in the district at the time, Roby had been pastor in Manchester since 1795. Born in 1766, he had been a minister in Lady Huntingdon's Connexion, but had moved to the Congregationalists due to disputes in the Connexion. Roby was instrumental in planting a large number of Churches in the Great Manchester area, and his presence at the opening of Hope Chapel would have helped to legitimate the young Church. His name would have ensured a packed chapel and a large collection; his support made the Church more than just a group of dissidents from the Tabernacle.

---

[19] Helen C. Colman, *Princes Street Congregational Church* (London, 1919) P. 51
[20] W. Gordon Robinson, *William Roby* (London, 1954) P. 108

Sadly most of the records of Hope chapel have perished, and so we know very little of the men and women who made up the Church. We can get some glimpses of the congregation from published records, but most of the people of Hope Chapel are now known only to God. They would have been much like any other Congregational chapel of the period, people from all walks of life, the congregation representing the working and middle classes, deacons drawn mostly from the ranks of the latter, including merchants and potters. Presiding over the church was the Pastor, a man educated in a Nonconformist Academy or College, whose responsibility was the spiritual oversight of the flock.

The Congregationalists laid a special emphasis on ministerial education. While they insisted on piety as the first qualification for the ministry, the Congregationalists believed in a learned ministry, which meant that it was expected that in general a Congregational pastor would have spent four or more years in a theological college. In this they differed from the Baptists, who laid less emphasis on learning, and many of whom were suspicious of formal theological education. The Particular (Calvinistic) Baptists had relative few Theological Colleges, only five at their height by the end of the 19th century, while the Congregationalists had nine by the same period. Even so, not all Congregational pastors were College-educated, though most Churches wanted a college man. Pastors were only rarely drawn from the congregation that they served; usually they were from another part of the country. None of the pastors of Hope were from Staffordshire.

What would a service at Hope Chapel in the early years have been like? The central position of the pulpit emphasised that the preaching of the Bible was the central part of worship in the Church, and as today the main place in the service would have been given over to a sermon preached from a Biblical text. One of the main differences that a modern member of the Church would notice between worship today and in 1812 is that rather than an organ, the singing would have been led by a precentor who would have used a pitch-pipe or a tuning-fork to give the opening note of the hymn and then led the congregation in singing without musical accompaniment. No doubt many of the hymns sung in 1812 are hymns that we still sing today, the praise of the church providing a link down the centuries.

Hope was a Congregational or Independent Church, meaning that the church was governed by the meeting of the church members. This would probably have been held monthly, after the Sunday evening service. The day-to-day affairs of the church would have been in the hands of a body of deacons who were elected by the membership from among themselves, and all was presided over by the pastor, when there was one. Deacons were usually respected members of the community; in the case of an industrial community like Hanley, they would have been merchants, factory-owners, shop-keepers, and sometimes (particularly in the early years) even brewers and innkeepers; beer was regarded as a wholesome drink in moderation, and favourably contrasted with gin, regarded almost as respectable people regard hard drugs today.

Doctrinally the church would have been like the Tabernacle, evangelical and Calvinistic. English Congregationalism at the opening of the 19th century was dominated by evangelical Calvinism, a situation that would not change until after the middle of the century.

For the first two years of its existence, the Church at Hope Chapel was without a pastor; services were presumably taken by visiting preachers, lay and ordained, and by any men in the congregation who were able to preach. Having a pastor of their own was something every Congregational church aspired to, so at least some of the visiting preachers would be there with a view to calling them to the vacant pastorate. Ministers would have supplied the pulpit from churches in Staffordshire, Shropshire, Derbyshire and Cheshire, and there would have also been young men from the Nonconformist colleges and academies sent to supply the pulpit during their college courses, hoping that the church would call them at the conclusion of the course so that they would not be forced to become teachers to make ends meet.

One of the men who supplied the pulpit of Hope Chapel in these early years was Rev. John Greeves, who had been pastor of the Independent Chapel at Buxton in Derbyshire since 1812, and before then a student at the Dissenting Academy at Hoxton. The church was so impressed by his ministry that they extended a call for him to become the first pastor of the new church. We do not know if he was the first man they had approached with a call, but he was the first to accept it, and so in 1814 Rev. John Greeves left Buxton and moved to the Potteries.

John Greeves was born in the sea-port town of King's Lynn, in north Norfolk, on May 28th 1791. He was converted through the witness of an old school-friend whom he had lost contact with but who he met again when he was nineteen. The friend had been converted through the Methodists, and Greeves joined the Methodist Society in the town; this was described as "meeting in class"[21], the class being not an educational class, but a meeting in which Methodists would share their religious experiences. To "meet in class" was to be a full member of the Methodist society in a place; only later would Wesleyan Methodism introduce church-membership as such.

Having been converted thorough Methodism and joined the Methodist Society, it would have been expected that, feeling called to preach, John Greeves would have progressed in the usual way to the Methodist ministry, beginning as a local preacher. However, in his case, due to "peculiar circumstances"[22] not described in his obituary, he instead became a Congregationalist and entered the Dissenting Academy at Hoxton to train for the Congregational ministry. It is probable that for some reason the King's Lynn Methodists refused to allow him to preach, or at least to recommend him for the itinerant ministry,[23] and he therefore sought another way into the preaching ministry.

The Academy that Greeves attended was founded in 1791, the year of his birth, as the Evangelical Academy, and occupied buildings in the London suburb of Hoxton that had previously been used by another Academy, also known as Hoxton Academy, that had closed due to a lack of funds and students. The intention of the institution was to train men for the ministry, and students were required to be "of evangelical Sentiments, possessed of good natural Abilities" and to have

---

[21] *Minutes of The Methodist Conferences* Volume 10 (London, 1848) P. 307
[22] *Minutes of The Methodist Conferences* Volume 10 (London, 1848) P. 307
[23] Because of its origins in the work of John Wesley, Methodism has two grades of preachers, local preachers who remain in secular employment and preach in their own local area, and the 'Travelling preachers' as they were known in Greeves' day, who were the ordained and full-time ministry. Methodist churches are organised into circuits, which consist of several churches served by between one and three ministers and the Local Preachers. Because there are two grades of preachers it could be that much more difficult for a man to enter the full-time ministry.

"experienced a divine Change".[24] The theological tutor at the Academy was the Rev. Robert Simpson, a Scotsman from a decidedly Calvinistic background in the Secession Churches, which had been established by the Erskine brothers, George Whitefield's associates in the northern kingdom. In addition to the various branches of theology, Simpson taught 'evidences' (what we today call apologetics), Biblical criticism and church history. He was assisted by John Hooper as the classical tutor, who also taught English grammar and geography. A third tutor, Henry Forster Burder, was appointed in 1810 and taught, among other things, pneumatology (the doctrine of the Holy Spirit), philosophy, mathematics, and elocution.

The reason for this mix of subjects was that the English universities were closed to all but Anglicans, and would remain so until 1871. The majority of prospective Congregational ministers were therefore privately educated, and the schooling they had received would have varied enormously. Because the Congregationalists valued a learned ministry, much of the necessary learning had to be imparted at the Academy or College, so that it was the equivalent of both a university course and a theological college. As the college had far fewer tutors than any university, they were often overworked, even as they worked their students hard.

The primary aim of the Evangelical Academy was to ensure a supply of trained pastors of evangelical sentiments, and so evangelical religion rather than academic training was the primary emphasis of the institution, something that would sit well with a young Methodist from Norfolk. Nevertheless, standards were high, and there were two scholarships to Glasgow University available for the most academically promising students. As with most of the Nonconformist academies, Hoxton students lived on the premises, and senior students were expected to take up preaching engagements, often assigned by the college. Indeed, it seems that Greeves was actually sent to Buxton by the Academy, which actively sought out churches in need of an evangelical ministry.

---

[24] *http://dissacad.english.qmul.ac.uk/new_dissacad/phpfiles/sample1.php?asearch=0&detail=academies&parameter=Academysearch&alpha=Hoxton&acadid=75*

As the first pastor of the Church, John Greeves had the opportunity of forming the tradition of Hope, but in fact he played relatively little part in this. Nevertheless, his obituary records that "he exercised his ministry with acceptance and usefulness" in the Potteries.[25] "He was a diligent student of the holy Scriptures, and was thus enabled to bring out of his treasury things both old and new." His preaching was fervent and evangelical, his style marked by animation in the pulpit. He studied to show himself approved unto God, as the Apostle Paul says a pastor should, "A workman who does not need to be ashamed, rightly handling the Word of God."[26]

The Church welcomed their young pastor, but he was unsettled. Perhaps there was still lingering ill-will between the Tabernacle and the seceders, or perhaps he just found the transition from Buxton to Hanley difficult; the contrast between the spa town and the Potteries would have been marked, and his congregation would have been very different. What was more, the Potteries have long been an area distinguished by Methodism, and Greeves once again came into contact with the piety in which he had begun his Christian life. Congregationalism was Calvinistic, Methodism was Arminian, and Greeves found himself drawn back to Methodism even as he ministered as a Congregationalist. Dissatisfaction with the Potteries and theological questions led him to reconsider his position.

In the event, Greeves did not stay very long at all in the pastorate at Hope. In fact he did not stay very long in the Congregational ministry, for in 1815 he resigned from Hope and offered himself as a candidate for the Wesleyan Methodist ministry. The Wesleyan conference immediately stationed him in the Buxton Circuit, perhaps thinking that his experience as a Congregational minister in the town would help the Wesleyan cause. The fact that he had studied at Hoxton also meant that he would have been one of the best-educated men in the Wesleyan ministry.

---

[25] *Minutes of The Methodist Conferences* Volume 10 (London, 1848) P. 307
[26] 2 Timothy 2:15

31

Fig. 3: John Greeves in later life. From the Wesleyan Methodist Magazine

If he had been unsettled in Congregationalism, he found his home in Methodism. John Greeves remained a Methodist for the rest of his life, serving many different circuits. In 1828-9 he was stationed in the Newark circuit, and in 1844 he was stationed in the Huddersfield circuit and served on the committee for the Woodhouse Grove School, an institution for the education of the sons of Methodist ministers, located between Leeds and Bradford. In 1845 he was stationed in the Bristol South Circuit and also held the post of Financial Secretary for the Bristol District and was on the committee for the Kingswood School, a similar institution near Bristol[27]. In the obituary of his son Frederic he is described as "an honoured Methodist preacher, whose faithful sermons and loving counsels produced a deep impression on his son's heart and conscience while still in early youth".[28] His own obituary recorded, "Mr. Greeves possessed a generous disposition and an elevated mind. As a friend, he was frank, cordial, and unwavering, being incapable of

---

[27] *Minutes of The Methodist Conferences* Volume 10 (London, 1848) P. 174
[28] *Minutes of Wesleyan Conference,* 1895

meanness or duplicity himself, he did not suspect them in others. His experience was scriptural and sound, his communion with God deep and constant, and his enjoyments were rich and uninterrupted."[29] It seems that he found what he sought in Methodism; a congenial sphere for his ministry. Though he suffered ill-health as he grew older, he remained a zealous evangelist and preacher. The Conference gladly remarked that "His ministry was always acceptable, and in many Circuits was extensively useful in the conversion of sinners, and still more so in the edification of the Church."

Greeves died relatively young, from a painful illness; his obituary records that "his sufferings were extremely severe, being seldom surpassed in acuteness."[30] He died on June 25th 1846, aged 56, leaving a widow and several children, including three sons. His eldest son was received on trial as a preacher at the Conference of that year, shortly after his father's death; though John Greeves would have been looking forward to his son's being received into the Wesleyan ministry, it was not to be.[31]

While Greeves died at a relatively young age, he founded a ministerial dynasty that lasted into the 20th century. His three sons all entered the Wesleyan ministry and enjoyed successful careers; all three held important Conference appointments, and his son Frederic was President of the 1884 Wesleyan Conference, held at Burslem, and Principal of Southlands Wesleyan teacher training college. Frederic's sons, John Henry and Edward also entered the ministry. Edward Greeves had three sons who were Wesleyan ministers, the most notable of whom, Frederic Greeves, was a founder of OXFAM and principal of Didsbury College, Bristol (latterly Wesley College). This Frederic Greeves delivered the 1954 Fernley-Hartley Lectures on *The Meaning of Sin*[32] and the 1960 Cato Lecture on *Theology and the Cure of Souls*.[33] Another great grandson, Derrick Amphlet Greeves, was minister of Westminster Central Hall 1955-64.

---

[29] *Minutes of The Methodist Conferences* Volume 10 (London, 1848) P. 307
[30] *Minutes of The Methodist Conferences* Volume 10 (London, 1848) P. 308
[31] *Minutes of The Methodist Conferences* Volume 10 (London, 1848) P. 296
[32] William Leary, article, 'Greeves Family', in John Vickers (ed.) *A Dictionary of Methodism in Britain and Ireland* (Peterborough, 2001) P. 141
[33] Both published by Epworth Press

Chapter 3: William Farmer

Rev. William Farmer[34], second pastor at Hope, came to the Church from Bethel Congregational Church, George Street, Leeds, where he had been the pastor since 1806. William Farmer was born in Nottingham in 1780, and baptised at St. Mary's Church. He was the eldest son of John Farmer, a chemist and druggist in the city. John Farmer was an irreligious man fond of fast living, who wasted his money on pleasures. His abused wife was left to run the business, while John enjoyed himself with his mistress. This obviously affected the children, and William grew up in a household that was the opposite of orderly and religious. He spent some time with his maternal grandfather on a farm in the parish of Osgathorpe, Leicestershire, and gained some of his education at a school nearby. His grandfather was a devout Methodist, and on the farm William experienced a very different and much more attractive world than the family home in Nottingham.

William's early life changed for the better with the death of his profligate father in 1792. His mother re-married; her second husband was Rev. Thomas Peet, a Nonconformist minister in the city. Given that William was later ordained as a Methodist New Connexion minister, it seems reasonable to assume that Peet was also Methodist. Farmer found a warm welcome in the world of Methodism; the Methodists welcomed lay-preaching, and he began his preaching career as a local preacher in Nottingham. After attending several sessions at Edinburgh university, though apparently without graduating, he was ordained a minister of the New Connexion at the age of about 19. Unlike the English universities, the Scottish universities did not insist on membership of an established Church for students to take Arts degrees.

The Methodist New Connexion had the distinction of being the first secession from Wesleyan Methodism, being formed in 1797 in

---

[34] My thanks to Professor Liz Farmer, direct descendent of William Farmer, whose work researching the life of her great, great, great grandfather has been a great help to me. Unless otherwise indicated, information of William Farmer comes from her unpublished work on him.

Leeds by a group of Wesleyans seeking lay-representation in the Methodist Conference and other reforms. They were most influential in the Midland and northerly industrial towns[35]; Hanley was a centre of the New Connexion, and Bethesda in Hanley the largest chapel in the denomination. In Nottingham a majority of the members of the Methodist Society supported the New Connexion, and they left the old Wesleyan body for the New Connexion, taking Hockley Chapel in Goose Gate, their meeting place, with them. The chapel remained in the hands of the New Connexion until 1818, when it was recovered by the Wesleyans in a legal case.[36] It would have been in this large town chapel that William Farmer first preached.

For some reason, Farmer did not remain with the New Connexion long. It seems that after being stationed in Leeds he came into contact with Edward Parsons, the eminent Congregational pastor of Salem Chapel in the city, who persuaded him to join that denomination. In 1806 he was ordained to the Congregational ministry, as reported in the *Evangelical Magazine*:

> Aug 27th 1806 Mr W Farmer was ordained to the pastoral care over the Independent Church assembling in George Street Chapel Leeds. Mr Parsons opened the service and delivered the introductory discourse &c Mr Moorhouse of Huddersfield engaged in the ordination prayer; Mr Bruce of Wakefield delivered the charge and Mr Cockin of Halifax addressed the people.[37]

Bethel Chapel was a small red-brick building that had been built by a dissident from Methodism for his own congregation, but when his cause declined, a Congregational Church bought the building. Though the church was small, they were relatively wealthy, and Farmer had no money worries. Not that he did not work hard; in addition to three services on a Sunday, unusual in city chapels at the time, there was a weekly lecture on Wednesday evenings.

---

[35] E. Alan Rose, article 'Methodist New Connexion' in Vickers (ed.) *Dictionary of Methodism* (Peterborough, 2001)

[36] Royal Commission on the Historical Monuments of England, *Nonconformist Chapels and Meeting-Houses in Central England* (London, 1986), P. 162

[37] Quoted in Farmer, "Rev. William Farmer" P. 5

Established securely in Leeds, he was able to marry in 1809; the service was conducted in St. Peter's Church on 7th August, as at the time it was illegal for weddings to be conducted anywhere other than in the Church of England. Their first child, named Mary after her mother, was baptised by Farmer himself on Christmas day 1810 at the George Street Chapel. In all Farmer and his wife Mary had nine children, four girls and five boys. Even in early 19th century England, this must have made for a noisy household at times.

With a growing family, William Farmer supplemented his income from private tuition. He also took up literary work, editing the works of the Puritan theologian William Bates (1625-1699) in four volumes for the publisher James Black. Farmer contributed a memoir of Bates for the edition. He also edited an edition of Bates' work *The Harmony of the Divine Attributes in the Contrivance and Accomplishment of Man's Redemption*. Both of these, in Farmer's editions, can be bought today. The modern publisher of this work, Reformation Heritage Press, has a quote from Farmer on the web-page for the book, "*The Harmony of the Divine Attributes in the Redemption of Man* has always been one of the most popular parts of Dr. Bates' works; it embraces all points essential to the gospel; exhibits the same amiable spirit as that which breathes through the whole of his writing; and is at once calculated, it is presumed, to advance the interests of religion in general, and to confirm and edify the individual Christian."[38]

Farmer's description of his subject Bates seems at times to mirror Farmer's own life: "He began to preach early, probably in the twenty-second year of his age, and soon became one of the most popular preachers of the day. Nor is it to be wondered at, since there was a happy and unusual combination of circumstances to render him so. His person was handsome and elegant – his countenance mild yet dignified, his voice peculiarly sweet – his style inimitably polite for the age in which he lived."[39] The only surviving portrait of Farmer shows a fair-haired, good-looking young man, and his style, while strange to us today, was

---

[38] *http://www.monergismbooks.com/The-Harmony-of-the-Divine-Attributes-in-the-Contrivance-and-Accomplishment-of-Mans-Redemption-p-19035.html* Accessed 28/7/2012

[39] William Farmer, 'Memoir' in *The Works of the Rev. William Bates* (London, 1815) P. vii

certainly "polite" in 1815. Farmer goes on, "But the breath of popular applause did not, as it too often does, inflate him with pride. Deep humility led him to lay all the honours he received at the feet of his Master, Jesus Christ." It is only fair to say that it seems that Farmer wanted to be as humble as Bates as well. He also assisted in editing the works of the Puritan Oliver Heywood (1630-1702).

By 1815, Rev. William Farmer was a rising star in Congregationalism and a protégée of Rev. Edward Parsons, the celebrated pastor of Salem Chapel, Leeds and a leader of Yorkshire Congregationalism; great things were expected of him. That he was one of the men chosen as trustees for a new chapel in York indicates how highly he was thought of. Though Congregationalism had no national representative body, there were local Associations and County Unions, and an able man could rise to be highly regarded in the Churches.

The year following the publication of his edition of Bates, Farmer received a unanimous call from the Church at Hope to succeed John Greeves. After their first minister joined the Methodists, it seems somehow poetic that their second should have begun his ministry among the Methodists, albeit of a different branch. The call to Hanley meant a move away from Leeds and Parsons, and into a sphere where he could further develop himself.

The year 1816 saw the arrival of two new Congregational ministers in Hanley, Rev. William Farmer at Hope and Rev. Ridgeway William Newland at the Tabernacle. While the Tabernacle was the senior Church, it was Farmer who was the older and more experienced man; he was in his mid-thirties and had been in the ministry since the age of nineteen, while Newland was a young minister fresh from Hoxton, and ten years younger.

The Hope Street Church was never more influential than during Farmer's pastorate, if the number of references to the Church and its pastor in the *Evangelical Magazine*, the *de facto* organ of Congregationalism, are anything to go by. One sign of Farmer's increasing importance is that he was called on to preach away from Hope quite often. May 1818 found him at Harrow on the Hill, at the anniversary of the Congregational Church there, one of many outside engagements he was called on to fulfil; more than any other minister of the Church.

Fig. 4: Rev. William Farmer of Hanley

From the beginning of his ministry in the Potteries, Rev. William Farmer was involved with the Staffordshire Association of Independent ministers. The precursor of the later Staffordshire Congregational Union, the Association was, as its name suggests, one of ministers rather than Churches. In 1818 Farmer preached at the Annual Meeting on "The importance of Village Preaching".[40] 1819 saw Hope playing host to the Annual Meeting of the Association, with Mr. John Fernie of Brewood

---

[40] *Evangelical Magazine* 1818 P. 312

taking the pulpit at the first public service on the 13th of April. The following morning an early prayer-meeting was held in the chapel. Mr. Newland at the Tabernacle hosted the second public service, where there was also a communion service held. At these meetings Farmer and Newland were elected joint-secretaries of the association, an extremely important honour as well as a major piece of extra work for the two men.

A New Connexion Methodist turned Congregational minister, William Farmer was no denominational bigot. Of all the other denominations, the Baptists were closest to the Congregationalists; in fact the only difference between the two groups was on the question of baptism, the Congregationalists baptising infants of believing parents, while Baptists baptised only believers, on a credible profession of faith. So in 1820 Rev. William Farmer and Rev. Ridgeway Newland took the service at the re-opening of the Baptist chapel in Hanley. The Church had clearly been in difficulties for some time, and had actually been dissolved. On Friday December 1st 1820 a new Baptist Church was formed in the old chapel. Newland took the first part of the service, the reading and prayer, and then Farmer exhorted the Church from Philippians 1:27 and closed in prayer. It is notable that a Baptist Church should have called upon Congregationalists to lead the opening services, and is a sign of how influential the two men were; rather than rivals, they were close friends. That they often appeared together on platforms, and were even joint-secretaries of the Ministers' Association, suggests that they were seen as a natural pair.

In 1820 Farmer published *A Sermon Occasioned by the Execution of R. Ellis*. In 1820 many crimes other than murder still carried the death penalty; Ralph Ellis' crime was burglary. He and his accomplice William Bucklington were caught, found guilty, and finally executed 16th September 1820, by hanging, at Chester Castle. Apparently Ellis had some connection with the Church at Hope, for William Farmer was called to visit him in prison while the young man awaited execution. Having visited Ellis in prison, Farmer had found him apparently penitent, and his sermon was one part warning to young men who might be tempted by a life of crime and another part chronicle of a penitent. It is a reminder that the world in which Hope Chapel began its life was one of extreme poverty and injustice, where theft was a capital crime.

Farmer also made connections in North Wales. In 1819 he spoke at the anniversary of the North Wales Missionary Society at Pwllehli, preaching in English. As a member of the society he also addressed the business meeting. August 30th and 31st 1820 saw Farmer at the fourth anniversary of the same Society. He took the English service opening the anniversary meetings on 30th August. In the evening he was in the congregation listening to the celebrated Rev. Rowland Hill of London's Surrey Chapel. Farmer also spoke at the afternoon meeting on the second day. The fact that he was sharing a platform with Rowland Hill suggests how important Rev. William Farmer was becoming in Congregationalism. On March 14th 1821 Farmer was called upon to speak at the ordination of John Saunders, a former student at the Carmarthen Academy, over the Church at Buckley, Flintshire. Farmer shared the platform with the famed Rev. Thomas Raffles of Liverpool on this occasion, and took as his text Exodus 17:12, the passage that speaks of Aaron and Hur holding up the hands of Moses and commonly used to encourage the Church and especially deacons to uphold their pastor. Later that same year he presided at the ordination of three missionaries from the Potteries who were being sent out to India.

The need for local Church extension was not forgotten either; there was a flourishing home-missionary effort supported by both Hope and the Tabernacle. One concrete result of this was the opening on August 8th 1822 of a new Chapel called Hope at Wetley Rocks. This was still a mission situation in the small mining community, intended to reach both the miners and the local agricultural workers. At the opening of the chapel, Farmer preached from Psalm 132:17 and 18, and Rev. William Roby of Manchester was called upon to deliver a second sermon. The name of the Church suggests that this was a plant from Hope in Hanley, and Mr. Roby would have been glad to see the young cause bearing such fruit. The third sermon was delivered by Mr. Ball, one of the Home Missionaries active in the county and one of those who had pioneered the work in the moorlands. The *Evangelical Magazine* recorded that, "The place was filled with attentive hearers, and the prospect of usefulness is encouraging."[41] Sadly the effort was ultimately unsuccessful, and the building was closed and sold, though a new and

---
[41] *Evangelical Magazine* 1822 P. 449

more successful chapel was built at Tomkin with the proceeds. The chapel still stands today, as a pair of cottages, but the inscription, "Hope Chapel 1822" over a partially blocked arched window on the gable end facing the road betrays the fact that these were not always cottages.

On October 2nd 1822 Farmer was the evening preacher at the opening of the new Congregational Chapel at Tean, addressing a crowded congregation.[42] All was going well; Farmer was a rising star, and could have expected within a few years to have become one of the leading Congregational ministers in England outside of London; indeed he might have received a call to a prestigious London pulpit. But in fact the Church was about to be profoundly shaken, and Farmer's career would take a terrible blow from which he would not recover.

In the autumn of 1822 Farmer was taken ill, and the church granted him some time off to recover. He left Hanley to spend some time staying with his sister and his brother-in-law, James Ogle Robinson, in Clapham. Robinson, a Congregationalist and a member of the Congregational Church at Grafton Square, was one of the wealthy evangelicals who lived around Clapham Common. While in Clapham Farmer had time to rest, to meet with friends in London, and even an opportunity to preach at the Grafton Square Church. Farmer returned from his break refreshed and ready to resume work, but a little over nine months later Farmer and the church received a nasty shock; a letter from the Clapham Petty Sessions court accusing Farmer of fathering an illegitimate child in the parish.

The accusation was in regard to a woman in her mid-thirties called Hannah Foster who had been in service with the Rev. James Phillips, pastor of Grafton Square Congregational Church; Miss Foster was from Leeds, and had been in service with Farmer during his pastorate at Bethel. The newspaper reports at the time described her as "a decent looking woman, although not possessing any peculiar physical attractions"[43]. Phillips had suspicions in early summer of 1823 that the unmarried maid-servant was pregnant, an accusation that she denied until she went into labour in July. She was taken to the local workhouse,

---

[42] *Evangelical Magazine* 1822 P. 450
[43] *Morning Chronicle* 28th August 1823

where she was delivered of a healthy boy who was baptised William after his alleged father. Miss Foster insisted that Mr. Farmer, a married man, was the father. The accusation was one that, if true, would have completely destroyed Farmer's career and his reputation. Farmer always vehemently denied that he had ever had such relations with Miss Foster.

Her whole testimony was highly damaging to Farmer's character, as she claimed that the events at Clapham had not been a mere lapse of moral judgement, but part of a history of immorality and hypocrisy. Miss Foster declared that the respected Nonconformist minister was in fact an adulterer. She told the court that he had seduced her while she was in his employ at Leeds and that they had had a brief relationship during that time, but then she had left Leeds and moved to Clapham. However, she had met Farmer once more in Clapham, and had fallen again as a result of his influence. Farmer had met her employer Mr. Phillips at Mr. Robinson's house, and his brother minister had invited him to visit at his home. She explained how on 5th November 1822 William Farmer had visited Phillips at his home and agreed to preach for him. According to Miss Foster he also met her at the minister's house, and according to the papers she said that "He appointed to meet her the next evening at seven o'clock, near the church on the common."[44] According to her testimony they had met and walked on Clapham common in the dark before a romantic liaison on the common which had resulted in her pregnancy.

For his part, Farmer vigorously denied the accusations. He claimed that, so far from having been on the common with Miss Foster, he had not even been in Clapham at the time, and had an alibi to prove it. He had spent the day that Miss Foster named in London with a friend, a respectable employee of a banking house, and could be certain of the time that he had left the city. He had witnesses of respectable character to support his alibi. Despite this, after an hour of deliberation the magistrates gave their verdict against Farmer. They adjudged him to be the father of the child and insisted that he pay 3s. 6d a week support. Farmer replied, "Gentlemen, I have very little to say on this subject. I am innocent of this charge; I cannot submit to any order of affiliation which you may think it proper to make, and I am determined to go to prison, rather than pay a single farthing towards the support of a child which is

---

[44] *Morning Chronicle* 28th August 1823

not mine; I am perfectly innocent." He steadfastly refused to pay.

That he was found to be the father by the court does not necessarily mean that William Farmer was actually guilty; there are reasons why the Clapham Petty Sessions might well have been biased against Farmer. Where the father was unknown, illegitimate children were charged upon the Parish for support, and so there was pressure to find a father to pay for the support of the child; a man accused of being the father of an illegitimate child might well find that, whatever principle might be in law, the burden of proof lay in practice upon him to show he was not the father rather than upon the court to prove that he was. Secondly, Farmer was a Nonconformist clergyman, and Anglican magistrates might well have been biased against him on that count.

Farmer returned to Hanley to find that the news from London had arrived first, and in a form that was not quite accurate. The London papers were reporting that Farmer had been brought to London by a summons, whereas in fact he had gone willingly. Writing to the *Staffordshire Advertiser* on 4th September, Farmer said,

> "The guilty shrink from public investigation; the innocent alone court it. On the first intimation of this affair, there would have been no difficulty in hushing it up, and keeping it from the public eye. A guilty person would have pursued this course, I pursued an opposite one. I fearlessly pursued the most open course, and formed an immediate determination, first, to confront my accuser face-to-face, and, if not thus able to bring her to a confession, to bring her before a public court. This I have done. It was at my own request that a Sessions was held for a more public investigation of this base allegation."

He went on,
"It will, I presume, weigh with the public mind when balancing between the opposite statements of the accuser and the accused – that I have been of an unblemished character for upwards of twenty years in the ministry; and I appeal to the public, to my neighbours, and to the whole circle of my acquaintance in the place, in which I have

been a resident for seven years, as to my moral conduct and general deportment; no stains have been fixed upon my name, nor moral slander breathed upon it; and I may venture to say, that in no instance has my veracity been impeached. But on the other hand, here is my accuser, a person so lost to virtue, that upon her own showing, she makes an assignation with a married man one night, and the next deliberately goes out and seeks him up and down on a common – a woman who has proved herself unworthy of a moment's credit, by the most glaring contradictions, and the most palpable falsehoods."

Farmer complained that the London papers' reporting of the case had been biased against him; it had favoured Miss Foster's cause, even though, as he pointed out, she had given a most unfavourable character of herself by confessing that she had been willing to commit adultery. The case was presented in two different ways; in London it was presented as the wicked seduction of an innocent woman by a hypocritical married clergyman, in Staffordshire as an immoral woman attempting to blacken the name of a virtuous clergyman for financial gain. At this date it is impossible to know what the true facts of the case were, but Farmer protested his innocence to the end of his days.

Having given his own account of events to the press, Farmer also gave it to the Church. On 8th September 1823 a meeting was held at Hope Chapel, chaired by Farmer's mentor, Rev. Edward Parsons. As well as the membership of the church, several local Congregational ministers were present, no doubt including Newland from the Tabernacle. While there is no report of this meeting in existence, we can safely assume that Farmer's report to the meeting was in substance the same as his letter to the press. He would have explained how,

"A number of gentlemen present (and among them was not one of my own relations) entered into a voluntary agreement to exonerate me from all charge; on the ground of a conviction that the allegation was false. I leave this fact to speak for itself. My determination was, and nothing could have induced me to swerve from it, to suffer any length of imprisonment, or death itself, rather than to have suffered my immediate connections to have done so, in a case in which I knew myself perfectly innocent."

The result of this meeting was that "the church were so satisfied of Mr. Farmer's innocence that by a *prompt* and *unanimous* show of hands, they wished him to continue their pastor."[45] He resumed his ministry the next Sunday. All did not however return to normal. Again, we are so far in time from the events, and the available records are so scanty that we cannot be sure exactly what happened. There are suggestions that the papers, as fond of a scandal then as they are today, continued to run stories about Farmer, suggesting his guilt; since he had in fact been found guilty, he could not silence them, and perhaps the fact that the story continued to run led some of the Deacons at Hope to reconsider their supportive stance. Despite the unanimous support Farmer received in the September meeting, there were those in the church not entirely satisfied with his protest of innocence, and that these gained a majority of the church membership to their side. Others remained firmly on the side of the pastor, creating friction in the church. Farmer's position at Hope became untenable, and he and his supporters were forced to secede. The *Evangelical Magazine*, in which Farmer had featured yearly since his time in Leeds, suddenly ceases to mention him from 1823, even as a subscriber; apparently the wider Congregational world decided that he was guilty. Matters of guilt and innocence, almost impossible to determine at the time, are now lost in the mists of history. In fiction the story would have had a conclusive ending; real life is rarely that neat, and real people like Farmer and Miss Foster are not caricatures; it is best to suspend judgement until the great day when all secrets shall be brought to light.

In 1824 the Rev. William Farmer ceased to be the pastor of Hope Chapel, and his departure was not peaceful. He and fifty members of the church seceded and formed a new church that at first met in a room in the earthenware factory of Mr. Simpson in Hanley. Among the seceders were some wealthier members of the congregation, and one of them, a Mr. Pawley, gave a plot of land at the bottom of Brunswick Street on

---

[45] *Leeds Mercury* September 21th 1823

which a chapel was built; this was a relatively small building, without galleries and with two small vestries. This building was christened Brunswick Chapel, and it still stands, much altered, and currently in use as a restaurant.

From 1830, William Farmer was associated with the Socratic School in Stoke. This was an institution of adult learning that was intended "To encourage virtue and discourage vice" by means of lectures, debates, publications and the provision of a library, and "By pecuniary and honorary awards for correct principles, good conduct, and long service."[46] In effect it was an early version of the public institutes that would become common in the Victorian era. Brunswick also established a Sunday school, and in 1831 the "Brunswick" friendly society was formed at the chapel.

Brunswick chapel was the scene of Mr. Farmer's labours until 1839. The church continued to exist, and in 1846 became part of the Presbyterian Church of England. In 1886 they moved to a new, larger Gothic chapel on Trinity Street, still remembered by many local people as Trinity Presbyterian Church and later (after the Tabernacle united with it) Trinity United Reformed Church. Farmer departed from Hanley at the same time as his friend Ridgeway Newland, who left to found a new cause at Encounter Bay, Australia

Brunswick was Farmer's last pastorate; the dissenting community seems not to have forgotten the scandal, and Brunswick was never welcomed into the Congregational fold. So long as he ministered to a faithful group of supporters at Brunswick Chapel, all was well, but every other door had been shut to him. After leaving Brunswick, he moved to Liverpool, where he worked as a secretary and librarian. By 1851 he had moved once more, this time to Bermondsey in the East End of London, where he was a "Railway merchant". Farmer died in Bermondsey on 12th January 1860, meaning he would have been about 79 at the time.[47] The scandal of 1823 ruined his career, and the man who had once seemed a future leader of the denomination ended his days in the wilderness.

---

[46] Quoted by Liz Farmer, P. 13
[47] http://www.findingwilliam.com/?page_id=7

Chapter 4: The First Missionaries

One of the most remarkable events of Farmer's ministry took place on Wednesday July 18th, 1821, when three men knelt at the front of a packed chapel to receive ordination. The three men were Mr. Micaiah Hill, Mr. James Hill and Mr. Joseph Bradley Warden. Two of the men were members of the Church, and all three were being ordained to the work of missionaries in Calcutta. Farmer led the service, Rev. Mr. Brook of Tutbury read and prayed, and Rev. William Roby of Manchester, back at the chapel he had helped to open in 1812, preached from Isaiah 6: 8, "Also I heard the voice of the Lord, saying, Whom shall I send, and who will go for us? Then said I, Here am I; send me." It was an appropriate message for the three men going from Staffordshire to India, and a challenge to those in the congregation to consider if they too would be willing to follow the calling of the Lord. Most of the leading Congregational ministers in Staffordshire took part in the service, but it was particularly Hope's service; the young Church sending two of its members off to bring the Gospel to heathen lands. One of the young men related how his mother had at first been resolutely opposed to his going to India, but had eventually changed her mind and supported him wholeheartedly. The final charge to the young men was delivered in Bethesda chapel, recently enlarged and the largest place of worship in the Potteries.[48]

All three missionaries were married men, and their wives were as committed to missions as they were. The six of them left Portsmouth on the ship *Ganges*, bound for Calcutta, on 10th October 1821.[49] They are the first missionaries the Church sent out.

The missionaries from Hanley joined a thriving work based at Union Chapel Calcutta. Their first task was to learn the local language so that they could teach the local people, although they also conducted services for English-speakers. Communication with England was

---
[48] *Evangelical Magazine* 1821 P. 398
[49] *Evangelical Magazine* 1821 P. 540

necessarily slow; a letter from the missionaries dated September 1822 only appeared in the *Evangelical Magazine* in October of the following year.[50] In it they reported that the Union Chapel congregation was growing, "An audience respectable and serious frequently exceeding 300 persons regularly attend the means of grace. Almost every month we have additions to the number of our church members, whose piety and zeal are our best epistles." The missionaries took turns preaching at Union Chapel. Although they were Congregationalists, they had good relations with the older Baptist Missionary Society work at Serampore and Calcutta, and jointly established a Bethel Society, that is, a missionary society for the benefit of sailors in the port of the city. They began by holding services, always with the permission of the captains, on board ships. When some of these objected, a small vessel was purchased for use as a floating chapel. Baptists and Congregationalists preached alternately, and since they kept their emphasis on the Gospel, there was no friction. The Governor-General of Calcutta agreed to become president of the society and to grant perpetual moorings for the Bethel ship. Commodore Hayes, Master attendant of the port, became vice-president of the Society. The Bethel ship was opened on 28th July 1822, Micaiah Hill led the service, but the preacher was the venerable William Carey, pioneer of the modern missionary movement, who had been at work at Serampore since 1793.

In the May of 1822 the missionaries, in company with clergymen and missionaries from the Anglican Church Missionary Society and the Baptist Missionary Society, took part in the formation of an Auxiliary Bible Association in Calcutta. Rev. J. Hill was chosen as one of the Secretaries of this organisation on 24th February 1823, replacing Rev. H. Townley, who had returned to Britain.[51] The speaker at the meeting was one of Carey's associates, Dr. Marshman. There was union on the mission field even if there was not uniformity. Among the Europeans, Christian soldiers at Fort William asked to have the missionaries preach to them, and again in partnership with the Baptists the Congregational missionaries from Hanley preached to the soldiers, both on Sunday and in the week.

---

[50] *Evangelical Magazine* 1823 P. 434
[51] *Evangelical Magazine* 1823 P. 520

Of course the primary aim of the mission was to reach the locals. The missionaries reported that they had a number of "bungalows" for preaching in the Bengali language, two in Calcutta, two and Kidderpore, and one under construction at Bhodanipore. The Gospel was preached in the open air in the streets, and in 19th century Calcutta things were no easier than they are in modern-day Hanley. The missionaries reported that; "The natives too seldom exhibit a desirable spirit of inquiry, and still less frequently conduct that inquiry with calmness or candour."[52] In other words, the locals liked to heckle the English preachers. They reported, "On one occasion, when a missionary was wearied by the innumerable foolish questions and remarks of a Hindu, the latter exclaimed, 'Do you preach forbearance, and yet become angry?' When the latter replied, 'Yes; I am a man like yourself, and my passions resemble yours, and therefore do not try to provoke me, because if I become angry I shall sin, and my God will be offended with me.' Which gentle expostulation silenced the offender, and fell with some effect on those who stood by."[53]

The missionaries conducted schools as well as preaching, viewing education as one way to bring the Indians out of Hinduism and to the truth of Christianity. They translated useful literature into the local languages, and lived closely with Indians so as to be able to reach them better.

The newly-arrived missionaries had to contend with Indian diseases. Micaiah Hill was struck down with a severe fever which almost killed him and forced him to take complete rest for two whole months. His wife gave birth in June, and although her child survived, the eldest child of Mr. Warden only lived two months.[54] In a postscript to the letter Hill recorded the death of Mr. Keith, one of the missionaries, who left a widow and children in India; his wife soon followed him, along with Mr. Bankhead, another of the missionaries. The Keith children were thus left without either parent. With England so far away, for many missionaries the trip to India was one-way, it was a commitment to live and die in a strange land.

---

[52] *Evangelical Magazine* 1823 P. 435
[53] *Evangelical Magazine* 1823 P. 435
[54] *Evangelical Magazine* 1823 P. 346

And it was a strange land. Coming from a country where the vast majority of the population professed Christianity to a land where most of the population were Hindu was a huge culture-shock. When the government had opened up India to the Gospel, some British Christians had assumed that the result would be the rapid conversion of India. In fact Hinduism had a much firmer hold of the people, and they were not as ready to see the superiority of Christianity as those in Britain had thought. Micaiah Hill observed: "Though when the British senate decreed the admission of the Gospel into India, thousands of British Christians imagined that to be the period of day-break to the sons of Hindustan; yet superstition, like the angel of death, spreads her raven wings over this immense territory, so that darkness covers this portion of the earth, and gross darkness the people. But we continue our exertions, knowing that, like the disciples at Jerusalem, we are required to wait for the descent of the Holy Spirit, when superstition with rapid flight shall escape from the abodes of men, and the crescent shall be eclipsed, and the darkness which renders it visible be scattered by the day-star from on high."[55]

On March 20th 1823 the missionaries from the Potteries were in Bhobaneepore to open a new Bungalow chapel there. The congregation was made up not only of Christians, but mostly of curious Muslims and Hindus who wanted to see what the English Christians would say. Rev. Micaiah Hill began the service by giving out a hymn in Bengali, and then Rev. J.B. Warden read from the Gospel of Luke, also in Bengali. The actual preaching was done by Rev. S. Trawin, one of the more experienced missionaries in Calcutta.[56]

Sunday April 6th saw the event that the missionaries from Hanley had been looking forward to since before they had been ordained in the crowded Hope Chapel; a local man called Ramhurree, formerly a Hindu, was baptised in public at Union Chapel. He was the first convert they had seen, and they saw him as the first-fruits of their work in Calcutta and the seal of God on their calling. They recorded, "The simple testimony which this convert bore to the power of the Gospel on his

---

[55] *Evangelical Magazine* 1823 P. 436
[56] *Evangelical Magazine* 1824 P. 76

heart, in the presence of a large European audience, and before the priests of Hinduism, was interesting to the highest degree."[57] Like many a convert, Ramhurree had to suffer persecution for his new faith; his friends rejected him, and his wife mocked him, "Tauntingly desiring him to go to heaven by himself."[58]

A Bengali-speaking convert having been baptised, it was necessary to go on with his discipleship. On May 9th 1823 the mission held its first Bengali communion service in the school-room of Union Chapel, Calcutta, with about thirty people including the missionaries. Not all of these were communicants; some were spectators, people who made no profession of faith but who were regarded as serious enquirers. Rev. J.B. Warden gave an address in which he recalled the parting words of his mother. He did not know if she was still alive, or dead, but she had told him, when they parted, that since he would not be present when she died, he wanted him to have a family silver cup that had been handed down through the generations. The cup had been used at family festivities when the "flowing bowl" had overflowed. Giving it to him, she had told him, "This I give you to employ for a very different purpose. When God shall graciously crown your labours or those of your dear companions, among the heathen, let this cup be employed as the sacramental cup from which the first convert may drink the emblem of the Saviour's blood."[59] So the family silver cup was presented to the Church to be used for the first time in its new role as a communion vessel. Warden only regretted that his mother could not be there to see the service.

Micaiah Hill was to be sent out to Tally Gunge, some five miles south of Calcutta, where a mission-house was being built to receive him in December 1823. One of his tasks there would be to present Persian Bibles to the Mysore Princes, the sons of Tipu Sultan, "the Tiger of Mysore" who had been killed at the Battle of Seringapatam in 1799. The Tally Gunge was a simple building with living quarters for the missionary and his family and a building that could function both as a school and a chapel. With the segregation of men and women in India,

---

[57] *Evangelical Magazine* 1824 P. 76
[58] *Evangelical Magazine* 1824 P. 76
[59] *Evangelical Magazine* 1824 P. 77

Mrs. Hill had the important task of running the female school. The station was opened on 24th October 1823, and in the first three months they never had more than 25 girls in the school.[60] Today we understand that the teaching of women is one of the most effective ways to influence a culture and improve living standards; the missionaries in the 1820s did not have the data we have, but did almost instinctively what anyone concerned for the good of India should have done.

The school-chapel was large enough for 200 boys, who would be taught the Bible there, and would learn to read and write in Bengali and English. The school-chapel would be in use all day, from morning until evening, for teaching and preaching.

An Indian Christian speaking at the opening of the station gave a sermon in which he made "several interesting observations." Among those which the missionaries thought interesting enough to translate into English was this: "When we are afflicted we sometimes go into the wilderness among snakes, jackals and tigers, to procure the juice of a tree by which we obtain a cure; thus that which we dislike to procure becomes salutary. It is so with religion. We do not like this house; yet it is for the worship of God, and the only true Saviour. We do not like the Bible *shastre*, yet it is the only *shastre* which brings salvation from sin. We do not like the *sahibs* (missionaries), yet, like the juice from the wilderness, they come from a far country, to heal the diseases of our hearts, and to turn us from idols and the devil, to the true God. Thus you see, good people, those whom we think friends are enemies, and those whom we consider as enemies are our best friends."[61] It is certainly honest about the general attitude of the Indians towards the British missionaries!

Tally Gunge was later willingly given up to the Anglicans who had been seeking to set up a school there for a while.[62] Miciah Hill was moved to the Mission at Berhampore. It was a difficult station; the local people did not appreciate the missionaries at first, and a retrospect of the work in 1838 records that, "For several years after the arrival there of

---

[60] *Evangelical Magazine* 1824 P. 458
[61] *Evangelical Magazine* 1824 P. 458
[62] *Evangelical Magazine* 1829 P. 156

our brother, Mr. Hill, whenever he attempted to preach the tidings of redeeming mercy, he was hooted and hissed by the people, his voice was drowned in tumult, clapping of hands, and shouts of 'hurree bol;' and men would even pursue him with clubs to do him personal injury."[63] He persevered, however, and opened an orphanage and a school in the town.

August of 1824 saw the Calcutta missionaries in the large village of Beallab, about three miles south of Kidderpore, opening a school for the Indians.[64] Most of the population of the village were Brahmins, the priestly caste; this meant that they were not exactly well disposed towards Christianity, which had not been taught in the village before as far as the missionaries were aware. "We expect, however, that the cheering tidings of mercy will now frequently sound in the ears of those idolatrous priests, as we intend to make the school-bungalow serve the purpose of a chapel, in which we hope frequently to preach to the people."[65] Although opposed to Christianity, the Brahmins understood the usefulness of education, and so a school was welcome where a chapel would not have been. Haldam, one of the leading men of the village, was a supporter of the plan for a school and sent his own children there. No doubt his main hope was that the education would enable them to get posts with the Colonial administration, but the missionaries were only glad that children would be attending the school.

On 30th July 1824, Rev. James Hill, who had been very unwell again, once again had the task of preaching a funeral sermon for one of his fellow-missionaries, Mrs. Mundy, wife of Rev. George Mundy of the Chinsurah mission; Mrs. Mundy died in childbirth; the child survived.[66] In November 1824, Hill was in Calcutta to welcome two new workers, Rev. John Edmonds and his wife, who were headed for the mission at Chinsurah. Edmonds, later to become pastor at Hope, observed of Rev. James Hill, that he had "A most important field of labour in attending to the respectable congregation at Union Chapel. He meets frequently with his young people, who justly appreciate his valuable labours, and evidently profit from them."[67]

---

[63] *Evangelical Magazine* 1838 P. 458
[64] *Evangelical Magazine* 1825 P. 208
[65] *Evangelical Magazine* 1825 P. 208
[66] *Evangelical Magazine* 1825 P. 124
[67] *Evangelical Magazine* 1825 P. 164

Mission work was a busy routine; the daily work of the missionaries was made up of teaching children in the mission schools, of translating works into Bengali and other Indian languages, and of preaching. Sundays were spent in the chapel, where the form of worship was much as it was in England. In the week there was open-air preaching in the bazaars in Bengali. There were services in English, attended mainly by British soldiers, and services in Bengali for the local inhabitants. While there was the breaking of new ground, and missionaries often visited other stations, very sensibly the emphasis was on building up churches rather than travelling around and preaching without following up the work.

In October 1825 the missionaries at Calcutta had the great joy of baptising nine converts from Hinduism, five adults and four children. Union Chapel in Calcutta was filled with interested spectators for the service. While the elder missionary Rev. Samuel Trawin, baptised, James Hill read and prayed and J.B. Warden preached from Matthew 13:16 and 17, "Blessed are your eyes, for they see: and your ears, for they hear. For verily I say unto you, that many prophets and righteous men have desired to see those things which ye see, and have not seen them; and to hear those things which ye hear, and have not heard them." The five adult converts were questioned to make it clear that they understood what they were doing, and then baptised. The four children were the children of some of them, and were baptised in accordance with the Congregationalist understanding of infant baptism. Trawin reported, "Thus we have seen one whole household, and parts of others, all baptised in the name of our adorable Lord: thus have we beheld the branches, and their little buds, cut out of the olive tree, which is *wild by nature* and *grafted into the good*; where, according to the apostolic testimony, they will together *partake of the root, and fatness of the root.*"[68] Since the missionaries were Congregationalists, the baptism was by sprinkling rather than immersion.

The converts remained firm in the faith despite the hostility of many of their neighbours, and on 3rd April 1826 four more Indians were baptised, including the mother of one of the converts baptised in

---

[68] *Evangelical Magazine* 1826 P. 209

October; she was nearly 80 years old. Initially she had been very much opposed to her son abandoning the religion in which he had been brought up, but she had seen how becoming a Christian had changed him, and she eventually followed him in baptism. The preacher on this occasion was Mr. Edmonds, who in his sermon insisted that "the sole purpose of the Missionary Society is to bring sinners to the Saviour, and that in the prosecution of this great work, we do not design to proselyte the heathen to any particular denomination of Christians, but to make them sincere followers of Christ."[69]

Rev. J.B. Warden did not last long on the mission-field. In a letter on 25th December 1825 Rev. James Hill wrote to the LMS headquarters in London that Warden was seriously and dangerously ill; by the time the letter arrived in London, Warden was dead. Despite the best efforts of the mission doctor, Dr. Vos, and of Dr. Twining, Sir Edward Paget's doctor, the missionary died in Calcutta at ten in the morning on 8th January 1826.[70] His illness had lasted six weeks, and was extremely painful. Hill wrote: "His sufferings were extremely great, to an extent which I have never witnessed in any other person."[71] Speaking to James Hill, Mr. Warden commented, "With regard to my own safety, I have not a doubt, and with reference to death, it appears to have lost all its terrors. I know I am a poor worthless creature; but the precious blood of Jesus! How perfectly it answers all my wants." As death approached the missionary met it bravely. Typically of Evangelicals of the period, Warden's fellow-missionaries gathered around his bed to comfort him. They were not unrealistic, however; they knew that Warden was suffering terribly. Hill writes, "Sometimes, when of account of his debility and great suffering, I have been reluctant to propose to pray with him, he has requested it with so much earnestness, and afterwards has appeared at a loss how to express his gratitude."

The day before his death, Warden asked James Hill to sit with him and to pray and read. Mrs. Warden and a female friend joined them, and they sang together the hymn, 'There is a Land of Pure Delight', by Isaac Watts, a hymn that looks forward to heaven. At first it was just

---

[69] *Evangelical Magazine* 1826 P. 529
[70] *Evangelical Magazine* 1826 P. 313
[71] *Evangelical Magazine* 1826 P. 313

those who were well who sang, but, "When we came to the lines, 'Infinite day excludes the night, and pleasures banish pain,' with all the strength he had, he joined us, and continued singing to the end of the hymn, and the ecstasy depicted in his countenance and expressed in his tones was indescribable."[72]

He did not regret the fact that he had gone out to India and was therefore dying far from his family, far from the mother who had bidden him a tearful farewell. He asked Hill to read Mark 16 to him, including the words, "Go and tell his disciples, and Peter." After reading verse two Hill said to his friend, "What, my dear brother, if early in the morning on the first day of the week, you should see the Sun of Righteousness rising upon the plains of heaven, and gilding the battlements of that city, where the Lamb is the lamp thereof?" Warden replied, "Ah, that was the prayer of my father – that he might be let loose on the Sabbath-day, and it was answered. Oh! To see Jesus, and see him as he is. What a glorious sight! And my poor father will then meet his wayward first-born of whom he had the least hope."[73]

When they came to verse 15, "Go ye into all the world and preach the gospel", Hill asked how the words struck his dying colleague now. "Oh, my brother... I have not one painful emotion, not a single uneasy feeling that I gave myself to the Lord's work among the heathens; nay, I bless, *I do bless God* that he put me into the ministry."[74] This was the piety of the 1820s face-to-face with death in a foreign land. We must admire Warden's faith; but also we remember that his God is the same as our God. Warden "spoke of the glories of Christ, and the wonders of redemption, in a manner which baffles all description." He believed what he preached, and was able to die still proclaiming the same message in death. Towards the end he cried out, "Spectators, hear my dying words. If you would be happy! - if you would be happy with God for ever, come to Jesus, trust in Jesus. O, let my poor dying voice give emphasis to my words, do come to Jesus." His last words were, "Oh, to be lost in wonder, love and praise!"

---

[72] *Evangelical Magazine* 1826 P. 314
[73] *Evangelical Magazine* 1826 P. 314
[74] *Evangelical Magazine* 1826 P. 314

Warden was buried in India, where he had been so determined to serve Christ. His wife and son were left behind, and Mrs. Warden was determined to remain and continue to teach the Indian women. She and her son therefore travelled to Berhampore to assist Mrs. Hill in the work of teaching Indian women and girls there. This was a pioneering situation, and it is a sign of her dedication to the work that she travelled there only twenty days after her husband's death.[75] She died in 1829.

The work went on; Rev. Micaiah Hill reported on March 14th 1826 that a group of Hindu converts had publicly renounced an idol which he calls "Sheeb", presumably Shiva. The worshippers at this shrine in Kidderpore decided to dethrone the image and convert the temple into a chapel. As was common, the image was sent back to England as a sort of trophy to encourage the supporters of the mission.[76]

In August 1827 Micaiah Hill had to report the death of another missionary, Rev. Samuel Trawin. Trawin had been aware that his health was deteriorating for some time, but rather than going back to England to recover, he felt that he could not leave India until there were more workers in the field to replace those who had died.[77] His dedication to the work led to his early death. Hill wrote of him, "A man more beloved, so useful, and more devoted to God, we have, I think, never had among our missionaries in Bengal."

James Hill was forced to return to England in 1834 as a result of poor health and became the pastor of George Street Chapel in Oxford, where he remained until 1838. He went on to Salford, and then to the prestigious Grafton Square Church in Clapham, where he served 1841-62. Hill served a few years at Hove in Sussex before his retirement from the pastoral ministry in 1866, and died in January 1870. Rev. James Hill served as Chairman of the Congregational Union of England and Wales in 1860, the highest honour the denomination could give.[78]

---

[75] *Evangelical Magazine* 1826 P. 353
[76] *Evangelical Magazine* 1826 P. 488
[77] *Evangelical Magazine* 1828 P. 125
[78] *http://surman.english.qmul.ac.uk/displaycards.php?id=13853*

Micaiah Hill's wife was forced to return to England with their children on 25th December 1836. The long sea-voyage seems to have helped her recovery, and it was reported that she "reached London, in improved health," on the 24th April 1837.[79] She had been in India for nearly sixteen years, and none of the children had seen England before. Micaiah Hill himself reported in 1837 that, "He has of late suffered much from bodily indisposition, induced, we doubt not, by unceasing exertion in the burning climate of the East."[80]

In 1839 Rev. Micaiah Hill temporarily returned to England to recover his health and to engage in deputation work. His heart was still in India, and so he returned there in 1842 and resumed the work in Berhampore. In 1847 he took over the work at Union Chapel, Calcutta, and was still labouring there at the time of his death on 3rd February 1849 at the age of fifty-eight.

His eldest son, William Henry, followed in his father's footsteps. Having trained at Spring Hill College, Birmingham and Western College, Plymouth, he went to Calcutta in 1848 and took up his father's work. Ill-health forced him to return to England in 1863, and from 1865 until his death in 1902 he was a minister in Faversham, Kent.

Micaiah Hill's second son, also called Micaiah, entered the Congregational ministry and after training at Spring Hill College in Birmingham was ordained at East Retford in Nottinghamshire in 1848. He was Secretary of the Birmingham Town Mission (now Birmingham City Mission) 1856-1884, when he died on 24th September, aged sixty.[81] A third son, Samuel John Hill, was also a Congregational minister.

---

[79] *Evangelical Magazine* 1837 P. 352
[80] *Evangelical Magazine* 1838 P. 458
[81] *http://surman.english.qmul.ac.uk/displaycards.php?id=13865*

Chapter 5: 1824-1845

Following the sad division over Mr. Farmer, the remaining members at Hope had to call a new minister. The man whom they chose was Mr. Samuel Jackson, a young man from Sheffield; Jackson was only 24 years of age, and fresh from another Nonconformist Academy, when the church at Hope Street called him to the pastorate.

Samuel Jackson was born on 2nd June 1800 in the Wicker, Sheffield, the youngest of five children. His parents were members of the Independent Church at Attercliffe, "Highly esteemed for intelligence and true piety."[82] Sadly they both died when Samuel was young, leaving the five children in the uncertain circumstances of orphans. Thankfully an uncle in Sheffield adopted all five of them as his own. He was a respectable businessman, and able to give the five orphan children a good education and trained them to take posts in his business. Not all of the children turned out as he would have liked, it seems, for Samuel Jackson's obituary records that the uncle was "tried and disappointed with some of his adopted children." Although he and his wife were not Christians when they adopted the children, they were later converted and became members of the Independent Church at Garden Street.[83]

Samuel was initially one of the more trying and disappointing of the children. Unhappy with the position he held with his uncle, he decided to make his own way in the world at the age of fifteen. He found a situation as an apprentice in the village of Wentworth, the other side of Rotherham from Sheffield, and his uncle gave him permission to go. For eighteen months he pretty much pleased himself when he was not working, "He was far from a gospel ministry, and from salutary restraint... his associates and pursuits widened his distance from all that was good." However, he was eventually brought under the ministry of Rev. James Bennett, the pastor of the Independent Church at Masbro', Rotherham. There he was converted remarkably. His obituary records,

---

[82] *Evangelical Magazine* 1851 P. 1
[83] The building still stands as the Croft House Settlement

"There was a rapid development of his intellectual and moral faculties. He seemed to spring into maturity at once."[84] He became a model Church member, and soon began to take on responsibilities in the large and active Church at Masbro', first in the Sunday School, and then preaching to adults in the villages around Rotherham and Sheffield. His work was much appreciated, and the result was that a number of people suggested that he should enter the ministry.

Masbro' Chapel was closely linked with the Rotherham Academy, which had been established in 1795 to train young men for the ministry of the Congregational Churches.[85] The first principal of the Academy was Rev. Edward Williams, who had been called to the pastorate of Masbro' and the position of Theological Tutor at the new Academy. A Welshman from Denbigh, Williams was a brilliant teacher and established an Academy that played a major role in the development of Yorkshire Congregationalism. It had opened in 1795 with ten students. James Bennett had succeeded to both the pastorate and the tutorship in 1813, following Williams' death.

Fig. 5: Ruins of Masbro' Chapel in 2012

---

[84] *Evangelical Magazine* 1851 P. 2
[85] For the Rotherham Academy, see Elaine Kaye, *For the Work of Ministry* (Edinburgh, 1999)

The Academy expected a certain level of prior education on the part of its students, and Samuel Jackson did not possess that education. Bennett, determined that the promising young man would not be lost to the ministry because of this, arranged for Jackson to spend six months studying with Rev. James Buckham of Finkley to bring him up to the standard the Academy required for entry. It was quite common for young men from less academic backgrounds to be sent to study with ministers to prepare for entry to academies.

Jackson would have known exactly what to expect when he entered the Rotherham Academy; the College was very closely linked with Masbro' Chapel, and of course the Theological tutor was his own pastor, Rev. James Bennett. The only other member of staff was Rev. Thomas Smith, the Classical Tutor. Like most Independent Academies of the early 19th century, Rotherham followed a four or five year course. In the first year students studied English, Latin, and the rules of composition. In the second year they tackled Latin, Greek, Moral Philosophy, and theology. In the final year students concentrated on theology and Church history. A fifth year was available to those students who showed particular ability, and was something of a post-graduate studies year.

Although it taught arts and science subjects, the Rotherham Independent Academy was a theological college dedicated to training ministers and missionaries. Senior students were expected to undertake preaching engagements in local towns and villages, while the junior students were expected to attend prayer-meetings in the villages around Rotherham, reflecting the fact that many students began their courses at a relatively young age. The Academy was located on what is now College Road in Rotherham, close to the curious old building of Masbro' Chapel, where Samuel Jackson and his fellow-students would have attended services when not preaching elsewhere.[86]

There would have been quite a mixture of men among the student body at Rotherham, ranging from young men still in their teens

---

[86] The Church is now closed, and the building was destroyed by fire early in 2012. I visited it a few days later, when the smell of smoke was still thick in the air. Figure 5 shows the front of the chapel

to mature students who had had a secular career before entering the ministry. The students lived on the upper floors of the Academy buildings, and each had his own study with a bedroom above. They had four meals a day, and while the domestic management of the college was in the hands of the tutors and their wives, a number of servants were employed to do much of the work. The Academy was funded largely by subscriptions from local Churches and their wealthier members.

Samuel Jackson was not one of those students who went on to take a fifth year of the course, but he did well. He suffered from ill-health, and his studies were interrupted by illness. The author of his memoir in the *Evangelical Magazine* records, "He is one of the few of whom it can be said, that his piety sustained no injury by passing through a collegiate course."[87] Jackson took great care over his devotional life at college and afterwards.

During the third vacation of his course at Rotherham, Jackson took an opportunity to spend three months as a pulpit supply at the Independent Chapel in Hamburg, where his congregation was largely made up of British people living in the city. His time in Germany was very successful, though he went to minister and not to study, as later Congregational students would. The young man from Sheffield was welcomed by the ex-pat community in the German port city, and his ministry was very blessed.

On his return to England in 1825 he supplied the pulpit at Hope Chapel, still vacant after William Farmer's departure. He proved popular with the people, and was unanimously called to the pastorate of the Church, which he took up as soon as his college course was over. His relatively short pastorate of just two years, 1825-7, seems to have been uneventful, though his memoir states that "His character and ministry are still [in 1851] cherished with grateful recollection."[88]

As was quite common, he assisted at the ordinations of friends from college. On August 21st 1828 he was in Whitchurch, Shropshire, taking part in the ordination service for Thomas Potter, who had studied

---

[87] P. 2. The same concern that academic studies can be harmful to piety continues today.
[88] *Evangelical Magazine* 1851 P. 2

with him at Rotherham. The main preachers were Rev. Thomas Smith, Classical Tutor at Rotherham, and Rev. Thomas Raffles of Liverpool, one of the leading ministers in the denomination.[89]

In 1827 Jackson was called to take up a joint pastorate with Rev. William Luke Prattman in Barnard Castle, County Durham, where he was extremely popular. As a joint-pastor, he had fewer preaching responsibilities at the main Church in Barnard Castle, which meant that he had more time to devote to the work in smaller village Churches. One of these, at Staindrop, was developed until they were able to call a pastor, and Jackson was the man they chose. He accepted, and spent almost four years as pastor of the Church there. In 1834 he moved to the struggling church at Walsall. While there a friend of his suggested that he should consider overseas work and go to Nova Scotia. Jackson went so far as to resign his pastorate at Walsall, and was close to securing a settlement in Nova Scotia when, at the last minute, the whole thing fell through. Suffering from ill-health, he returned to the city of his birth.

While he was in Sheffield, Mount Zion Chapel, being without a pastor, approached him as a pulpit-supply. He proved popular, and so in June 1845 he became the pastor of the Church. He remained there until December 1847, when he was called to become pastor of the Congregational Church in Northallerton. He began his work at Northallerton in April 1848, expecting several more years of usefulness. The struggling Church looked forward to progress under the leadership of this gifted and experienced preacher. He worked very hard to build up the Church, and this was probably partly the cause of his death in February of 1849. The December of 1848 was full of hard work, preaching for friends, speaking at public meetings, addressing Sunday schools and laying the foundations of a new chapel at Gainford, a village where he had begun the work. On his return home, he was taken ill and declined rapidly, dying on February 20th 1849. He left a widow and eight children, and a Church that mourned a promising beginning that had been tragically cut short. He was not yet fifty years old.[90]

---

[89] *Evangelical Magazine* 1828 P. 13
[90] *Evangelical Magazine* 1851 P. 4

John Edmonds

Rather than being a young student fresh from the academy, Samuel Jackson's successor was a returned missionary, Rev. John Edmonds, born in Poole, Dorset in 1798. When he was still a boy his parents moved to Portsea, where he was converted under the ministry of Rev. John Griffin. An early conversion led to his early entering on church work as a teacher in the Independent Sunday school in Portsea. Griffin was impressed by his ability and evident gifts for the ministry and encouraged him to enter full-time Christian work. These were the early days of foreign missions among English Christians, and Edmonds' imagination was fired by the prospect of preaching Christ among the pagans. He applied to the London Missionary Society for training, and was accepted as a student at the Society's training college at Gosport Academy.

Gosport Academy had been founded in 1777 by Rev. David Bogue, Independent minister at Gosport.[91] Initially it was simply Bogue taking on men one at a time to train for the ministry in a kind of apprenticeship, but in by 1789 Bogue was taking on three new students a year and running a three-year course. In 1800 the Academy was taken over by the LMS, who had learned as a result of a number of missions failing that zeal was not enough; missionaries had to be educated and prepared for the work.

Gosport was unusual for the era in that for most of its life it had only one tutor, David Bogue, and it had had no buildings of its own; students boarded with members of Bogue's congregation, and teaching was done at his chapel. Although the course was formally three years, Bogue often allowed missionaries to leave the academy early if convinced that they were ready. He did not, however, allow any students to leave before finishing the course; rather, a student leaving early had to finish the course in the time he had. Bogue remained sole tutor until 1817, when his son, David Bogue Jr., became classical tutor. The younger Bogue resigned in 1821, when he was succeeded by Rev.

---

[91] *http://dissacad.english.qmul.ac.uk/new_dissacad/phpfiles/sample1.php?asearch=0&detail=academies&parameter=Academysearch&alpha=Gosport&acadid=61* Accessed 30/7/2012

Theophilus Eastman. This allowed David Bogue to concentrate on the theological and missionary training aspects of the course.

Gosport students were not expected to begin preaching as soon as they reached the mission field. Since the Academy (and every other English Academy at the time) lacked provision for teaching the languages of the nations to which the students were sent, their first task on arrival was to master the native language. They were to translate the Bible into the native language, prepare linguistic tools such as grammars and dictionaries for future missionaries, and produce certain theological texts, the nature of which Bogue prescribed, in the native language. They then opened schools in which they could engage the natives intellectually.

The Gosport method took seriously the work of discipleship. Each Gosport student had at the end of his course a set of lecture-notes that had been corrected by Bogue himself, and these notes would form the basis of their work on the mission field. Where a Gosport man went, he set up a school that taught the same curriculum as every other Gosport school. The emphasis on education is also striking; Gosport missionaries were primarily educators, their missions schools where the natives received education that was not available elsewhere.

Edmonds then stood firmly in a tradition that emphasised rigorous education and worldwide mission; if the average Congregational minister in the 1820s was educated in a rather narrow field, he was certainly not ignorant, and it would have been a disgrace for such a man to be illiterate. The men who were sent overseas were certainly not sent off with a second-rate education. Edmonds had married at some point before this, and he and his wife left for India in 1824, sent by the LMS to Chinsurah, near Calcutta, an existing mission station of the Society. They entered enthusiastically into the work of the mission, but the Indian climate and tropical illnesses took their toll on the health of them both, and by 1827 they were unable to continue the work, and returned to England to recover. There were few remedies for tropical diseases, which were not understood then as they are today; many missionaries died on the field, and although Edmonds and his wife recovered their health in England, they were unable to return to the mission field. Instead Edmonds sought a pastorate where he could employ his talents and training in reaching the people of his own nation. This led him to Hope Chapel, where he exercised a happy ministry from 1828 until 1841, when he accepted a call to the pastorate at St. Helen's, Lancashire.

Trained to view education as a vital tool of missions, Edmonds never lost his appreciation of the importance of Christian education; the same methods that had been used to reach the pagans of India would be used to reach the pagans of Hanley. The existing Sunday school was strengthened, and a new building able to accommodate 300 children built at the rear of the chapel. From the 1840s until the 1890s, this was also used as a day school in the week. Both of these were primarily educational institutions and only secondarily evangelistic.

As education was seen by the Church as a way to bring children under the influence of the Gospel at an early age, it was also seen by some of the poor as a possible route out of poverty. Arnold Bennett's father was simply following a route taken by many when, as a poor potter, living above a pawn shop in Hope Street, he spent what spare time he had studying to become a solicitor. The ability to read and write could give a child from a background of grinding poverty a passport to a better paid job as a clerk or shop-worker. As the school he had presided over in India had given Indian children an education that their parents could not have dreamed of, the school that Edmonds presided over at Hanley opened up a new world of knowledge to the children of the poor.

Like most Nonconformist schools, the school at Hope taught both boys and girls; nonconformists were early in recognising the importance of educating girls, who would be the formative influence on their children. Popular books for Nonconformist children emphasised female piety, and often education as well. The mother of the hymn-writer John Newton had been a Nonconformist, and she was celebrated as the main Christian influence in his upbringing[92]; the story of Philip Doddridge being taught the Bible by his mother from Dutch tiles in the fireplace of the family home was also a popular story of female piety in

---

[92] See Richard Cecil, *Memoirs of the Rev. John Newton* (London, 1817)

which the mother as educator loomed large.[93] Susanna Wesley, Mother of John and Charles Wesley and the daughter of a Congregational minister, also exemplifies this pattern of the mother as educator.[94] If today people regard such an idea as limiting, in the 19th century it was liberating, for it meant that girls were taught to think.

For the Nonconformist, education was also necessary to fully participate in worship. The central part of early 19th century Nonconformist worship was a sermon, often an hour in length, delivered by a man who ideally had been trained in philosophy, science, mathematics, classics, English, theology, history and Biblical studies for at least three years and more usually four. The worship was centred on the teaching of Scripture by a trained scholar; every member was expected to be able to read the Bible, and heads of households were expected to lead family worship. Ignorance was the enemy of Nonconformist devotion, and rather than turning away the uneducated, the Church at Hope was determined to educate them.

A Nonconformity with working-class roots that were still very apparent, and at Hope were never lost, educated the children of the poor, and rather than inculcating a conservatism that told the poor their place, it taught them to seek to be better. The Congregationalists were the backbone of the Liberal Party in politics, and some of them could be quite radical. Their ministers shared platforms with those Liberal leaders calling for political reform and extension of the franchise, they spoke against unjust taxes and dared to challenge the Church of England. A Congregational school was as likely to be a hotbed of radicals as it was to be teaching due submission to authority, and some conservatives suspected them of being hotbeds of sedition. After all, in the Bible the Nonconformist found that all men were descended from the same father, and that all men were brothers. Not only was the African "a man and a brother", but so was the collier. At the 1836 anniversary of the Staffordshire Association of Congregational Churches, held at the Tabernacle in Hanley on June 18th and 29th, Edmonds moved that "It is the opinion of this Association, that at the present time Dissenters are

---

[93] See Alan C. Clifford, *The Good Doctor* (Norwich, 2002)
[94] Susanna Wesley is beloved of biographers. Among the best are Rebecca L. Harmon, *Susanna: Mother of the Wesleys* (London, 1968) and Arnold Dallimore, *Susanna Wesley* (Grand Rapids, 1993)

called upon to make very decided efforts to obtain the redress of those civil grievances under which they labour; and that this Association also deliberately recommend the pastors and Churches of this society to pay no more Church rates, as the best, and as it appears to this meeting, the only practicable means of obtaining the utter extinction of this unjust impost." The motion was unanimously carried.[95] The 'grievances' in question not only included the payment of Church Rates, by which they were forced to contribute to the support of the Church of England as well as their own ministry, but also the fact that only those willing to declare themselves members of the Church of England could graduate from Oxford and Cambridge, the only two universities in England at the time. Other laws barred nonconformists from certain positions in both national and local government.

Contrary to expectations some might have concerning ministers who get involved in politics, Edmonds never lost either his evangelical zeal or his missionary passion. He was an earnest preacher who devoted his annual vacation to deputation work for the London Missionary Society, speaking at meetings of the Society's auxiliaries in many places. Nor did his call to St. Helen's end his connection with the church at Hope Chapel. During a ministerial vacancy in May of 1852 we read that he officiated at the wedding of Mr. Edward Holt Diggles, of Toxteth Park and Mary Anne Downs, the daughter of James Downs, Esq., Corn merchant of Shelton and Barlaston.[96]

The Downs family were, it seems, one of the leading families in the church at Hope, and their connection with Hope can be traced through several generations. By 1866 they were resident in a substantial house called Chatterly House in Old Hall Street, and still connected with Hope Chapel. Chatterley House was definitely a superior residence, having been home to mayors and other leading men of the town. Though we cannot be certain, it is reasonable to assume that the Downs family supplied deacons to the church. They were the sort of people who counted in the new industrial cities; not old landed gentry, but merchants whose position came from their trade.

---

[95] *The Examiner* July 10th 1836
[96] *Liverpool Mercury* May 28th 1852

John Edmonds remained in the pastorate of the St. Helen's Church until his death on March 21st 1858. That morning he preached on the subject of "Access to God through a Mediator" from Ephesians 3:12. That evening, his obituary records that he "went to realise it by falling asleep in Jesus."[97]

Charles Fox Vardy

Following Edmonds' departure, the church called the Rev. Charles Fox Vardy as his successor. Vardy was one of eight sons of the Rev. Joshua Lambert Vardy; his mother was a daughter of Matthew Wilks, a leading evangelical preacher and minister of Whitefield's Tabernacle on the Tottenham Court Road in London. Vardy was born in 1806, and his mother died when he was just two years old. He was brought up in a decidedly evangelical and Calvinistic atmosphere, and early on committed himself to the cause of Christ. He became a teacher in the Sunday-school at an early age, and was appointed superintendent of the school when still a young man. By all accounts he was a gifted teacher, and as with others his ability in the school led to his being directed towards the ministry.

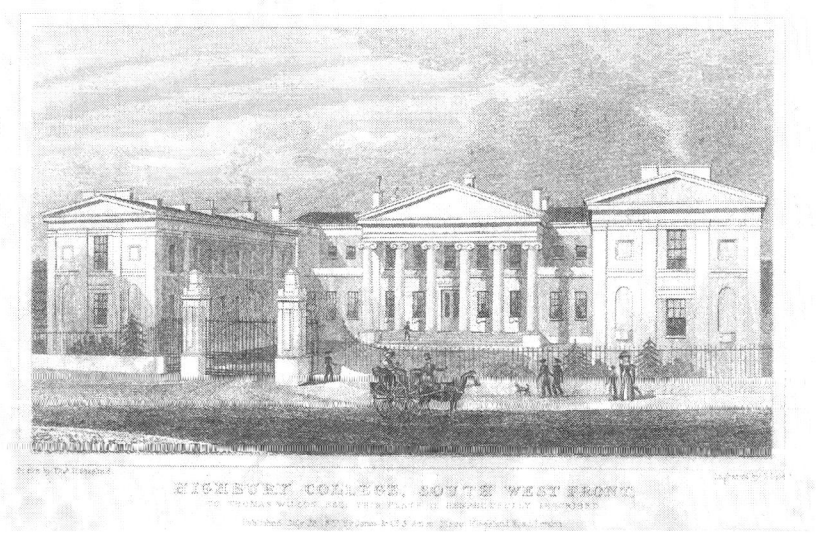

Fig. 6: Highbury College

---

[97] *CYB 1859*, Pp. 195-6

In 1831, Vardy entered Highbury College; this was in fact the same institution in which John Greeves had trained, but in 1824 it had moved from the old buildings at Hoxton, which were then turned over to the LMS to house their training-school, to a new purpose-built home at Highbury (Figure 6). Though the college now had a more modern building, this did not mean students were necessarily more comfortable; Baldwin Brown, a student who entered Highbury in 1841, wrote that at the College he learned "patience, and how to shave with cold water."[98] The college was now affiliated to the University of London, and students could earn degrees, though the University of London was not authorised to give degrees in theology. The staff included Robert Halley, classics tutor, and Ebenezer Henderson, theology tutor.

Following four years of study, Vardy was successful in his examinations to take the London arts degrees. We do not know if he secured one of the two scholarships to Glasgow University that the Dr. Williams' Trust had in connection with Highbury College, but at the conclusion of his course Charles Fox Vardy went north, to study at the University of Glasgow. Unlike the historic English universities, which were closed to all but members of the Church of England, the universities in Presbyterian Scotland were open to all, regardless of denominational adherence, and so those English nonconformists who were able to do so travelled to Scotland to study at old-established universities. The recently-established University of London was no more than an examining body for a variety of institutions, and would remain such until the late 19th century. Vardy studied for three more years at Glasgow, taking his BA in 1837 and his MA the following year.

Equipped with one of the best educations of any Congregational minister of the period, Charles Fox Vardy returned to England to begin his ministry. He was ordained pastor over the church at Hounslow, Middlesex, where a new chapel had recently been built. Whatever doubts any might have had over his evangelistic fervour or evangelical convictions were swiftly dissipated. He preached the Gospel in its fullness, and during his first year in the pastorate some 40 people were converted under his ministry.

---

[98] Quoted in Mark D. Johnson, *The Dissolution of Dissent, 1850-1918* (New York and London, 1987) P. 67

He resigned the pastorate in 1842 because he had become engaged to a lady in the congregation. The general opinion of Congregational churches at that time was that the pastor should not marry one of the people under his charge. While the Hounslow Church implored him to stay, Vardy did not feel it possible, and so he resigned his charge so that he could marry the woman he loved. It was at that time that he accepted the call to the pastorate of Hope Chapel.

Charles Fox Vardy and his new bride arrived in Hanley in 1842, to a church that seems to have given them a warm welcome. The author of Vardy's obituary writes that he laboured in Hanley, " for four years, honoured and beloved for his work's sake."[99] In 1842 his name is found among a large number of Nonconformist ministers congratulating Queen Victoria on the birth of a son, the future King Edward VII.[100] Certainly his ministry was a time of stability, and his preaching would have been much appreciated by a congregation who had been used to Edmonds' evangelical ministry.

Hope continued to assert itself in opposition to the laws that made nonconformists second-class citizens. In 1843 the church put its name to a petition protesting against the education clauses in the factory act that would have compelled the children of Protestant Dissenters to be educated in Church of England schools. The newspaper report records that both "Protestant Dissenters worshipping in Hope Chapel, Shelton" and "Protestant men Dissents [sic]" as signatories to the petition, apparently referring to the church as a whole and then the male members of the congregation. The fear, not at all unreasonable, was that the law was meant to not only undermine the Nonconformist schools, but also to draw the children of nonconformists into the Church of England. Thus a law that was supposed to make sure that children working in factories were educated had been turned into a sectarian measure, one which Vardy and his Church were determined to resist.

Vardy left Hanley in 1846 when he accepted a call to the Church at Kentish Town. However, he had worked himself too hard, and soon after he began the work there his health collapsed. He was forced to

---
[99] *Congregational Year Book 1890*, pp.195-7.
[100] *The Standard* 11th April 1842

resign in 1847 and never held another pastorate, instead devoting himself to serving the interests of Congregationalism and Protestantism in other ways. In 1848 he was appointed a school inspector with responsibility for the south of England for the British and Foreign Schools Society, which ran Nonconformist day-schools. He also served as Secretary to the Congregational Pastor's Insurance Aid Society, and the Protestant Union. The Protestant Union was a society founded for the benefit of widows and children of Protestant ministers, and intended to provide aid for them in the event of hardship. The Insurance Aid Society was a life insurance company for Congregational pastors, and so of a similar nature.

Charles Fox Vardy continued to serve the churches, even though he was unable to serve as a pastor, a fact that suggests his breakdown was mental as well as physical. He did however serve as a deacon at Grafton Square Chapel, Clapham, under the ministry of Rev. J. Guinness Rogers. Coincidentally, it was in this very chapel that William Farmer had preached during his fateful visit to Clapham in 1822, and where James Hill had ministered after his return from Calcutta. Vardy died at his home in Clapham on July 9th 1889.

Chapter 6: 1845-1864

Robert Macbeth

The minister called to take Vardy's place at Hanley was Rev. Robert Macbeth. Born 4th July 1816, a native of Auldwick, Caithness, he was a sturdy Highlander. His father, a stalwart of Caithness Congregationalism, was an engineer in charge of the construction of the first harbour at Wick, a harbour that contributed enormously to the prosperity of the town and the establishment of its herring fishery. The elder Macbeth was also a farmer, and insisted that each of his sons not only learn a trade, but also that they should all be able to work on the farm. Robert Macbeth was therefore apprenticed to a cabinet-maker, and also worked for four years on his father's farm. Yet Robert's vocation was neither as farmer nor as cabinet-maker, and so in 1841, at the age of 25, he entered the Blackburn Independent Academy, which had been established in the year of his birth.[101]

Blackburn Academy was established particularly for training Congregational pastors for Lancashire and its neighbouring counties, particularly Cheshire, Cumberland, Westmoreland, Derbyshire and north western Yorkshire. When Robert Macbeth entered the Academy it was located in Ainsworth Street, Blackburn, and had an intake of about 10 students per year. The course lasted four years, with a discretionary fifth year for students desiring to go on to further study. While we cannot be sure why Macbeth chose Blackburn over the Theological Hall of the Scottish Congregationalists, one of the factors may have been the Academy's President and theological tutor, Rev. Gilbert Wardlaw, a native of Glasgow and nephew of the Scottish Congregational leader Ralph Wardlaw. Gilbert Wardlaw had been the pastor of Albany Street Congregational Church in Edinburgh for several years, and editor of the *Christian Herald*. He was a popular preacher particularly among the younger members of the Scots Congregational Churches. It seems reasonable to suppose that this Scottish link is what drew the young man from Caithness to Blackburn.

---

[101] For Blackburn, see Kaye, *For the Work of Ministry*

When Macbeth entered the Academy, plans for it to relocate to the growing metropolis of Manchester were already underway. It would move without Wardlaw, however; his eyesight had begun to deteriorate rapidly, and he was unable to continue his work. We know that Macbeth found the academy unsatisfactory; Wardlaw's failing sight and a concentration on the impending relocation left leadership largely in the hands of the students themselves, particularly Alexander Raleigh and Watson Smith.[102] The library was in a poor condition, and deficient in many areas, and the institution was seriously under-funded.

In August 1843 Robert Macbeth and twelve other students from Blackburn arrived at the splendid new Lancashire Independent College at Whalley Range, Manchester. It was a magnificent building in the Tudor Gothic style, with a tall central tower 92 feet high flanked by two long wings of three stories each. There were three Professors, Robert Vaughan, formerly professor of history at University College, London, was the Theology Professor; Samuel Davidson, from the Belfast Academical Institution, taught Biblical Languages, and Charles Peter Mason held the Classical Chair. While it was technically a continuation of the Blackburn Academy, the Lancashire College was practically a new institution, with a far better course. Davidson, however, was influenced by the 'Higher Criticism' emanating from Germany, a fact that would eventually lead to his leaving the College in 1857. Macbeth continued at Manchester to the end of his course in 1845, when he received a call to Hope.

Robert Macbeth was ordained pastor of the Congregational Church at Hope Chapel, Shelton, on Tuesday April 29th 1845. The first speaker was Rev. Dr. Samuel Davidson, Professor of Biblical Criticism and Oriental Literature at the Lancashire Independent College. The burden of his sermon was the Biblical doctrine of the Church. The Rev. S. Butler of Stone offered the ordination prayer, and the charge to the newly-ordained pastor was given by Rev. S.T. Porter of Darwen, Lancashire. There was a lunch held at the school-room, and Rev. Dr. Robert Halley of Moseley Street Chapel, Manchester presided over a

---

[102] *http://dissacad.english.qmul.ac.uk/new_dissacad/phpfiles/sample1.php?asearch=0&detail=academies&parameter=Academiessearch&alpha=B&acadid=18*

lunch that was followed by "various interesting addresses" according to the *Evangelical Magazine*. Halley was also the preacher at the evening service, where the address was to the congregation. His subject was "the duties that devolve upon an Independent Church at the present eventful crisis." Other ministers, including the pastors of the Churches at Tean and Newcastle-Under-Lyme participated in the service.[103] The crisis in question was the rise of the Oxford movement in the Church of England. John Henry Newman was teetering on the brink, about to go over to the Roman Catholic Church, while E.B. Pusey, still resolutely a member of the Church of England, was under suspension for preaching a sermon on the Eucharist that was regarded as frankly Roman Catholic in its doctrine. The Oxford men were regarded as a threat to the Protestant character of the Church of England, and the end of the movement was regarded as the reversal of the Reformation in England. The responsibility of the Independents was of course to teach true Protestant principles.

Fig. 7: Rev. Robert Macbeth in later life

---

[103] *Evangelical Magazine* 1845, P. 480

Not long after, it was Macbeth's turn to take part in the ordination of one of his college friends, Stephen Hooper, who was ordained pastor of the Church at Heaton Mersey, near Manchester, on June 4th of the same year. As a newly-ordained minister, Macbeth took only a minimal part in the service.[104]

Macbeth remained at Hanley for six years; like many nonconformists of the period he was an advocate of the disestablishment of the Church of England, and he spoke at the first triennial Conference of the British Anti-State Church Association (later renamed the Liberation Society, an example of putting a more positive spin on an initially negative name). In the course of his address he said that the Wesleyan Methodists in Hanley, despite the official position of the conference, were for disestablishment "to a man."[105] The pastor at Hope had moved from calling for an end to the disabilities suffered by nonconformists to calling for the disestablishment of the Church of England; equality between the churches by the removal of the Anglicans from their privileged position as the state Church. Quite naturally the Church of England viewed this as Nonconformist aggression.

It was a part of Macbeth's character to take an interest in wider movements; he would later be involved in the work of the Hammersmith Institute, an educational venture for working people which began in the Broadway Chapel under his ministry there. His obituary records, " In social and political matters involving any moral issue he was always at the front with a note of definite guidance, caring little or nothing at such seasons for the opposition and sometimes the opprobrium to be encountered. He was, indeed, identified with a variety of enterprises, and made it his duty to watch from without, if he could not conscientiously assist from within, every great movement of the day. He was not only prepared but eager to step in at any stage in the development of these movements, and endeavour to get his Master's interests recognised."[106] In Hammersmith he was involved in a public debate with socialists which a

---

[104] *Evangelical Magazine* 1845, P. 481
[105] *Liverpool Mercury* May 11th 1847. This, if even slightly accurate, shows the tensions developing in Methodism, for the leaders of the denomination were against disestablishment.
[106] *Congregational Yearbook 1900*

hearer recalled "developed rather stormily"[107] His own background, involving work on a farm and an apprenticeship, helped him to identify with working men, and with young men in particular, and he was always willing to help those who came to him, something which was often witnessed to by those who had received help from him.

While at Hanley Mr. Macbeth was married to Miss Mary Cotton, daughter of Mr. John Cotton of Congleton. They were married at the Independent Chapel in Congleton on 8th March 1849 by Rev. R. M. or the rest of his life. Davies of Oldham.[108] Mrs. Macbeth, like most Nonconformist ministers' wives, was the silent support and unpaid assistant of her husband.

Macbeth left Hanley in 1851 to take up a pastorate in Darlington. He remained there only a short time before moving to the historic Broadway Church in Hammersmith, Middlesex. Though the church had a long and honourable history, it had an uncertain future. By 1853 the elders were considering selling the building to pay off the debt that had accumulated on it and winding up the church. The call to Mr. Macbeth was their last hope, and in the providence of God they were not disappointed. The fervent Scotsman threw himself into the task facing him. The historian of the church records:

> "His powerful personality and earnest eloquence soon filled the church. In ten years the number of the congregation had increased to such an extent that it was found necessary to build a larger church next door to the old one, and in 1863 it was duly opened. For forty years he exercised a large influence on the neighbourhood. He was not only a strong personality but a ripe scholar."[109]

Macbeth remained at Hammersmith for the rest of his ministerial career until his retirement, a period of nearly forty years. During this time he was a popular and influential pastor, as well as a figure of some importance in the wider church.

---

[107] Rt. Hon. Sir William Bull, Bart., MP: *A History of the Broadway Congregational Church, Hammersmith* (London, 1923) P. 42

[108] *Manchester Times* 10th March 1849

[109] Bull, *A History of the Broadway Congregational Church*, P. 36

"One cannot imagine a finer type of a real genuine Scots Nonconformist divine," Sir Edwin Cornwall, who was brought up in the Broadway Chapel under Macbeth's ministry reflected of his former minister. "He was always beloved, respected, and admired by those who were privileged to know him. Although a very learned man, he would perhaps not be considered a great preacher, but seemed to prefer simple religious Bible teaching, applied consistently and reverently."[110] Another former member of Macbeth's Hammersmith congregation, Mr. Peck, reflected, "The good old Scottish formula, 'Let us worship God', with which he prefaced all his services, seemed to indicate that he had entered the Holy Place and was inviting his hearers to do the same."[111]

As a pastor, he was willing to help however he could. E.J.B. Spearing, secretary of Broadway Church in 1923, wrote of Mr. Macbeth, "I have seen him at one time busily engaged repairing a broken magic lantern for the Sunday scholars and at another helping a little girl with her home-work arithmetic. And in times of real trouble I never met anyone who could make you feel as he could, that, whatever the sorrow, the Everlasting Arms were about you."[112]

Macbeth retired from the ministry in 1891 due to his increasing age, recognising that the time had come for a younger man to take the pastorate at Hammersmith. A town meeting was called in his honour, and there he was presented with an illuminated address which read in part: "At the close of your ministry at the Broadway Chapel, Hammersmith, many of your friends and neighbours, representing all shades of opinion, desire to record in this address their high sense and appreciation of the faithful and self-denying labour that has distinguished your long pastorate of 38 years."[113]

Robert Macbeth continued to preach for several years after his retirement, and to take part in a variety of events. At last he died quite unexpectedly on January 16th 1899 after an illness lasting only four days. At his funeral in those who took part included J. Guinness Rogers,

---

[110] 'Recollections of the Broadway Chapel' in Bull, *A History of the Broadway Congregational Church* P. 39
[111] 'Notes by Mr. Peck' in Bull, *A History of the Broadway Congregational Church* P. 41
[112] In Bull, *A History of the Broadway Congregational Church* P. 46
[113] The full address is reproduced in Bull, *A History* opposite P. 36

Andrew Mearns and C. Silvester Horne, all leading men of the denomination. The benediction at the grave itself was pronounced by the Rev. Prebendary Snowdon, Vicar of Hammersmith. He is commemorated by Macbeth street, Hammersmith, W6. The Broadway Congregational Church that was built during his pastorate was demolished in the 1920s, and its replacement building on the other side of the road has now also been demolished. After many years using St. Paul's Anglican Church, the Broadway Church itself recently united with the Methodists.

James Deakin

The next pastor at Hope was the Rev. James Deakin. While Macbeth had been fresh out of college, Deakin was at the other end of his career; he was fifty-eight years old and had already served pastorates in three other churches.

James Deakin[114] was born in the village of Preston Brockhurst, where his father was a farmer. He was converted early in life and joined the Independent Church in the nearby town of Shrewsbury. He was led to consider the ministry, and the church recommended him as a student to Rotherham Academy, where he studied 1819-23, a contemporary of Samuel Jackson. He had the same tutors, and lived in the same old-fashioned building close to the Masbro' Church. He was a good student, and in August 1823 he received a call to the pastorate of the Independent Church at Lutterworth, Leicestershire. He seems to have spent less than a year there before accepting a call to the Hollinshead Street Church in Chorley, Lancashire, where he settled in the summer of 1824. He remained in Chorley until 1828, when he moved to Stand Chapel, Manchester. Deakin remained at Stand some twenty-three years. He devoted himself to the congregation, even declining a call from the Church at Dewsbury.

In 1851 he received a call to take the pastorate at Hope, and accepted it. Due to his age and increasing infirmity, Deakin remained at Hope only until 1855, when he retired from the ministry and moved to the village of Egerton, not far from Bolton, Lancashire. There he bought

---

[114] Most of the information about Deakin is taken from his obituary in the *Congregational Yearbook 1881*

a house called Moss Cottage, where he died on 20th May 1880. He was buried in the family vault in Walmsley Churchyard, and a funeral sermon was preached in the Independent Chapel at Egerton by Rev. Robert Gorbutt Leigh of the nearby village of Farnworth. Leigh had been pastor at Egerton 1862-69, and so had been Deakin's pastor for most of the length of his retirement.

Deakin was a committed Calvinist and a lover of the old Puritan and Nonconformist theology. His obituary states, "He was well read in our old Nonconformist theology, and took great pride in his library. His conversation was clear, cheerful, and replete with memories of men whom he had known in his earlier days, and side-by-side with whom he had fought in his master's cause. He was a staunch Nonconformist, a cordial hater of all modern innovations and courageous in the defence of his opinions."[115] He was in other words an old-fashioned pastor-scholar of the early 19th century type.

John Kay

James Deakin was succeeded by Rev. John Kay. Since he had no obituary published by the Congregational Union, little is known about him apart from the outline of his career. Kay had held pastorates in Hinckley, Londonderry and Warrington, and he came to Hope in 1855 from Wycliffe Congregational Church, Warrington.

He took part in the usual activities of a minister of the period. On Thursday 28th May 1857 he was one of the ministers who took part in the ordination of Josiah Hankinson over the Church at Union Street Independent Chapel in Leek. This was a Church formed by a group of seceders from the Derby Street Church in 1829 over a disagreement with the minister, Rev. James Morrow, who had established a private school on the Church premises, effectively shutting out the congregation.[116] The seceders had built a chapel in Union Street, which had become by 1857 the only real Congregational Church in Leek. The main preachers at Hankinson's ordination were Rev. S. Bowen of Macclesfield, Hankinson's old pastor, and Rev. Robert Vaughan, President of the

---
[115] *CYB 1881* P. 370
[116] The full story is told in Woodhouse, *The Story of a Leek Church*

Lancashire Independent College, where Hankinson had studied. Kay was among the three other minsters who took part in the proceedings.[117].

Today we are so used to the idea of the weekly offering taken up on Sunday that it is a surprise to learn that it was only introduced in the 1850s. Prior to this point the income of the Church was derived from a number of sources including seat-rents, subscription and quarterly collections. In about 1856 Kay introduced the weekly collection at Hope Chapel to replace all of these methods of obtaining income. In 1856 he wrote to the *Evangelical Magazine* in reply to questions on the subject, "I have lately taken the opportunity of conversing with the members of the congregation respecting the working of the 'weekly offering'. I am glad to find that, after nearly two years' experience of it, they like it. I have not met with a single exception."[118] This meant that pews were now all free, and people could, within reason, sit where they wanted in the chapel. Of course, then as now the regulars had their own accustomed places.

Kay continued the traditional links with the LMS, and on 12th December 1858 he addressed an LMS meeting in Middlewich.[119] In 1857, the *Evangelical Magazine* recorded that Miss Downs and a Miss Parry from Cobridge, both members at Hope, gave money that they had collected to the North Staffordshire Auxiliary of the LMS. Miss Downs collected £8.10/6d, while Miss Parry collected £2.10/10d.[120]

Kay remained at Hope from 1855 until 1860, when he accepted a call to the Congregational Church at Thirsk. He did not remain long at Thirsk, staying there only 1861-2. In 1862 he moved to Great Ayton, also in the North Riding of Yorkshire and about 30 miles from Thirsk. Neither Kay's date of birth nor the date of his death are known, though he resigned his last known pastorate in 1864.

---

[117] *Evangelical Magazine* 1857 P. 496
[118] *Evangelical Magazine* 1858 P. 496
[119] *Cheshire Observer* 18th December 1858
[120] *Evangelical Magazine* 1857 P. 315

Richard Henry Smith

Perhaps the most interesting of all the pastors to serve at Hope, Rev. Richard Henry Smith, is perhaps best described as a force of nature. His father, also called Richard Henry Smith, was the Congregational minister at Upminster at the time of his birth, and later moved to Marlborough in Wiltshire. Though the son of a minister, Richard Henry was not initially intended for the ministry, but apprenticed to a bookbinder and printer at Bicester. Smith, however, experienced a call to the ministry which he could not ignore, and entered Highbury College to train for the Congregational ministry in about 1840. There he was particularly influenced by the teaching of Rev. John Hensley Godwin, who taught Philosophy, Logic and Biblical Criticism. A former Highbury student himself, Godwin had served as pastor of the Old Meeting-House Congregational church in Norwich for two years before returning to Highbury as Professor of Philosophy.

While many students left the college with a call to a vacant pulpit waiting for them, Smith was one of the small but significant number who did not. While he waited for a call, he took up residence in Brading, Isle of Wight. There was a small Congregational church there, which Smith became involved with. His activities soon led to a call in 1845 from the Church for him to become their pastor; this he readily accepted, even though the church was poor and located on a bad site. It was to be a characteristic of him; Richard Henry Smith never refused a challenge.

Smith was a firm believer in evangelism and education. At the time he became pastor at Brading, the only school in the area was Church of England, and this created difficulties for nonconformists. Pupils were required to learn the Church of England's catechism, and to attend services at the Anglican Church, and which it seems the local Vicar took full advantage of this to try to influence the children of Nonconformist parents to become Anglicans. Smith set himself to rectify to situation, and led a movement to establish a Nonconformist school where the pupils would be taught according to the tenets of their parents' religion. A house was built for the school, with separate houses for a master and mistress. The school became a well-known institution, and served the town for many years. Having built a school, a new chapel and manse followed. The opportunity was taken to move the Church from an obscure location in the village of Brading to a more prominent location in Shanklin, about four miles away. Shanklin was growing as a fashionable resort, full of smart villas. The Isle of Wight had become a popular place for the rich to take holidays since Queen Victoria's purchase of Osborne House as a holiday home in 1845. He secured a prominent location at the centre of the small but growing village for the new chapel.[121]

These were days of friction between the Church of England and the nonconformists, and this led to a situation where the local Vicar, a high-church Anglican, refused to bury a child baptised by Smith on the grounds that a dissenting baptism was, in his view, no baptism at all. Richard Henry Smith was not one to take such action lying down; if the vicar would not bury nonconformists, then he, the Congregational pastor, would bury them. Since he was not allowed to officiate in the Anglican churchyard, he immediately set about obtaining a plot of land for a Nonconformist burial-ground. At the end of his pastorate there, Smith left a flourishing Church and school. This twin emphasis on religion and education was to characterise his ministry.

He left the Isle of Wight in 1850 to take up the pastorate at the Congregational Church in Halesworth, Suffolk. In the event this small, historic market-town did not provide him with the sort of challenge that he relished, and so in 1853 he left and went to Surbiton, Surrey, to start a new church. The growing town presented a definite challenge; not only was there no chapel, but there was not even a public hall or even a room in an inn where a church could meet. Smith solved this difficulty by beginning services in a room in his own house, and later by building a small meeting-room in his garden. His efforts drew support from a number of sources, and soon a small church was formed, and a small chapel built to replace the room in the garden. The church that he founded came to be called Surbiton Park Congregational Church.

Having laid the foundation for the church in Surbiton, in 1860 Smith received a call to the pastorate at Hope. This was a different sort of church again, a large chapel in a working-class district of an industrial

---

[121] The Church, still on the same site, is called Shanklin United Reformed Church today

city, surrounded by the poverty that characterised the Victorian age for the working classes. It was after all in Hope Street, at the other end from the chapel, that Arnold Bennett was born in a flat above a pawnbroker's shop in 1867, and that flat was one of many above the shops in Hope Street, some of which can be seen today across from the church car park. Next to the chapel Sunday school was the Borough Exchange pub, the main place of entertainment for the inhabitants of Hope Street.

In this congenial environment, Smith once again threw himself into the work. He went from church-planter in a London suburb to pastor of a town-centre church almost fifty years old with remarkable ease. He addressed himself in particular to the question of how to reach the working classes of the town; those who worked in the small shops, factories and workshops that surrounded the chapel. One of the devices he set up was a Sunday afternoon lecture for working men, a sort of precursor to the national Pleasant Sunday Afternoon movement that would be founded in the 1870s in West Bromwich. He could not have done any of this successfully alone, but was blessed by a number of deacons who were supportive and other willing workers. Their names we do not know, though it is likely that there was a member of the Downs family among them.

The author of his obituary in the 1885 *Congregational Year Book* wrote: "Mr. Smith's preaching was remarkable for its suggestiveness and great spiritual power. He had formed a high ideal of the Christian life, and he condemned departures from that ideal with a pungency of expression which sometimes gave to his ministry an air of sternness and severity. He had a dread of mere religious conventionalities and mechanical contrivances to secure religious ends, and insisted on the necessity of living by principle, and not by expediency. As a consequence, he attracted many who were repelled by ordinary religious methods, and powerfully influenced for good minds which had been untouched by other agencies."

His concern for the working-classes went far beyond Hanley and the Potteries. The period of his pastorate coincided with the American Civil War and the resulting cotton-shortages in the Lancashire mill towns caused by the Union's blockade of the South. Smith appealed in a special sermon to the church for them to send aid to Lancashire to support those who were out of work because of the shortages. In working-class Church like Hope, this was a powerful appeal not only for working-class solidarity, but also for Nonconformist solidarity, for many of the Lancashire mill-workers were also nonconformists. For an English Congregationalist the American Civil War was a difficult matter; the nonconformists were overwhelmingly opposed to slavery, and yet the cotton which the Lancashire mills relied on was produced in the American South, by slaves. This was a point where radical politics came rather sharply into conflict with the need for work and bread. On the one hand, *Uncle Tom's Cabin* told the pious Nonconformist that slavery was an intolerable evil and the struggle for its abolition a righteous cause, on the other, the war against the slave-owning Southern Confederate states threw thousands of British labourers out of work.

In many ways Richard Henry Smith was ahead of his time; he was doing at Hope in the 1860s what others would rediscover in the 1870s. He was a true pioneer, and left the Church greatly strengthened by his pastorate. Smith was one of the first orthodox Nonconformist ministers to re-discover the power of art; a gifted amateur artist himself, he painted a large picture illustrating one of the parables of Christ every week for the Sunday afternoon meetings, a device to liven up the Bible-study for those who found them dull. He had invented the PSA some fifteen years before the PSA existed. He was a pastor for the working man, and maintained Hope as a working-class Church in a working district.

Smith did not just paint pictures; he realised that the lives of many of the working-classes were degraded and drab. With the town full of smoking pot-banks, buildings black with soot, there was little colour in the lives of the workers. Nor was there much culture available to them; free libraries were still relatively rare, as were workers' institutes where there would be lectures and classes available. Smith believed that Christ cares for the whole person, not just the soul, and therefore he recognised that education and culture was as important in its own way as collections for starving cotton workers. It was while at Hanley that he began to publish a series of popular books on fine art; in these volumes Smith used his interest in the Old Masters to introduce not just the

Gospel, but also culture. The first of these books, published in 1861, was *Expositions of the Cartoons of Raphael*, followed in 1863 by *Expositions of Great Pictures*, and in 1868, after he had left Hanley, *Expositions of Raphael's Bible*. These lectures had the double advantage of exposing working people to the riches of fine art and bringing the Gospel to them pictorially.

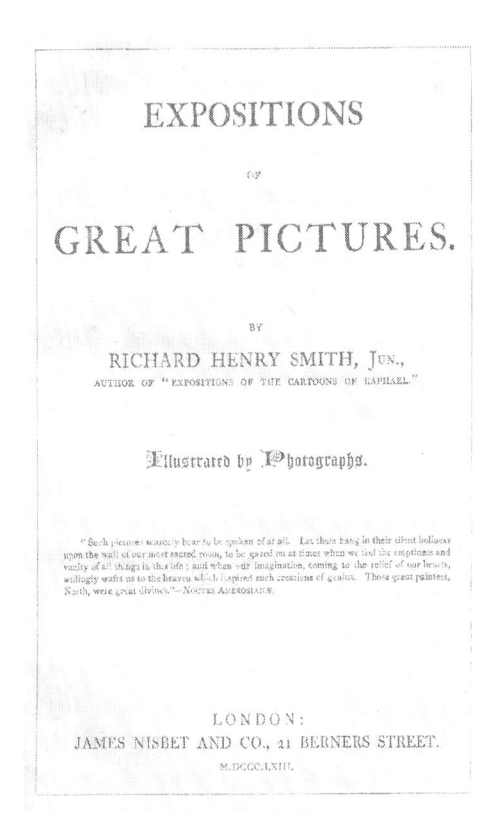

Fig. 8: Title Page of Expositions of Great Pictures

In the preface of *Expositions of Great Pictures*, his second book on art, Smith writes: "The revival and growth of the public interest in Sacred Art has encouraged the Author to continue his comments on Bible Pictures; and he has written, under the conviction, that an expositor may render real service to his fellow-laymen, by offering the results of his long and loving study of the great works of the Great Masters." The reference to "fellow-laymen" is puzzling because he wrote it, Smith was a theological college graduate who had been in the pastoral ministry for over fifteen years, and only the Anglican vicar on the Isle of Wight and those like him would have considered him a 'layman' in any sense. Perhaps it shows that even the new-found "public interest in Sacred Art" had not yet rendered it quite acceptable for a minister to publish on the subject. It says something for the deacons at Hope that they supported a man whose ideas about outreach were so radical. No doubt the fact that his new departures attracted the working classes had something to do with it, but it gives the lie to the caricature of the conservative deacons who sat on every attempt to innovate. In general, in fact, deacons supported their pastor so long as he respected them, and Smith certainly respected the Hanley deacons. He must have, otherwise they would not have approved of a man who published books that were regarded as not quite proper for a Congregational pastor.

The books themselves mixed history, art-criticism and Biblical teaching. They contained photographs of engravings of the pictures under discussion, followed by a discussion of the picture itself in its historical context. Other pictures would be brought in, and something of the life and career of the artist mentioned. Finally the meaning of the picture would be brought out, the Biblical story explained, and the practical implications given. One gets the impression that these 'expositions' began their lives as lectures given in the old chapel in Hanley, aimed at bringing art and the Gospel together. The fact that these were pictures based on the Bible certainly made it easier for Smith to talk about them; purely secular art would have been frowned on as an unsuitable interest for an evangelical minister. So, writing on 'La Madonna Della Seggiola', he says something about the Roman Catholic veneration of Mary, and then brings in Christ as the corrective; "As we come unto God by Him, weary and heavy laden, we have the greatest confidence and comfort in the compassionate intercession of our merciful and faithful High Priest. As our Mediator, He is, as in everything else, all and in all. His advocacy with the Father leaves nothing to be desired. The worship of the Virgin is superfluous."[122] While

---

[122] Smith, Richard Henry, *Expositions of Great Pictures* (London, 1863), P. 11

the audience of Smith's lectures on paintings would have come away informed about art, they would also have come away better-informed about the Bible and Christianity. In his obituary we read: " He used art as a means of preaching as well as the pulpit."

Smith continued the Nonconformist tradition of educating the masses. While on the Isle of Wight that had taken the form of opening a school for nonconformists, in Hanley, which was already well-provided with schools, it took the form of teaching adults about art. By the Victorians, education was seen not only as the imparting of information, but the forming of character. The Victorian Nonconformist would have looked askance at the idea that education can ever be 'values' neutral'; the imparting of values was a central part of education for him, and in that he was wiser than we are today. The fact is that education always imparts values, even when it is not meant to. The Victorians, in explicitly seeking to inculcate Christian values in teaching, were wiser than we are when we think that teaching can be done without imparting any values at all.

Forming character meant more than teaching morality; it meant teaching an appreciation for the true, the real and the beautiful. Of course the Bible took the first place; the Authorised Version of 1611, commonly called simply "the English Bible" in the period, was regarded as one of the pre-eminent monuments of English. The Victorian Congregational historian Dr. John Stoughton wrote of it: "There can be no reasonable doubt that the pre-eminence which distinguishes the history of England among the states of Europe for the last three hundred years is to be attributed largely to the wide circulation of this volume, and the Bible-reading habits of the people. It has proved a pillar of strength, bearing up and giving stability to public and private virtue – to patriotism, loyalty, obedience, and domestic affection. It is a fountain of light and love, illuminating the intellect and purifying the heart."[123] Obviously the patriotism that Stoughton referred to was not a mere slavish obedience to government, for the Liberals and their Nonconformist allies were at the forefront of political reform, but it meant seeking the good of the nation. If the Bible was the book that made England great, then all Englishmen and women ought to read it.

---

[123] John Stoughton, *Our English Bible* (London, no date) Pp. 258-9

Where Smith departed from the older nonconformists was in teaching the ennobling power of religious art. The older Puritans, like the Calvinist Reformers, banished art from the Churches, though not from the home. There had however grown up a view among some evangelicals that pictures of Biblical subjects were not really proper. There are still many Evangelicals for whom a picture of Jesus is, at least potentially, a breach of the Second Commandment; Smith would not agree. As new engraving techniques had brought art within the reach of even the poor, cheap prints of Biblical scenes and subjects like 'The Good Shepherd' became widely available and came to decorate many a poor family's home. Art was ennobling as far as it conveyed truth; the best art was "addressed... to the mind, rather than the eye,"[124] It was not simply a pleasing picture, but it made the viewer think. Raphael's *Transfiguration*, for example, would convey to the educated mind, the message of "our deliverance from evil by a *divine* redeemer."[125] And the educated mind was not the mind of a person of a superior class educated at public school and university, but the mind of a working man educated in an urban chapel on Sunday afternoon. Smith's meetings and those like them were a sort of little university for the workers, a mutual improvement class as well as a Church service.

Bringing his message to the working people of Hanley, Smith insisted on the *ordinariness* of the Bible characters. While Jesus is the divine redeemer of men, he was a true human being, and the people he mixed with were *ordinary*, working men and women like the Hanley congregation. The picture he chose for the Virgin Mary in his little art gallery, *La Madonna Della Seggiola* was chosen precisely because in it Mary was not depicted as an ethereal, otherworldly saint, but as a pretty young woman, an ordinary human being like them. "It reminds us that we are the children of God, and that our Saviour was the Son of Man,"[126] he explained. "It preaches to us in a language which we can all understand, the Fatherhood of God and the thorough humanity of our Saviour, by placing before us a child upon a mother's knee."[127] This insistence on the humanity of Jesus and the reality and ordinariness of the Biblical history certainly tried to bring Palestine to Hanley, and it

---
[124] Smith, *Expositions of Great Pictures* P. 15
[125] Smith, *Expositions of Great Pictures,*. P. 16
[126] Smith, *Expositions of Great Pictures,* P. 6
[127] Smith, *Expositions of Great Pictures,* P. 7

told the working people who sat in the free seats in Hope Congregational Church that they mattered to God. This is perhaps one of the great benefits of Congregationalism; evangelical preaching, joined with the fact that the labourer in the kiln had the same authority as his employer in the Church meeting, conveyed the great truth that "In Christ there is neither Jew nor Gentile, bond nor free."

Although much has been written about the Victorian era which caricatures evangelical preaching as "hell-fire and brimstone", probably a more accurate description of it is given by D. Basil Martin, when he writes of the preaching he heard as a boy in the 1860s, "The fact is that although the doctrine of an everlasting hell was preached and accepted... All the emphasis was laid on the love of God in providing a way of escape. The leading theme was the sacrifice of Christ. Over and over again I was told how the Son of God had left the happy mansions above, and the company of holy angels, and had come down to earth to suffer and die on the cross in order that I, a little boy named Basil, living nineteen hundred years later, might be saved from sin and misery. The doctrine of hell was a dark background on which was painted a lovely picture of heavenly bliss. I often wonder whether there will ever be anything else which can excite the same sense of gratitude and devotion."[128]

Smith also took a keen interest in children's work, for which his artistic talents and interest in art were well suited, writing a number of illustrated children's books including one of family worship. He contributed works to *Little Children's Hymns and Songs*, and *The Sunday Magazine*. In the slums of Hanley, little children were expected to go to work early, in the pot-banks or the mines, to contribute their own share to the often meagre family finances. An illustrated book as a Sunday-school prize would have been a treasured possession, and a book of family worship with attractive pictures would have been very welcome.

The five years that Richard Henry Smith spent at Hope were

---

[128] D. Basil Martin, *An Impossible Parson* (London, 1934) Pp. 16-17. This is all the more striking, since Martin, the son of a Congregational minister in Oxford, after holding Congregational pastorates became a Unitarian. His son, Kingsley Martin, was editor of *The New Statesman and Nation*.

very productive. A call to plant a new Church in Gospel Oak fields, Hampstead, however, drew him away and back to pioneer work. The man who loved a challenge would remain at Gospel Oak until his retirement in 1881, which was forced on him by declining health. He hoped to spend several years in writing and itinerant preaching following his retirement, but it was not to be. A stroke in October 1883 caused widespread paralysis, and a second stroke in March of 1884 worsened things considerably. He suffered greatly, and died on the 13th of November; his last words were, "It is all right!"

Chapter 7: David Horne

Smith's successor was to be the longest-serving pastor of the church in the 19th century, though his obituary suggests that a lack of drive to get a 'better' pastorate may have had something to do with that. The Rev. David Horne was a quite different character from his artistic and pioneering predecessor; a quiet, rather shy and studious man, Horne was born in Keighley, Yorkshire, in September 1828. His parents were from Largo Bay, in Scotland, and his mother was a friend of the Scottish missionary Robert Moffatt, who always made a point of visiting her when he was in England. Moffatt owed a great deal to her family, and the great missionary's connection with the family must have made David quite familiar with the importance of mission.

David was educated at Keighley, and his intellectual ability resulted in his becoming a pupil-teacher at Alnwick College, a private Nonconformist school run by Mr. Blyth, the Congregational pastor at Alnwick. It was while away from home that his thoughts were turned towards the ministry as a future vocation, but before he was able to express these thoughts to anyone he was called back to Keighley to take up a teaching post in the school where he had been educated. After two years teaching in his home town, he entered Airedale College, located at Undercliffe. near Bradford, to study for the ministry.

Airedale College was one of two Congregational colleges in Yorkshire, the other being Rotherham. Airedale began in 1756 with the old Heckmondwike Academy; the first in Yorkshire to be intended solely for theological education. The tutor was the Rev. James Scott. Following his death in 1783, it was transferred to Northowram under the care of Rev. Samuel Walker. Walker was not gifted as a tutor, and the old Academy was closed in 1794. The four remaining students were placed with Rev. William Vint, pastor of the Congregational Church at Idle, near Bradford, to complete their training. While the intention was for them to finish training and then for Vint to return to ordinary pastoral work, Vint actually proved to be a good tutor, took on more students and thus founded the rather unfortunately-named Idle Academy (though Idle students were never allowed to be idle, for Vint was a great believer in hard work). In 1834 the institution was moved to a new site just outside Bradford and renamed Airedale College. While the students at Idle had boarded out, the new building was a residential college with studies and bedrooms for the students.

In common with other Congregational colleges, Airedale College was not intended to make preachers, but to improve them, and so there was a rule that no student would be accepted who did not have experience as a preacher. This meant that every candidate had to prepare a sermon to read for the committee. The building itself was an impressive structure; Rev. James S. Drummond, who studied at Airedale almost twenty years later, described it, "Airedale College was an old rambling building, standing on top of a hill overlooking the city of Bradford."[129] When Horne entered the College, the "rambling building" was not quite so old, having been built in 1831, but it was certainly rambling. Built to the designs of John Clark of Leeds, in the Greek style with a large central portico, it has been likened to Emily Bronte's fictional Wuthering Heights.

Fig. 8: Airedale College, Bradford

---

[129] James S. Drummond, *Charles A. Berry, D.D.* (London, 1899) P. 16

When David Horne began his studies at Airedale, the teaching staff consisted of three professors; Rev. Walter Scott, the Principal, Rev. Henry Brown Creake and Rev. Daniel Fraser. As the Theological Tutor, Scott taught theology, Homiletics, Hebrew, German, Old and New Testament, and Church History; Creake taught Mathematics and Philosophy, and Fraser taught Classics. Scott in particular had a reputation for working his students hard, though never harder than he worked himself. His son, Caleb Scott, later principal at Lancashire, was a fellow-student of Horne at Airedale. Scott's conservatism is apparent in the fact that he published a book arguing for the existence of evil spirits and another in favour of the death penalty for murder. His successor, Rev. Daniel Fraser, wrote of him, "Strong and vigorous in body and mind, there was less manifestation of sympathy and tenderness in his manner than could sometimes have been desired."[130]

The division of labour at Airedale highlights the great drawback of the Congregational Colleges in the Victorian era; subjects that in the Universities were divided between several professors were all taught by one man. Although some were remarkably gifted teachers, most were very able in one department only; in Scott's case he was primarily a preacher. In a college that was expressly intended to prepare men for the pastoral ministry, this was not a great handicap, and the historian of the College in the 1950s observed that "He produced many good preachers and good ministers."[131] Airedale's three tutors were an advance on Idle's single tutor, and allowed the students to be involved in more academic study. Still, the course offered was regarded by some as lacking in scholarship. As long as students had to study arts courses at the Congregational theological colleges, the situation would continue.

Scott, a gifted preacher, sought to gather a church connected with the college where he could continue to preach and where students also preached. Located on the Undercliffe side of Bradford, this church, called the College Chapel, was the scene, on Sunday afternoons, of weekly sermons delivered by students before Scott and a special congregation. These sermons would be discussed in the homiletics classes during the week.

---

[130] Quoted in K.W. Wadsworth, *Yorkshire United Independent College* (London, 1954) P. 112
[131] Wadsworth, P. 113

The course at Airedale was supposed to be adapted for the London BA. While not all students took the degree, Horne did. The London BA, as a recognised academic degree, gave an academic respectability to the course, though some felt that it had the disadvantage of distracting from the more theological part of the course and leading the tutors to "teach to the test". The suggestion raises a smile when we consider that the same is said about the effects of school league tables today. Scott's successor, Daniel Fraser, discouraged students from taking the London degree because he felt it had a negative effect on their ministerial studies; the aim of the college was, he maintained, to train preachers, not to produce men with degrees.

At his graduation from Airedale, Horne was called to Lower Chapel Congregational Church in the Yorkshire town of Heckmondwike. Lower Chapel was the lesser of two Congregational causes in the town, and the sort of church where a student recently graduated would expect to begin his career. The people at the church loved him, and it was here that he met and married the daughter of one of his Congregationalist neighbours, Rev. James Potter of Honley.

Heckmondwike had another attraction for the studious young pastor; it was the home of the Heckmondwike Lectures, an annual occasion that dated from the days of the old Academy in the town. It had its origins in an attempt to keep the disruption to the work of the Academy from visitors to a minimum; rather than visitors being allowed to come to the Academy during the normal course of the sessions, it was decided to set aside a day for supporters of the Academy to come together; this combined an open day with a series of public lectures. Although the Academy moved on, the Lectures had become a major event in the life of the town, and continued, with students now brought in from Airedale. Having begun as a single day, the Lectures eventually came to occupy a whole week of preaching and special meetings. They were held at Upper Chapel, and students at Airedale were expected to attend. The Lectures were so popular that special trains were laid on to take people there, and students from Manchester took advantage of the opportunity.

Two years at Heckmondwike were followed by five years at Villiers Street chapel in Sunderland, another happy ministry, this time in an industrial city. From Sunderland Horne was called to the very similar Richmond chapel in Salford, where he remained for just a few years before his call to Hanley in 1865. It was to be his last move before his retirement, for he found in the Potteries a home and a sphere of ministry that was most congenial to him. The industrial towns and cities of England were the main power-base for Congregationalism, and it was there that their most prestigious pastorates were located. It was no accident that Airedale College was located just outside the rapidly expanding industrial town of Bradford. Many of the industrialists and factory owners responsible for the wealth of these cities were Nonconformists, and these funded large and wealthy chapels as well as backing the colleges. Both Leeds and Bradford had many Congregational chapels, several seating almost 2000 people.

While he was never a man who drew crowds like the great men of the Victorian pulpit, David Horne was a thoughtful preacher, and his obituary admits that "There was, indeed, a subtle, metaphysical strain in his mind that perhaps necessarily limited the range of his influence." He seems to have been the only one of the Hope pastors to have had a tendency towards the liberal theology that was growing in popularity in the period, "While faithful to evangelical truth, he breathed the atmosphere of modern thought," says his obituary.[132] He lectured on one occasion on 'Darwinism and Evolution', drawing a large audience, and probably attempted in some way to synthesize Darwin and the Bible. Although the popular modern narrative is that the Churches violently rejected Darwin, in fact the evidence is that on the whole Darwinian evolution, agreeing as it did with the Victorian emphasis on progress, was fairly quickly assimilated into theology and did not undermine faith as much as atheists might like to think it did. It did however introduce a weakness into popular theology; if progress was not inevitable after all, popular Christianity would fall with the myth of progress.

Like many shy and scholarly men, David Horne was at his best among friends, and loved to discuss the theological topics of the day with them. At the same time, this was the era of the university extension

---

[132] *CYB 1906*

movement, and the era when lectures on Darwinism could draw packed audiences to lecture halls and chapels. Victorian Nonconformity was beginning to feel the need of a more educated ministry, and so a scholarly pastor like David Horne was an asset.

David Horne was the uncle of Rev. Charles Silvester Horne, who became a famous Congregational leader, and champion of the Pleasant Sunday Afternoon movement. One of Silvester Horne's hymns, 'Sing We the King Who is Coming to Reign' is in the new *Christian Hymns* book[133]. Since he grew up at Newport, Shropshire, it is practically certain that the young Charles Silvester Horne worshipped in Hope Chapel on some occasions during his uncle's ministry, and perhaps his thoughts were in part turned to the ministry by his uncle's words and example.

Although on the whole David Horne's ministry at Hope was both long and happy, his time at Hanley was also marked by personal tragedy. His first wife died on July 22nd 1868,[134] and both his children by that marriage died during his pastorate at Hope. His son had joined the Indian Civil Service and had just begun a very promising career when he died in India, while his unmarried daughter died in Hanley. Horne married a second time, to a Miss Wollaston, of Shrewsbury, in 1870, and also had a son and daughter by her, both of whom survived him.

Horne very nearly lost his own life in what came to be known as "The Hanley Tragedy" of 1881. On Wednesday February 2nd, 1881, an actor called Mr. Siddons was returning from Hanley, where he had been performing in a play, along Bucknall New Road. It was a dark, foggy night, and the actor was horrified to discover, lying across the pavement, the body of a man. The dead man wore the garb of a Nonconformist minister; the cause of death was quite obviously a nasty head-wound. The police were called, and they found a hat and umbrella lying in the road. These did not belong to the dead man, who was identified as Rev. Thomas Cocker of the Congregational Church in Copeland Street, Stoke-upon-Trent, but bore the name of Rev. David Horne. Going to Horne's house in Birch Terrace, they found him with a serious head injury, and unable to recall what had happened that night.

---

[133] Number 481
[134] *The Christian Witness and Congregational Magazine* 1868 P. 432

When the news became known the local rumour-mill went wild, as can be imagined. The first report of the incident suggested that the two men had been attacked by some unknown person or persons, who had killed Mr. Cocker and almost killed Mr. Horne.[135] A second rumour began when it was noted that Mr. Horne had been instructed to keep the police informed of his movements. While this was in fact simply so that he was available for the inquest, local rumour turned this into Horne being "under police surveillance"[136], and from this was evolved a rumour that the two men were suspected of having got into a fight that ended in Cocker's death. Being both lurid and violent, this speculation spread widely.

The facts were much less sensational; the two men were in fact the victims of an accident caused by negligence on the part of the council. Once Mr. Horne had recovered enough to be able to make a statement, he cleared up everything. He and Mr. Cocker had been at dinner at the home of a mutual friend in Northwood, and had stayed long into the night discussing the Revised Version of the Bible, at the time a great topic of conversation in religious circles. Mr. Cocker was intending to give a paper on the subject, and so the three men talked about the matter into the night. At midnight the two ministers left the house to walk home. They missed their way in the fog, and instead of joining Bucknall New Road as they intended to do, they turned down the now-vanished West Street.

West Street was located roughly where the footbridge on Bucknall New Road is today. As today, the level of Bucknall Old Road was considerably higher than Bucknall New Road at this point. Rather than a bridge, however, West Street in 1881 ended abruptly in what the *Sentinel* described as "A sharp descent of broken ground, at the bottom of which there is a dead wall, and a sheer drop of about ten feet down to the pavement." There was no barrier of any kind to prevent people going over the edge. While a number of accidents had happened there in the past, this was the first that resulted in a fatality. The newspaper went on to report that "Mr. Horne, being a strong-limbed, robust man, barely

---

[135] *Staffordshire Sentinel*, February 5th 1881
[136] *Staffordshire Advertiser*, February 5th 1881

escaped death; Mr. Cocker, the more fragile and delicately constituted, died from the shock." Medical evidence supported this, and the verdict of the inquest was accidental death. The blame lay squarely with the council, which, the *Sentinel* reporter stated, "allows one of the streets of the borough to be nothing else than a fatal trap and pit-fall for the unwary pedestrian."[137] It expressed the hope that "The public of Hanley will be indignant that what seems to be a culpable negligence should have occasioned such a terrible calamity, and will no longer tolerate" such a state of affairs. "Human wisdom will be asserted in its usual method of taking precaution when it is too late and the precipice will be railed in. But it will be long before this tragic incident is forgotten."

Cocker's death must have affected Horne deeply. Thomas Cocker was one of his few very close friends; the two men had both come to the Potteries in 1865, and it seems that they shared many of the same interests. Both were scholars who took a keen interest in the thought of the day, both churches were located in town centres, surrounded by poverty, and both men worked hard to draw people into the churches over which they were pastors as well as taking an interest in the wider life of the Potteries. Born in Ashton-under-Lyne in 1840, Cocker was converted under the ministry of J. Guinness Rogers at Albion Chapel. He came to the Copeland Street Congregational Church in Stoke straight from his course at the Lancashire College. Horne, having been in the ministry for some six years already, would have been able to support Cocker and encourage him in the early, difficult years at Copeland Street before the church recovered some of its strength and the work became a little easier. The *Sentinel* recorded that, "For sixteen years the deceased minister has spent himself, sacrificing all personal aims, in the endeavour to build up the Congregational Church at Stoke. He has been snatched away at the moment when his labours were crowned with success, when the Church and school buildings were paid for, and every part of the organisation freed from debt."[138] Cocker had also served on the Stoke-on-Trent School Board. With Cocker's death, Horne lost a man who was a very close support to him, and who would have helped him after the loss of his first wife.

---

[137] *Staffordshire Sentinel*, February 5th 1881
[138] *Staffordshire Sentinel*, February 5th 1881

As is often the case, the tragedy that befell David Horne drew out the very real affection of the Church and the town towards him. The *Sentinel* reported on February 15th that "On Thursday afternoon a deputation waited on the Rev. David Horne, at his residence, Hanley, to present to him the following letter of sympathy: - 'To the Rev. David Horne, M.A., Hanley. - Hanley, February 12th 1881. - Reverend and dear Sir, - We, the members of your Church and congregation, together with other friends and fellow-townsmen, as undersigned, take the present opportunity of expressing to you our affectionate regard and esteem. The late sad disaster which has deprived you and us of the presence of a dear friend, and which has inflicted on yourself most serious physical injuries, and, as we fear, even greater mental suffering, impels us to assure you of our deep sympathy in this overwhelming trial. We pray that the Divine consolation which you have so often imparted to others in the long course of your ministry may be abundantly granted to you now, and that you may be speedily restored to perfect health and strength, and spared for many years of increasing usefulness."[139] The report went on to say that, "The reverend gentleman, although recovering from the effects of his recent accident, appeared greatly shattered and enfeebled by the bodily and mental suffering which he has endured." He was forced to take a prolonged absence from the pulpit to recover his mental and physical health, but did eventually return to his pulpit at Hope.

David Horne laboured on for a few years after the accident, but it was increasingly clear that he was going to have to retire. He seems to have been the only pastor in the history of the Church who planned his retirement in advance and took charge of the work of finding a successor for him. The result was that there was a swift and orderly transition. He remained in the pastorate until 1886, and so in October 1885 he was at the meetings of the Congregational Union in Hanley. In particular he would not have missed the paper by Principal A.M. Fairbairn of Spring Hill College, Birmingham on *The Sacerdotal and the Puritan Idea*[140] read before the Union in the Tabernacle.

---

[139] *Staffordshire Sentinel* February 15th 1881
[140] The paper was later reprinted in Fairbairn, *Studies in Religion and Theology* (London, 1910) Pp. 109-141

It is almost impossible for us today to realise the optimism that reigned among the delegates who gathered from all over England and Wales for the October meetings of the Congregational Union in 1885. Looking back, we realise that the 1885 Assembly was in some ways a high watermark of Congregationalism. Fairbairn was about to lead the Congregational invasion of Oxford as the first Principal of Mansfield College. He had already revolutionized Horne's old College at Airedale, abolishing the arts courses and making it purely a theological college. He had now just been appointed to lead Spring Hill College as it moved to the seat of the oldest English University. It was to be the flagship Nonconformist College; a purely theological institution headed by one of the greatest Nonconformist scholars of the age. The relocated institution was to be named Mansfield College, after the family who had given the Spring Hill Estate to be used as a theological College back in the 1830s.

Fairbairn's paper was not only a manifesto for the College he was leading to Oxford, but for Congregationalism as it entered the last quarter of the 19th century. "In England today two opposed conceptions of the Christian church stand face to face... According to the one conception the Church is an organised society, with a political constitution it owes to its Founder and his apostles – visible, historical, a veritable corporate divine state, so instituted and guided of God as to be possessed of divine authority and invested with divine rights. According to the other conception, the Church is the kingdom of God, or of the truth, created and governed directly by Christ, composed of his saints, with vassals, but without princes, civil or ecclesiastical... On the one theory certain offices and orders are held to be so necessary to the very being of the Church, that where they are not it cannot be, and where they are they represent a regulated and continuous succession which has, through the centuries, been the chosen channel for the transmission of Apostolic grace; but on the other theory there are no official sanctities, no inalienable orders, no persons that must be, in order that Christ may be, in his Church. All depends on the indwelling Spirit, and the truth he reveals, in order that it may be preached by pure and spiritual men."[141] These were the battle lines; between the Sacerdotal, represented by Catholicism, Roman and Anglican, and the Puritan, as represented by the Nonconformists, and particularly Congregationalism. "Sacerdotalism

---

[141] Fairbairn, Pp. 109-10

makes the worship of God depend on its own institutions and modes, and on the ministers it creates and controls. Puritanism believes that spirit and truth are the only things essential to worship, and godliness the mode in which God most loves to be honoured."[142]

Though Fairbairn was a Scotsman, he identified himself completely with English Congregationalism, "We who are sons are also heirs of the historical Puritanism of England; and our position creates our responsibilities and defines and enforces our duties."[143] What were these duties? "At the very moment when the Providence of God has so ruled our history as to leave us free to realise our characteristic religious idea, we are confronted with its very antithesis – a resurgent Sacerdotalism."[144] Sacerdotalism, he went on to explain, is ecclesiological – it regards the Church as central. On the other hand, Puritanism is theological; the centre is the doctrine of God in Christ, not the doctrine of the Church. The Congregationalists were therefore to *be* theological, "Our work... to be effective, must be creative, not controversial."[145] As the Anglo-Catholics made so much of the Church and of the Bishop, the Congregational Churches must make much of Christ, "Over against their doctrine of the sacraments place the faith in the personal and reigning Christ."[146] Where the Anglo-Catholics made much of the priesthood of the clergy, the Congregationalists must make much of the priesthood of all believers. The false had to be counter-acted by the true, the traditions of the Anglo-Catholics by the teachings of the Bible.

The Puritan ideal had no place for the Sacerdotal priest; it rather needed ministers trained in the interpretation of the Bible, the history of the Church and the science of theology, to teach the people their true high calling. "If we believe in our mission, we must not leave its fulfilment to chance; we must make it our special concern, and work like men who mean to have their idea realised. If the Sacerdotal idea is to be superseded, it must be by an idea sublimer, truer, and more spiritual, and so our need is men who not only believe this idea, but are able so to present it as to win to faith and obedience our cynical and sceptical age.

---

[142] Fairbairn P. 110
[143] Fairbairn, P. 110
[144] Fairbairn, P. 117
[145] Fairbairn, P. 137
[146] Fairbairn, P. 138

You know what is meant; on the ministry of the next generation the future of our Congregational Churches depends."[147] And that was where Fairbairn's new work in Oxford came in.

The address was received with frantic applause, and R.W. Dale, who was chairing the meeting, turned to Fairbairn on the platform and said, "There now, you have built Mansfield College, top-stone and all."[148] He had certainly given a good rationale for the institution, and the College got off to a good start on the address. But in truth, Mansfield never lived up to its promise; like Congregationalism as a whole, by the end of the 19th century it really had no distinctive message to bring, no prophetic voice in a changing world.[149] Though he called for the Church to bring truth to bear against error, Fairbairn was regarded by many of his students as rather weak on the positive side of his own teaching. But all this was ahead and unknown in that hopeful autumn of 1885.

Though the main meetings were held in the newly-built Tabernacle Church with its soaring spire and sanctuary seating over 1000, one of the sectional meetings was held in Hope. On the afternoon of the 7th of October the Rev. James Paterson Gledstone of Streatham Hill Congregational Church spoke at Hope on the subject 'Home in its Relation to Social Purity'. In the course of his address he concentrated on the importance of a Christian upbringing for children, and the beneficial effects this would have on society.[150] It was all quite positive, and indeed in many ways the best years of Congregationalism were still ahead.

1885 was also the year that the Staffordshire Congregational Union was re-organised and reconstituted, with David Horne as a founding member. At the second annual Assembly in 1886 the Union recorded his retirement in the following words:

"Rev. D. Horne, B.A., who ministered to the Hope Church at Hanley for nearly twenty-one years, and who,

---

[147] Fairbairn, P. 140
[148] Sir Albert Peel: *These Hundred Years* (London, 1931), P. 293
[149] For Mansfield, see Elaine Kaye, *Mansfield College Oxford* (Oxford, 1996) and Johnson, *The Dissolution of Dissent*
[150] Report in the *Birmingham Daily Post* 8th October 1885. Gledstone was the author of a biography of George Whitefield

during that time won the respect and esteem of his brethren, whether ministerial or lay, by his varied gifts, his genial disposition, and his sterling Christian worth, deemed it his duty to resign his charge."[151]

Though it is couched in the typical language of Victorian sentimentality, there is a very real appreciation for the man there. He was certainly a popular preacher, and perhaps the accident in 1881 that nearly cost him his life increased that appreciation.

David Horne did not immediately leave Hanley, but remained in his home in Birch Terrace for a while to help his successor settle in. By 1887 he was living in Alsager, where he had been asked to take the temporary oversight of the Congregational Church after Rev. William Richard Attwood had left to take up a pastorate at Correy, Pennsylvania. Horne helped the church through the transition and no doubt helped to find a new pastor in the person of Rev. Joseph Fry, who had been a pastor in Berkshire. Following Mr. Fry's settlement, Horne retired to Bowdon, Altrincham, then as now a leafy suburb, and then a popular retirement location for nonconformists; the Rev. William Chambers of the Congregational Church in Newcastle-Under-Lyme had already retired there in 1870. Horne became a member of the prestigious Bowdon Downs Congregational Church, and no doubt took as full a part in the life of the church as he was able. Rev. Alexander Mackennal had been pastor at Bowdon Downs since 1879, and remained pastor there until his death in 1902.[152] The Church also maintained a number of mission stations and branch Churches, in the Manchester suburbs and in the Cheshire countryside. Surrounded by intelligent and often wealthy Congregationalists, and with continued outlets for his considerable abilities, David Horne passed a happy retirement. His last years were however full of pain, and his obituary records that his death on December 23rd 1904 was "after long suffering."[153] The funeral was at Bowdon Downs Church.

---

[151] *Report* P. 22
[152] For Mackennal, see D. MacFadyen, *Alexander Mackennal, B.A., D.D., Life and Letters* (London, 1905)
[153] *Congregational Yearbook 1906* P. 217

Chapter 8: William Lansdell

David Horne led the church in their search for a successor. Alongside him would have been a man who had been chosen as a deacon, Mr. William Bennett. Bennett was an earthenware manufacturer who operated the Cleveland Works in College Road, Shelton, close to St. Mark's Church. He seems to have been one of the leading men in the Church, and his contributions to the Staffordshire Congregational Union were often the largest single contribution from any individual at Hope.

The church would have considered a number of men, both those already in the pastorate and college students. We do not know how many students came to "preach with a view" at Hope, but it is reasonable to suppose that students from Airedale and Rotherham as well as Lancashire and the London colleges would have occupied the pulpit under the critical eye of the diaconate.

When there is a succession in a church the church is likely to go in one of two directions; on the one hand they may look for a man who is a like their old pastor as possible, or on the other a man entirely unlike him. Perhaps it is an indication of how beloved David Horne was that the church chose a man who was quite similar to the retiring pastor, though a student and not an experienced minister.

The choice of the Church at Hope fell on Mr. William Lansdell. Born in the City of Norwich on September 26th 1859, his parents were Congregationalists and attended Princes Street Congregational Church, the leading Congregational cause in the city. The young Lansdell had been converted under the preaching of Rev. Dr. George S. Barrett, the church's distinguished and influential pastor. Barrett had come to Princes Street as a student straight from college in 1866 and had rapidly become as influential as his predecessor John Alexander.[154] Three times chairman of the Norfolk Congregational Union, Barrett earned the nickname "The

---

[154] Colman: *Prince's Street Congregational Church*

Nonconformist Bishop of East Anglia."[155] He was involved in the reformation of Free Church worship as well; when Barrett came to Princes Street the singing was, as in most other Nonconformist places of worship, led by a precentor who would set the pitch with a tuning fork. In 1860 a harmonium was introduced into the Church, and in 1875 a magnificent pipe organ. Barrett was in the lead in the use of musical accompaniment; other churches were content to remain without accompaniment for many more years.[156] He also sought to introduce a more reverent attitude in worship. In the 1860s the attitude of the congregation in prayer was decidedly varied, "The men of the congregation mostly stood, turning with their backs to the pulpit; children knelt on the seat or on a hassock; the women were rather free lances, many of them sat bolt upright, others, more reverent, leaned forward on their book rails."[157] Barrett introduced a uniform tradition of kneeling in prayer.

This concern for worship reached to hymn books as well. Dr. Watts' book was still a standard in Congregational churches, and although a new book was introduced in 1859, it was still dominated by Isaac Watts' compositions, and began with 250 psalm versions, mostly taken from Watts' paraphrases of the Psalms. When this book became too outdated to continue in use, the Congregational Union of England and Wales turned to Dr. Barrett for an editor. The book he produced, *The Congregational Church Hymnal*, contained not only 775 hymns drawn from a wide variety of authors ancient and modern, but also a selection of litanies, chants and anthems for churches with more sophisticated musical tastes. Authors of hymns ranged from the 4th century Latin Father Ambrose of Milan to Horatius Bonar, still living at the time the book was issued. Hymns came from men and women of all Churches, from the high Anglican Sabine Baring-Gould to the Quaker John Greenleaf Whittier, from John Henry Cardinal Newman to the 18th century High Calvinist Joseph Hart. Nor were the hymns all from the English speaking world; German writers were very largely represented. The book was a great success, and received much praise.

---

[155] *CYB 1917* P. 163
[156] Colman, Pp. 52-3. The present author personally witnessed the introduction of an electric organ into a small Baptist chapel that had never had musical accompaniment before, in about 2005.
[157] Colman, P. 52

Fig. 9: Rev. G.S. Barrett

Barrett was a theological conservative; his obituary records, "the central theme of his preaching was ever the atoning work of his Lord, and whatever might be the text of his sermon he seldom, if ever, closed it without a personal appeal for fuller service to those who were already servants of the Lord Jesus Christ, and for those who knew Him not to make the great decision and yield their lives to Him."[158] "Dr. Barrett was a great believer in a definite creed of faith."

This, then, was the man who was William Lansdell's pastor, and through whom he was brought to Christ and to a decision to enter the Congregational ministry. The English universities were still closed to Nonconformists, and not being from a professional background, Lansdell was apprenticed to an engineer. Though he was a diligent apprentice, Lansdell was a studious young man, and after serving his apprenticeship, he took the London BA degree. Sensing a call to the Christian ministry,

---
[158] *CYB 1917* P. 163

he approached Dr. Barrett for advice as to what he should do. Barrett agreed that the young man was a suitable candidate for the ministry, and, being a graduate of the Lancashire Independent College, Manchester, he directed Lansdell to that institution for training.

When Lansdell entered the Lancashire College in 1880, it had recently been expanded to provide more accommodation for students and teaching space, creating among other things a magnificent assembly-hall for examinations, worship and other important events. The president and theological tutor was David Horne's old class-mate Caleb Scott, quite probably a factor in students from Lancashire coming to Hope to preach as prospective successors to Horne. Scott was in his theology quite conservative, but in other ways he was quite radical; he was an advocate of university education for women, and his daughter Charlotte was a mathematician and one of the great women scholars of her day.

The other tutors at Whalley Range were George Lyon Turner, who taught Philosophy and Church History and Alexander Thomson, a conservative scholar who combined teaching with the pastorate of Rusholme Road Congregational Church. It is recorded that Thomson, who taught Old Testament and Hebrew, kept the college's copy of Wellhausen's *Prolegomena to the History of Israel* in his study so that no student would be corrupted by its radical destructive criticism.[159] Finally James Muscutt Hodgson, formerly pastor at Uttoxeter, taught 'science of religion' and apologetics. Lansdell, described as a studious man seems to have profited from his time at Lancashire, and at the end of his course received the A.T.S. Diploma from the *Sentatus Academicus*, the Nonconformist body that validated theological training.

Lansdell was welcomed enthusiastically by the Church at Hope, and by the wider Staffordshire Congregational community. He took a full part in the life of the denomination; in 1889 he was appointed Missionary Secretary for the northern district of the county. This meant that he co-ordinated deputation speakers and missionary services for overseas work, especially the LMS. In 1890 he was one of those who offered prayer at the opening of the annual Assembly of the Staffordshire Union.

---

[159] Elaine Kaye: *For the Work of Ministry* (Edinburgh, 1999) P. 95

William Lansdell was a committed Congregationalist, and when Congregational leaders said un-congregational things, he spoke out. In 1902, while chairman of the Congregational Union, Joseph Parker, the celebrated pastor of London's City Temple and perhaps the most famous British Congregationalist of his time, used his chairman's address to recommend sweeping changes to the Congregational Union. He proposed that what was a voluntary union of independent Churches should become "The United Congregational Church". This would be, not a union of Churches, but a centralised denominational body with control over colleges, missions and even Church property.[160] Lansdell was one of many Congregational ministers who were furious at the idea, and he seconded a motion at the Staffordshire Assembly condemning the proposal as opposed to the spirit of Congregationalism.

This did not mean that he was an isolationist opposed to all closer links between Churches, only that he would not see such links established at the expense of the principle of Congregationalism. Indeed, in 1890 he was elected to the Executive Committee of the Staffordshire Union. That same year at the Northern District meeting it is recorded that Lansdell "Gave a thoughtful and suggestive address on 'The Spiritual Unity of Independent Churches.'"[161] A discussion followed the paper, and from the discussion there arose two main practical results. The first was 'The Potteries' Ministers' and Deacons' Association', which was intended to bring the leaders of the churches in the Potteries into closer contact. The second was a half-yearly pulpit exchange between the churches in North Staffordshire. This and Lansdell's deep involvement in the work of the Staffordshire Union indicate that he was a Congregationalist of the old type who believed that unity was first of all spiritual, and should come from the ground up, not down from central committees. All of his work in the wider sphere of Congregationalism and the Free Church Federation movement shows this in various ways. In 1893 Lansdell was one of those involved in the creation of the Potteries Congregational Association, which was an association of churches rather than of individuals.

---

[160] Peel, *These Hundred Years* Pp. 349-53
[161] *Report of the Staffordshire Congregational Union 1890* P. 21

Lansdell had, like many men of his era, an historical consciousness. In 1892 he spoke at a Northern District meeting held in the old Dresden Congregational Church (on the site now occupied by Longton URC) held to commemorate the Pilgrim Fathers on the lessons that modern Congregationalism could learn from the Pilgrims. Sadly none of his District addresses seem to have survived; they would have been very enlightening had they done so. A pastor first and foremost, Lansdell did not write for publication himself, but he did translate several volumes of German philosophy for a London publisher, presumably to supplement his income.

His involvement in the Union continued throughout the rest of his time in Staffordshire. In 1895 he was appointed to the Staffordshire Union's 'Council of Reference', the men who had oversight of the Union's affairs between the annual Assemblies. That same year he was elected chairman of the Union for 1896-7, which was held in what is now Trinity Church in Leek. The primary task of the chairman was to preside over the annual Assembly and to give an address. He took as his subject 'The Kingdom of God', expressing a high Congregational Churchmanship in the course of the address. His reading is displayed by his references to James Orr's seminal work, *The Christian View of God and the World*.[162] Published in 1893, this book may be said to be the first major British work to discuss the idea of 'worldview'. Orr, a conservative Scottish scholar who taught Church History in the United Presbyterian College in Edinburgh and would later contribute several articles to *The Fundamentals*, sought to bring the German concept into English, and he succeeded.

There were, Lansdell noted, three factors that had contributed to the prominence of the idea of the Kingdom of God in the last decades of the 19th century; this was a hopeful development, as it presented the Church with "glorious possibilities."[163] In the course of the address he gave what is probably best described as a fairly typical late Victorian orthodox Nonconformist address, influenced by Dr. Barrett's views. The conception of the Kingdom that it presents is largely outdated; more recent work in scholarship has recognised that the idea behind it is the

---

[162] Edinburgh, Andrew Elliot, 1893
[163] *Report of the Staffordshire Congregational Union 1896* P. 20

rule of God, rather than any sort of society.[164] Still, the address is worth examining as one of the few examples we have of the theology taught at Hope in the Victorian era.

The first influence that had led to the concept of the Kingdom of God becoming prominent in theology, Lansdell noted, was "What is sometimes called *The Return to Christ*." This was the movement in the Victorian era that contended that Christian theology had become sterile and academic and that Jesus himself should be the centre of our teaching. While true as far as it went, it sometimes led to a theology being constructed on the Gospels alone, the rest of the Bible being marginalised to all intents and purposes. Lansdell himself was not so naïve, and had been taught better by Barrett and his tutors at Manchester.

The second factor was the recognition of the need for a Christian worldview to meet the attempts by philosophy to develop a comprehensive and non-Christian worldview. Christianity of course *is* a worldview, but it needs to be recognised as such as it had not been previously. The term 'worldview' itself, a translation of a German word, entered the English language about this time. "It is this idea, that the whole range of Christian truth can be brought under one great generalization, and that the whole history and life and destiny of man, and of nature are to be viewed from the same standpoint, that is the almost wholly new conception which is shaping theological thought to-day, and is to shape still more that of the future."[165] It was the concept of "the Kingdom of God" that was the central pivot of this worldview.

The final factor Lansdell referred to was that of evolution. Since the publication of Darwin's *Origin of Species* in 1859, Christians had been wrestling with the issue of how to respond to it. While there were those who rejected the whole idea of biological evolution outright, there were in fact many more who accepted it and sought to bring the idea into Christian theology. Lansdell, like many of his day, held to a version of what we would call "Theistic Evolution", the idea that God was behind evolution, directing it in the path that he had laid out; in other words that evolution was the means God used in creation. Among the various

---

[164] So, for example, Harold Roberts, *Jesus and the Kingdom of God* (London, 1955)
[165] *Ibid.* P. 21

responses to evolution there were two books Lansdell drew the attention of the Assembly to; Professor Henry Drummond's *Ascent of Man* and Kidd's *Social Evolution*. Both of these books, though otherwise very different, sought to find in evolution itself an element of altruism; rather than a ruthless individual struggle to survive, evolution included a *social* element (hence Kidd's title); what survived was not just individuals, but societies, populations. As well as the struggle for life, there was "The subordination of personal good to the good of society or of generations yet unborn. For this subordination there is no rational ground, its possibility depends upon supra-natural sanctions, in other words, upon religion."[166]

With a typical Victorian optimism, Lansdell could say, "There is in the hearts of men an anticipation that the Kingdom of God is coming nearer to us, and a longing to see and realize more of the glory of the Golden Age."[167]

What, then, was the Kingdom of God? While modern scholarship would regard his idea of the Kingdom as hopelessly outdated, we cannot fairly judge Lansdell by what expositors say in 2012, or even in 1970. He was up-to-date in 1896, and he spoke like a typical man of his age. He criticised two false ideas of the Kingdom. First of all, implicitly opposing the Plymouth Brethren and their premillennial dispensationalism, he said, "Some think of it solely as in that spiritual and eternal life which lies beyond the present; they have no thought of, and so little care for, its realization upon earth." At the other extreme were those who, "Would identify it merely with social aims and ideas; and, altogether forgetful of its spiritual and eternal character, work as though it were possible by some new 'Morrison's Pill', by nationalization of land and capital, by change of economic conditions, to cure all the ills of human life and to bring about the ideal." It is evident that he here has the Socialists in his sights. So what is the truth? "Must we not say that there is truth and error in both of these, and that only by the union of these two conceptions can the true ideal be set before us."

---

[166] *Ibid* P. 22
[167] *Ibid.*

The Lord's prayer says, "Thy Kingdom Come", and therefore it follows, Lansdell said, that the Kingdom must come on the earth, otherwise we would not be told to pray for it. "Jesus does not speak of this earthly life and this world of ours, as though they were altogether apart from the kingdom which he came to establish. It is no devil's world to which he comes. He came unto his own." Appealing to history as only one living before World War 1 could, he appealed to the 'facts' of history; that the Church had formed society and had made the world a better place. "In history the progress of the Kingdom is marked by two main features,- on the one hand it has been the expelling from society forms of injustice and sin that were hardly recognised as such, and on the other hand it has been claiming whatever has been of good, and filling that good with deeper and purer meaning."

On the other hand, the socialist is far worse than the Plymouth Brother, "If then we err when we forget that the Kingdom of God has thus its meaning for this life here on earth, still more disastrously do we err if we go to the other extreme and seek it only here, and solely or chiefly in social aims and economic reforms." The Social Gospel was not to Lansdell's liking any more than the dispensationalist teaching that the Kingdom is only future. "We must not forget that if the Kingdom is to be on earth, it must be a kingdom having some kind of social organisation," he notes. But the "Labour Church" movement, which identified Christianity with socialism, was a caricature. We should not forget that there was a Labour Church in Newcastle-Under-Lyme, using the Old Meeting-House, at the time these words were spoken. "Whilst, with all earnestness, we seek the uplifting of human life in society, we must not forget the source of the one elevating power – it is in the spiritual and eternal forces that have been brought nigh to us in Christ Jesus. Our ideal is to be a kingdom of God; a kingdom in which God is no vague abstraction, but a living, righteous king, a gracious and loving Father of his people." Socialism, even Christian socialism, neglected this fact.

Socialism was a major issue in the nation at the time. The Independent Labour Party had fielded many candidates in the 1895 general election, but they got no-where. George Slayter Barrett, Lansdell's mentor, had spoken from the chair of the Congregational Union in 1894 on "the Secularization of the Pulpit" and "the secularization of the Church", in which he had torn into the preaching of politics, especially socialist politics, in the pulpit, and the treating of the Church as an instrument of social rather than spiritual change. Lansdell was therefore doing on a local level what his mentor was doing on a national level. In retrospect, Lansdell's warning was hardly needed at the time; the high-point of socialism in the Congregational Churches was already past, and the Labour Church in Newcastle-Under-Lyme did not survive long after the disastrous showing of the Socialist candidates in the 1895 General Election.

"We combine, then, these two truths into one conception of the Kingdom of God. First and supremely it is a spiritual kingdom, not a product of merely human forces or tendencies, but one that has come to us from above. It is made up of those whom Christ has redeemed to himself, and to whom he has given the Divine life. Every soul that owns allegiance to God in Christ belongs to that kingdom; and so it is a spiritual kingdom even on earth, extending invisibly into every land, ignoring all barriers of race and custom, and bringing into one communion of saints all who share the one life, and obey the one Lord." At the same time, "This new spiritual life, just because it is a real life, must clothe itself in outward form." It must change society to make it more heavenly, abolishing all that is sinful in culture, "the good leaven permeating the whole lump." Finally there would be a time when all the world belonged to this kingdom. We have here a typical late Victorian postmillenialism, a vision in which the Church would transform the world and only then would Jesus come again.

The tendency of the modern Evangelical at this point is to say that, since Lansdell believed in a form of theistic evolution, and taught postmillenialism, he must have been a liberal. That would be an oversimplification. He is quite clear that it is by the Spirit of God working in and through the Church, not by mere social reforms, the world shall become the Kingdom of God on earth. Lansdell's evangelical postmillennialism is a reflection of the theology that his mentor, George Slayter Barrett, taught in his 1896 volume, *The Intermediate State and the Last Things*.[168] Given how closely Lansdell follows Barrett, it is reasonable to conclude that Barrett's eschatology

---

[168] George S. Barrett, *The Intermediate State and the Last Things* (London, 1896).

was shared by his protégée. Barrett stands firmly in the Evangelical mainstream in his work, rejecting the Premillennial scheme for one in which at some future point in the world's history, Satan will be bound; not that he will cease to act, but that his activity will be largely restricted; and that, "there will be a considerable and widespread conversion of the Gentile and heathen nations."[169] This did not mean that everyone would be converted, but that large numbers would be. The Jews would be restored to faith and, "With this conversion of Israel will come their restoration to their own land."[170] There would be an era of blessedness in which the Gospel would dominate and Christianity would influence the world for good. At the end of this millennium there would be a falling-away, and then Christ would come again to usher in the eternal state. The final consummation of the Kingdom is brought in by the literal, physical, bodily return of the same Jesus who died on the cross, rose from the dead and ascended into heaven. While we, living on the other side of two World Wars, can see that the optimism of 1896 was illusory, Lansdell could not. His address made some sense when the Churches were still growing, and new congregations being established.

What, then, he asks next, is the relation between the Kingdom and the Church? "The ideal Church and the Kingdom are one. This cannot be said of the actual Church and the kingdom. The kingdom here is often wider than the Church, and men may be recognised as belonging to the Church who are far from the Kingdom. But are we not wholly right when we say that the Church should be the visible expression of the spiritual life and unity of the Kingdom; and that it is only as this spiritual life and unity of the kingdom are fostered within the Church, that we have the possibility of the continued growth and progress of the kingdom?" As a result, it was absolutely vital that members of the Church should know what the Church really is. This unity was not a matter of outward organisation, which can exist without any spiritual life at all, but it is, like the life, spiritual. We shall find the true conception of the Church, he said, "In that form of Church life which tends most to spiritual life and unity, which makes the individual Christian realise most clearly his dependence on Christ for spiritual life and power." This was of course evangelical Congregationalism. "A man may be a good

---
[169] Barrett, P. 128
[170] Barrett, P. 130

Christian without being a Congregationalist, but a man cannot be a true Congregationalist without being a true Christian... The true meaning of our independence is not, for the individual, liberty to think and do as you please, and not for the Church, isolation but something infinitely higher and nobler – a personal loyalty and devotion to Christ and his will, and closest sympathy with all who own him as Saviour and Lord... Other Churches have their organisation, their ritual, their priesthoods; *we have nothing, we are nothing, unless we are everything* – communities in which the very life of God dwells, and in which the presence of Christ is continually realised. In endeavouring to realise this ideal we shall most fully set forth the spiritual life and unity of the Kingdom of God." This high conception of the Church is vital for Lansdell, who may then be regarded as, like Barrett, a high-Church Congregationalist.

The Church then has to labour to extend the Kingdom of God, "Whilst we recognise the fact that the Church and the kingdom are not identical, we must not forget that the spiritual forces which make the kingdom can only come into our human life through the Church; and by the extension of the Church we shall be doing our best work toward the extension of the kingdom." Yes, the social conditions in Britain, particularly in the slums, were dreadful, and something should be done to help improve the condition of the poor. But it was vital to remember that the Church's first work was spiritual, not social. "We need to-day to keep before ourselves the fact that the kingdom is not made by social conditions, but by spiritual life, which in its turn will shape the social conditions. It may seem the slower and less showy way, but it is the surer and more lasting, because it touches human life, not simply upon its surface, but at its very heart and spring, bringing into the man a life which is eternal." This was the fact that the Congregational ministers and laymen assembled in Leek should take away with them; that mission is always first and foremost spiritual, and it is the spiritual that will change the world.

That was not to say they could be complacent about the state of the nation and the world, "Nothing indeed that is of human interest can be alien to the Church. She still has to wage unceasing war against social injustice and immorality." So the Church had a part to play in local politics and even in national politics. In an age when the majority of

Congregationalists belonged to the Liberal Party, even when the Liberal leadership at times regarded their Nonconformist MPs as only a sort of lobby fodder, this was only to be expected.

Concluding his address, Landsell said, "In one word, it is the work of the Church, whilst living ever near to her Lord, and seeking ever to extend his kingdom as a spiritual domain, at the same time to bring the spirit if Christ – his righteousness, gentleness, truth, and love, into every relation of human life." All the while looking for the personal coming of Christ.

It is important to deal with this address because it reveals to us the spirit of the age and the theology that underpinned the ministry at Hope. It was an optimistic postmillennial theology, but a spiritual rather than socialist postmillennialism, evangelical rather than liberal.

It must be emphasised that the millennium expected by Barrett and Lansdell was the result of mass conversions to Christ, not to political, social or economic programmes; what would make the millennium a period of blessing and plenty would be the fact that Christ ruled spiritually in the hearts of so many. As a result of this, they viewed the Gospel as the primary engine of social transformation; because of the Gospel, the Church was interested in the end of social evils. The end of political and social disabilities for Congregationalists did not lead to their withdrawing from politics, but to a broadening of their social concerns. Lansdell recognised the danger of secularisation latent in such a move, and his insistence on the priority of the spiritual is a response to that danger which was seen most glaringly in the Labour Church movement.

As Chairman of the Union at the 1896 Assembly, Lansdell welcomed into membership Rev. Dugald MacFadyen,[171] newly called to the pastorate of the Tabernacle in Hanley. MacFadyen was one of A.M. Fairbairn's Mansfield men, a member of the new elite of Congregationalism. Possessing an Oxford degree from Merton College, MacFadyen personified the hopes of the denomination for the fast-approaching new century. It is therefore perhaps fitting that the First World War ended his ministerial career.

---

[171] Biographer of Alexander Mackennal

The call of the kingdom required a Christian response to the challenges of the age. On the positive side this meant encouraging young people and teaching them the faith, helping them to transition between Sunday school and the church. Among the agencies he used was a Hope Young People's Guild at his own church. He commended the Young People's Society of Christian Endeavour from the chair at the 1896 Assembly. This was an organisation formed in 1881 in the United States in a Congregational church in Portland, Maine, intended to bring young people into the church as workers. It was decidedly evangelical, and had an evangelistic focus.

On the negative side, the call of the kingdom could lead to a critique of government policy. In 1897 Lansdell seconded a motion condemning the events in South Africa that would lead to the war with the Boers in 1899. The motion, "Referred to the state of things in South Africa, and expressed strong disapproval of the use of the nation's prestige and power to promote the selfish aims of capitalists and companies, and deep regret and alarm in contemplation of the words and deeds that tend to lead to a racial war." It is not known if he continued to be a critic of the government's policy in South Africa, a policy which introduced the term "Concentration camp" to the English vocabulary, but consistently he ought to have.

Though he was a decided and principled Congregationalist with a high view of the local Church, Lansdell was no more a denominational isolationist than he was a local church isolationist. He was an enthusiastic supporter of the Free Church Federation movement. This was a movement that promoted co-operation between Nonconformist churches on a local level without compromising their independence or denominational identities. In 1899 Lansdell resigned from his work with the LMS to take up the post of secretary to the local Free Church Federation. A practical example of the work of the Federation was that it discouraged churches from replicating work being done by other denominations in an area.

As a high Church Congregationalist, Lansdell's first commitment was to the local Church, and of course that meant Hope. While figures for the membership do not become available until later in his career, there are many clues that the Church was still quite poor. It was the second church in Hanley, after the Tabernacle, and a comparison of the donations that Hope gave towards the Staffordshire Union with those from Tabernacle reveals that not only were the amounts given by individuals at Hope smaller than those given at the Tabernacle, but the church itself gave considerably less. So in 1891 there were ten members at the Tabernacle who gave amounts over one pound to the Union, while only one member at Hope, William Bennett, gave a pound, in contrast to the £20 that was the largest donation from a Tabernacle member. The general collection for the Union at the Tabernacle was £7.9/10d, while that at Hope was £1.1/. Lansdell lived at 29 Rectory Road in Shelton, an ordinary terraced house that is in striking contrast to the nearby spacious Rectory, which was set in its own grounds. The fact bears further testimony to the fact that the Hope Congregation was never rich, and the pastor lived as the people did. While little is said about his wife, Martha Spatchett, she was no doubt his faithful companion through his ministry and subsequent retirement.

Having himself begun to preach as a young apprentice, Lansdell interested himself in the welfare of the young people in the Church, especially in the matter of education. He established a Young People's Guild at Hope and was one of the main promoters of the Young people's Society of Christian Endeavour in the Potteries. He encouraged those young men who sought to become lay preachers and sought out opportunities for them to try their gifts. It was in 1888, during his pastorate that Hope Chapel took pastoral oversight of the chapel at Tomkin in the Moorlands, giving some of the young men at Hope opportunities to minister to the small rural congregation there.

Tomkin Chapel[172] had been founded in 1837 by the Tabernacle Church in Hanley, following the failure of Hope Chapel at Wetley Rocks. It was one of fourteen new Congregational causes established in northern Staffordshire between 1825 and 1850.[173] Rev. Ridgeway William Newland of the Tabernacle, Rev. Samuel Barton Schofield and Rev. Samuel Jones of the Caroline Street Church in Longton were among the

---

[172] For further information on Tomkin Chapel see Irene Turner, *Tomkin in the Staffordshire Moorlands* (Leek, 2006)
[173] Turner, *Tomkin*, P. 39

first trustees of the Tomkin chapel. The original building was replaced in 1865 by the present brick chapel. While initially Tomkin was under the oversight of Tabernacle, new ventures in church planting and the establishment of a town mission hall in Hanley itself meant that Tabernacle was only too glad to give the oversight to Hope, while Lansdell was more than willing to take on the task.

Fig. 10: Tomkin Chapel in 2010

In 1891 the church at Hope felt confident enough to completely renovate the chapel, making it more attractive and more suitable for late Victorian worship. While the exterior was not significantly altered, £1000 was spent on the interior work. The old pews and pulpit were replaced, a pipe organ mounted in the rear gallery and the seating capacity reduced to 500. The report of the Staffordshire Union records, "It is to be devoutly hoped that, favoured with a place of worship of greater convenience and attractiveness, our good and zealous brother, reinforced by his too-small band of fellow-helpers, may be enabled to strengthen his hold on the large surrounding population; and so bring it more directly under the ennobling and hallowing influence of the Gospel of the grace of God."[174] We can therefore safely say that it was felt that Hope was not having the impact desired upon the masses living around

---

[174] *Report of the Staffordshire Congregational Union 1892,* P. 27

the chapel. The opening of the Tabernacle Town Mission in Union Street in 1879 would not have helped, as the mission was attempting to reach the very people Hope relied upon and was seeking to reach.

The list of members at Hope who gave donations to the County Union gives us the first serious idea of what the leading members at the chapel were like. The first thing that strikes the reader is that, compared to the more affluent Tabernacle, there were fewer people at Hope who were able to give to the Union, and second that they gave less per person. Still, the list can be cross-checked with trade directories to reveal that there was something of a 'shopocracy' at Hope. Among Lansdell's "too-small band of fellow-helpers" were deacons William Bennett and John Lowe. While Bennett was a potter and owner of a factory, Lowe is described in the trade directories of 1900 as "General and family grocer, tea dealer, provision merchant and Italian warehouseman."[175] He was also appointed a local magistrate. Other leading church members who gave to the County Union were Mr. William Stedman, builder and joiner, Birch Terrace, also probably a deacon, and Mr. William Henry Mitchell, hatter and hosier, Tontine Street. Skilled craftsmen and shop-owners were the leading members of the chapel, contrasting with the more aristocratic Anglicans, and the captains of local industry at the Tabernacle. While an aristocratic Anglican resented the idea that a group of grocers, hatters and potters were able to hold a college-educated minister to account, the fact was that the relationship between most deacons and ministers was extremely good, even when there were disagreements. In Churches where there were no tithes levied for the support of the ministry, it was the grocers, the hatters and the potters who ensured that the college-educated minister was supported in the midst of a poor working area where some streets were no better than slums. It is a curiously snobbish attitude that regards the patronage of a duke who rarely if ever attends the church whose minister he chooses as a great blessing, but the patronage of a potter who sits in the front pew every Sunday as a bane.

This small number of tradesmen in the congregation was all the more important because of the poverty of the majority of the congregation. The mass of the membership were not able to give to the

---

[175] *Kelly's Directory, Staffordshire* 1900

121

Union themselves; they were the poor who lived in the streets of crowded terraces about the chapel and above the small shops on Hope Street. If the church had its share of shop-keepers, the membership figures and the low level of giving suggests that at Hope the church had not lost touch with the working-classes, a fact that paradoxically created its own problems, for the poor were really poor then, and had trouble enough feeding themselves and their children, let alone keeping up a large chapel. Even the modest terraced house in which Lansdell lived would have been seen as luxurious by those who lived in tiny flats above shops, and in terraced houses where whole families lived in single rooms.

A new trust deed for the church property was drawn up in 1890. This also functioned as the Church constitution, providing for the running of the Church on congregational lines, placing the finances in the hands of the deacons, and requiring that any future pastor be appointed by a two-thirds majority of the members of the Church provided the man chosen was neither immoral nor heretical.[176] Following trouble with Unitarians taking over chapels built by Trinitarian churches in the 18th century and settled on trust deeds that did not specify the doctrines to be taught in the chapel, the 1890 Hope deed contained a schedule of doctrines that the minister of the Church had to maintain. Seen in the light of contemporary controversies, they are decidedly Evangelical and conservative. There are six doctrinal articles in the deed, and they are worth quoting in full:

> "1. The Divine and special inspiration of the Holy Scriptures of the Old and New Testaments, and their supreme authority in faith an practice." The second article is of the Trinity
>
> 2. The Unity of God. The Deity of the Father, of the Son, and of the Holy Ghost.
>
> 3. The depravity of man, and the absolute necessity of the Holy Spirit's agency in man's regeneration and sanctification.
>
> 4. The incarnation of the Son of God, in the person of the Lord Jesus Christ; the universal sufficiency of the atonement by his death, and free justification of sinners by faith alone in him.
>
> 5. Salvation by grace, and the duty of all who hear the Gospel to believe in Christ.

---

[176] Copy of deed in Church archives

6. The resurrection of the dead, and the final judgment, when the wicked "shall go away into everlasting punishment, and the righteous into life everlasting."

The first of these articles relates to the controversy over the inspiration of the Bible that had reared its head in the 19th century. At the same time that these articles were written, C.H. Spurgeon was warning the Baptist Union of the "down-grade" in theology that began with a destructive criticism of the Bible that in practice reduced it to the level of a merely human document, and indeed often treated it with a suspicion that no other document suffered from. The third article is against Pelagianism and Semi-Pelagianism, which teach that the Holy Spirit is not absolutely necessary to conversion and that human nature is either not injured at all by the Fall in Adam, or that it is only slightly bruised. "Depravity" does not mean that everyone is as bad as they could be, but that we all tend towards evil. The fourth article insists that Jesus is God incarnate, and that his death is sufficient for all; this is not Arminian, but moderate Calvinism. Article 5 is against Hyper-Calvinism, which teaches that it is not the duty of all who hear the Gospel to believe, but only of those who know that they are of the elect. The final article, made up largely as it is of a Biblical text, deals with the debates over the Eternal State of man. It begins by affirming the Resurrection, which some people denied, and then the reality of eternal punishment. Some leading figures in Congregationalism had embraced a teaching known as Conditional immortality, which said that all those who were not saved would be snuffed out of existence. The Hope deed makes plain that this is not the Bible's teaching.

In 1900 Lansdell was appointed secretary of the Northern District of the Staffordshire Union. Part of his responsibility in the role was the planting of new churches to serve the expanding Potteries conurbation. The first of these Churches was established on the Park estate, between the newly laid-out Hanley Park and Stoke railway station. Even before his election as Secretary, Lansdell had been deeply involved in the scheme to open a new Church on Cauldon Road, and in 1898 he was one of those present when an iron chapel seating 250 was opened, one of the first buildings near the Park. The iron church was located behind the present site of Park Evangelical Church, but the

Congregational Union purchased the whole site facing onto Boughey Road between Cauldon Road and Avenue Road, intending to construct a permanent brick building on the site. This hope was realised in 1902, when the present building was opened, facing onto Cauldon Road. The Park building was a multi-purpose hall seating 450 in chairs rather than pews, and it was hoped that the Church would eventually be able to construct a grand chapel on the site that the iron church had occupied, facing onto Hanley Park.

The chapel and hall were designed at the same time by Wood and Hutchins of Tunstall. Curiously, the Kelly's Directory of 1912 describes the design for the chapel as if it had been built, but we know from old maps that this was not the case. It is described as "The Park Congregational Church in Avenue Road... an edifice of red brick with stone dressings, in the Gothic style... [It] consists of clerestoried nave, with aisles, deacons' and minister's vestries, and a tower rising above the north-east porch."[177] Clearly there was a serious intention to build the Park Church as soon as possible, but although the designs were drawn up and accepted, financial trouble and World War 1 meant that the church was never built, and the empty site was finally sold in the 1970s. A house now stands where the church was intended to be.

The first pastor at Park was Rev. Harry Gaywood Lewis, a graduate of London University and Hackney College. The church began with sixteen members transferred from the Tabernacle and twelve added by profession of faith. In its early years the church grew rapidly, going from the initial 29 members in 1900 to 89 in 1906, helped by converts from a united Free Church mission led by Gipsy Smith.

With the opening of the brick building at Hanley Park, the iron church was dismantled for use elsewhere. Leading local Congregational layman G.W. Garlick, seeing the development of Wolstanton as a suburb of Newcastle-under-Lyme, bought a piece of land for a chapel site that he leased to the Union for an annual rent of a shilling for five years. The iron chapel from Park was moved to Wolstanton, a loan from the Staffordshire Union financed the setting up of the venture. Lansdell was approached to take up the work of pioneering a Congregational Church

---

[177] *Kelly's Directory, Staffordshire* 1912. The same description is repeated in 1928

in the new estate, and he accepted. It was with some sadness that the Church at Hope released him, but they had the consolation that he had left them for a harder and not an easier task, for hard work rather than greater comfort.

We have no figures for membership at Hope before 1900, when the annual *Congregational Yearbook* began to give membership figures, and so we cannot tell what the membership was when Lansdell began his pastorate, though the comments in the 1892 report suggest that the membership was then regarded as too low. We do know that when he left Hope the church had 123 members, three lay-preachers, over three hundred children in the Sunday school, and 22 Sunday school teachers. A report to the Staffordshire Union estimated an average Sunday congregation of 250, meaning that the building was only at half capacity, even after the seating capacity had been reduced.

Lansdell began work at at Wolstanton on 17th November 1902. It was hard work pioneering the cause, but the work was successful. In 1908 the iron chapel was replaced by a brick chapel, which was replaced in 1922 by the present building, now the home of Wolstanton United Reformed Church, opened by R.F. Horton of Lyndurst Road Church, Hampstead. In 1913, having established the Church at Wolstanton, Lansdell went to take oversight of the work at the Cadishead and Partington Congregational Churches, either side of the Manchester Ship Canal. The older Church, Cadishead had been founded in 1875. The newer cause, Partington, had been a branch of Bowdon Downs before being united with Cadishead in a joint pastorate as the first stage on the way to becoming an independent cause. Lansdell's aim was to get the Partington Church on a sound enough footing for it to have a pastor of its own rather than the joint pastorate with Cadishead, and he succeeded, becoming in 1917 pastor of Partington alone.

William Lansdell retired from the pastoral ministry in 1927 and moved back to his home county of Norfolk, where he settled in the north Norfolk market town of North Walsham, close to his brother Alfred. He became a member of the Cromer Road Congregational Church in the town. Though retired from the pastorate, William Lansdell continued to preach in the county's congregational churches. He died on June 22nd,

1943. His grave bears a quotation from the Commentator Matthew Henry, "A life spent in the service of God and in communion with him, is the most pleasant life that any one can live in the world." His wife Martha died December 11th 1959.

Fig. 12: William Lansdell's grave in North Walsham

William Lansdell was a hard-working pastor and one of the leaders of North Staffordshire Congregationalism in his day. Despite the increasing challenges of urban ministry, he remained at Hope, and never chose the easy path of seeking a wealthy congregation. Though he is buried in Norfolk, Lansdell's memory lives on in Lansdell Avenue, Porthill, Newcastle-under-Lyme, close to the church at Wolstanton which he established.

Chapter 9: The Edwardians

John Green Gascoine

While Horne had organised a smooth transition to Lansdell because he had retired, Lansdell's call to Wolstanton meant a more traditional Congregational transition; a vacancy during which various men were called to "preach with a view." These would have been the usual mixture of men already in pastorates and college students. Eventually the choice of the Church fell on an experienced and popular preacher who was almost fifty years old and had never attended a theological college.

Rev. John Green Gascoine was born at Newton, near Rugby, on April 8th, 1854. His parents soon moved to Wellingborough in Northamptonshire, and he was brought up in the old Salem Congregational Chapel in that town. It was while at Salem that he received the call to preach, first of all as a lay preacher serving the smaller chapels of the district that were unable to support full-time pastors or were seeking a pastor. One of these, the small Congregational church in the nearby village of Badby, was so impressed by the young preacher that they called him to serve as lay pastor, working a secular job in the week and preaching to them at the week-end. This was not an unusual way in which young men entered the ministry, bypassing theological college and getting a practical start in the work.

From Badby, Gascoine was called to the Church at Coton Road, Nuneaton, and there, in 1886, he was ordained pastor and entered full-time Christian service. In this working-class town setting he began a series of PSA meetings that became so popular that as many as 500 working men were gathering in the chapel for Brotherhood meetings every week, and many later testified to his inspiring leadership.

The Pleasant Sunday Afternoon or Brotherhood movement, usually shortened to PSA was a men's fellowship movement launched in 1875 by Mr. W. Blackham, a deacon at Ebenezer Congregational

Church, West Bromwich.[178] Its aim was to foster fellowship among working men, and as the name suggests its main activities took place on Sunday afternoons. It began with an effort to enliven the traditional Sunday afternoon Bible classes, and took as its initial motto, "Brief, bright and brotherly."[179] The PSA with its varied activities provided a Christian alternative to the various 'worldly' amusements that existed in the industrial cities. It was phenomenally successful, and soon many Congregational Churches had PSA or Brotherhood groups.[180] Hope Chapel was among these churches, though we cannot tell when the Hope PSA began. C. Silvester Horne, David Horne's nephew, was one of the greatest supporters of the movement, and it was only his sudden and premature death during a visit to America in 1914 that prevented him from giving the rest of his ministry entirely to the PSA movement.[181]

Despite the rather innocuous-sounding name, PSA brotherhoods, as venues where working class men could get together and better themselves, could be hotbeds of Socialism, something George S. Barrett noted back in 1894, disapprovingly, as might be imagined. A more sympathetic author at the opening of the 20th century wrote, "The attempt is nothing less than to teach a 'democratic religion' leading to a 'practical Christianity' full of love and good works. The ultimate aim is a social state which shall bring upon earth the Kingdom of Christ, and whose benefits shall be universally distributed".[182] They have been linked directly to the rise of the Labour movement; another writer suggests, "The Pleasant Sunday Afternoon movement of the Congregationalists may have been instrumental in moving working-class men in the direction of socialism."[183]

Locally led, though centrally connected, PSA meetings varied in character from place to place, according to the character of the Church with which they were associated; if the Church was an evangelical one (as Hope was), the PSA was religious first and democratic (or even socialist) second, if the Church was more liberally inclined, then the

---

[178] *http://www.blackcountrysociety.co.uk/articles/sundayafternoon.htm* Accessed 31/7/2012
[179] Leonard Smith, *Religion and the Rise of Labour* (Keele, 1993) P. 54
[180] *Matthews, P. 241*
[181] *Smith, P. 68*
[182] Frederick DeLand Leete, *Christian Brotherhoods* (Cincinnati, 1912) P. 272
[183] *http://www.derbyunitarians.org.uk/rise_of_labour.html*

democratic element predominated. They had a tendency to take on a life of their own apart from the Churches with which they were associated, and that association could become very loose indeed, to the point where the PSA at Ashton-Under-Lyme had its own building.[184]

The church at Hope called Gascoine from Coton Road in 1903, and his obituary says that he spent "a fruitful five years at Hanley".[185] The statistics returned to the Congregational Union of England and Wales certainly bear this out; when he arrived the church had 134 members, when he left in 1908 the church membership had grown to 190. Membership, of course, does not give the size of the congregation, which was in this period frequently much higher. If the proportion of 123 members, a congregation of about 250 in 1900 is any guide, then we can estimate that an average Sunday congregation would have been a respectable 400 or so. The increase was partly connected with the Gipsy Smith mission in 1905. By this time Smith was connected with the Free Church Council, and it is nice to think that he may have preached at Hope in the course of the mission; certainly Gascoine would have supported the work. In the working-class setting in Hanley, Gascoine continued to hold PSA meetings that were extremely successful. Hope remained responsible for the church at Tomkin during his pastorate.

Gascoine was a man who earned the love and respect of his congregations, a warm-hearted evangelical. He was a man of one book, the Bible, which he knew intimately and which he loved heartily. "He was a real man, a true man, a simple man, great in his love and in his work, and no man can be a better minister of the grace of God than that," reads his obituary.

Unlike Lansdell, he was not much involved in the wider life of Staffordshire Congregationalism, restricting his work to the local congregation where he served. The old deacons, Bennett and Lowe, disappear from the records after Lansdell, and other men take their place, Mr. W. Steadman of Newcastle Road and Mr. H. Hammersley of Bucknall New Road, a coal merchant.

---

[184] Smith, *Religion and The Rise of Labour*, P. 68
[185] *CYB 1943*, P. 427

After five years at Hope, Gascoine was called to the pastorate of the Octagon Church, Manchester, in 1908, where he remained for 17 years until his retirement in 1925. He died on February 3rd 1942 at Moulton, Northamptonshire, aged 88.

Mark Bairstow

In 1908 the area in which the church was set remained poor, and the flight of those better off to the rapidly-growing suburbs continued. It was therefore felt best to call a man who was an evangelist and who understood the challenge of urban ministry. With these qualifications in mind, the choice of the Church fell upon Rev. Mark Bairstow of Salem, Great Bridge, West Bromwich.

Mark Bairstow was born on February 28th 1859 in Castleford, Yorkshire. His father died when he was only seven years old[186], and Mark became a glassblower. Early in life he became attached to the United Methodist Free Church in Castleford, where at the age of 17 he was accepted as a local preacher. Though today the Methodist Church is a single body, in the 1870s Methodism was divided into a number of groups. The largest of these were the Wesleyan Methodist Church, the parent body; the Primitive Methodist Church, formed in 1811 after Hugh Bourne and William Clowes were excluded from the Wesleyan church in Tunstall; the Methodist New Connexion, the oldest splinter group, formed in 1797 because of disagreements over the direction that Methodism should take after the death of John Wesley, and the United Methodist Free Churches. Other groups included the Bible Christian Methodists, based largely in Cornwall, and the Wesleyan Reform Union, based in Sheffield, which continues to this day.

The third largest Methodist group after the Wesleyan Methodists and the Primitive Methodists, the United Methodist Free Churches (UMFC) was formed in 1857 by the union of a number of small groups that had divided from the Wesleyan parent body over the question of the role of the laity in the church. While it retained a connexional or denominational structure, local congregations had a much greater degree

---

[186] This and other information about Mark Bairstow kindly supplied by his great-granddaughter, Mrs. Helen Sharpe

of autonomy than in the Wesleyan denomination, and laymen had much more say in the running of the churches. It tried to combine a denominational structure with a form of Congregationalism at the local level, and succeeded remarkably well.[187]

From local preacher, Mark Bairstow became an evangelist, working full time in Gospel ministry but not yet ordained. He formed his own evangelistic organisation called the Red-Ribbon Army, probably in imitation of William Booth's Salvation Army and opened a mission-hall known as 'Bairstow's Tabernacle' in Knottingley, Yorkshire, where he preached for Christ and against the Oxford Movement. What he may have lacked in formal education, he made up for with sheer determination and hard study.

Though the UMFC had a Theological College at Victoria Park, Manchester, not all of its ministers were required to receive training there; all that was required was for a prospective minister to pass an examination set by the annual Assembly. Bairstow took this while still at Knottingley and graduated to the status of a fully-accredited UMFC minister. In 1883 he laid the foundation stone for the UMFC chapel in Knottingley, which was opened the following year.

In 1886 he was called to Birmingham to lead UMFC work there; based at first in a chapel in Bond Street that had been bought from the Baptists in 1886, and from 1890 in a new chapel in Well Street. He drew great crowds to Sunday afternoon lectures held in the Town Hall, and this brought the gifted evangelist to the notice of Rev. Nicholas Knight, a local Congregational pastor. Knight had been a Wesleyan Methodist minister, trained at the Wesleyan College at Headingley, Leeds, but had entered the Congregational ministry in 1884, becoming pastor at Ebenezer Chapel, Steelhouse Lane, Birmingham. He persuaded Bairstow to follow him into the Congregational denomination in 1889.

Though he had become a Congregationalist, Bairstow was not immediately brought into the ministry, but taught for a time at the Middle Class School in Frederick Street, Birmingham. In the meantime

---

[187] Anyone interested in further study of the UMFC is directed to Oliver A. Beckerlegge, *The United Methodist Free Churches* (London, 1957)

he applied to the Staffordshire Congregational Union for acceptance as a minister. On November 1st 1890 the Executive Committee of the County Union received Bairstow's application, accompanied by testimonials from ministers of the UMFC. The support of Rev. Charles Berry, the influential pastor at Queen Street, Wolverhampton, ensured that Bairstow was accepted, and he was placed on the list of accredited ministers available for a call to a vacant pastorate.

It was by no means unusual for Methodists to become Congregational pastors; a report in 1890 revealed that no fewer than 10% of Congregational ministers had previously been in the ministry of another denomination. Since Methodism and Congregationalism were the two largest Nonconformist denominations in England, it was natural that most of these men had been Methodists; theology had long since ceased to be the barrier that it had been for John Greeves a century before. Nor was it simply that ministers moved from one denomination to another; those brought up in one communion might find themselves ordained to the ministry in another. Perhaps the most noted of those who went from Methodism to Congregationalism was Rev. G. Campbell Morgan, who on being rejected by the Wesleyan Methodist ministerial training committee in 1888 turned to the Congregationalists and became pastor at Stone. Yet he was able to say in 1928, "During these forty years and still my ecclesiastical home is in Congregationalism, but my spiritual home has been, and still remains, in Methodism."[188]

The move from the UMFC to the Congregationalists was not as radical for Mark Bairstow as it might have been had he been a Wesleyan or a Primitive Methodist. The UMFC churches were largely independent, and he remained committed to evangelism in the context of the local Church. At this time the old city and town centre churches were beginning to suffer from the movement of the middle classes to the suburbs; city and town centre chapels built to seat hundreds were beginning to be embarrassingly empty. Men like Bairstow were therefore in great demand as missioners to revive flagging causes; it was felt that their affinity with the working-classes would help to bring those who still lived in the inner cities into the churches whose doors too many of them rarely darkened. Thus Bairstow's first Congregational pastorate was

---

[188] Quoted in Jill Morgan, *A Man of the Word* (London, 1951) P. 62

the historic Salem Chapel in Great Bridge, West Bromwich, which had been established in 1839, but which was struggling as the new century began. He served there with great success from 1894 until 1908, when he was called to Hanley to succeed Gascoine. His obituary records proudly that Bairstow kept the church self-supporting.

Bairstow took up his residence at 4, Salisbury Avenue, Hanley, close to Hanley Park. While the Church did not see spectacular growth during his ministry, it did grow; in 1908 when he arrived the membership was 176, by the time of his departure in 1912 it had grown to 195, the highest figure since the Congregational Union began to give membership figures in 1899. Above all other qualifications, a Nonconformist minister had to be able to preach, and in an age of preachers, Mark Bairstow was certainly a gifted preacher; it was said that "He had a wonderful dramatic power, being able to have his audience in laughter and tears within the short space of five minutes."[189] As to his personal character, he was described as "a devout Methodist with Puritan tendencies."[190] Given the heritage of Hope Chapel, he must have fitted in very well.

1908, the year Mark Bairstow arrived in Hanley, was also the year in which English Congregationalism reached its peak in terms of membership and number of churches. Denominational hopes were high as a whole, but town centre chapels were already beginning to close; in some places this process had already been going on for some time. Villages chapels were also feeling the pressure of the continuing drift of the population from rural areas to the cities. Soon this decline would be noticed in earnest.

Bairstow was more involved with the wider Congregational community than Gascoine had been. At the 1909 Assembly of the Staffordshire Union, held at Handsworth, then just outside Birmingham, he offered prayer at the opening of the Assembly. In 1911 he was a member of the Executive Committee of the Staffordshire Union, and on 28th March at the 1911 Stoke Assembly he led the prayer-meeting that was held between ten and ten-thirty. He served on a number of committees of the Union, including the Temperance Committee and the

---

[189] *CYB 1928* P. 129
[190] Personal e-mail from Mrs. Helen Sharpe

Youth Committee, a reflection of his own varied interests and his working class Free Methodist background.

Fig. 12: Rev. and Mrs. Mark Bairstow. Image supplied by Mrs. Helen Sharpe

Mark Bairstow was an evangelist, a preacher, a lecturer and a writer. As a writer, he was the author of a novel called *The Village Blacksmith and the Squire's Daughter,* published in 1903. The book is now incredibly rare, though the title suggests that it was a rather conventional late-Victorian tale with more than a little romance about it. It was published by Arthur Stockwell, a religious publisher, indicating that Bairstow was hoping to appeal to the large numbers who bought the novels of the Hocking brothers, United Methodist Free Church ministers.

After leaving Hope, Bairstow went on to minister to churches in Hindpool Road, Barrow-in-Furness, where he was pastor from 1912 until 1916, and Rainhill, Lancashire, where he remained until his retirement from pastoral ministry in 1925. He died on 8th September 1927 in Liverpool, aged 68. His eldest son, Rev. Arthur Bairstow, followed in his footsteps as a Congregational minister; at the time of his father's death Arthur Bairstow was pastor at Wycliffe Church in Alfreton, Derbyshire.

Chapter 10: War and Decline

Tom Longcaster Moore

Hope Chapel may have had almost 200 members when Bairstow left in 1912, but it seems clear from the state of the church's finances that they were almost entirely in the lower income brackets. On one level this is a testimony that the church had not lost touch with the working people round about, but on another level it presented a serious problem. Churches need money, and a building 100 years old needs to be maintained. Though Congregational pastors were not as a class greedy for gain, and the ministers of Hope lived in terraced houses, they still needed support. Lacking a manse, Hope had to be able to pay a minister enough to rent or buy a suitable house, and this was becoming increasingly difficult. The church had been running a debt for some years; in itself this was not unusual, many churches in the period did so. What was at issue at Hope was the church's ability to service that debt. The church's annual income was not enough to meet all its financial obligations and had not been enough for some time, and so the debt, instead of being gradually reduced, was actually increasing, and had reached the worrying sum of £918. To put it into perspective, in modern-day terms that would be a debt of £39,530. The church's annual income was about £150, £6,460 in modern money. Bairstow's departure left the church with the very real possibility that they would simply not be able to call a man to succeed him. Hope was no longer able to support the cause at Tomkin, and so in 1913 Tomkin once more came under the oversight of the Tabernacle Church.

The officers at Hope applied to the Staffordshire Union for financial assistance, and an inspection on behalf of the Union revealed just how bad things were; the decision to apply for help was only taken because the church officers could see no other way to keep going. The report stated:

"For some time the work here has been carried on under great difficulties, and with the utmost devotion of the officers. We have been in continual intercourse with the deacons for many months and have appreciated their steady sacrifice and doggedness. The overpowering burden of debt would have caused less devoted and faithful men to abandon hope and effort."[191]

In 1914 a proposal was brought before the committee of the Staffordshire Congregational Union that the small, struggling, yet still viable churches should be grouped together in a North Staffordshire Federation. They would all pay agreed amounts into a central fund to support the ministry. The proposal for the Federation explained, "The object of this scheme is the federation of certain Churches mentioned in the schedule which shall be united under a central committee for the purpose of securing ministerial service."[192] As none of the churches were able to support a pastor individually, they would be grouped together with two or three churches sharing a pastor. Federation Churches would still be independent; this was a scheme for mutual aid, not for union. It was agreed that Hope would be grouped with the church at Silverdale, under the joint-pastorate of Tom Longcaster Moore, a lay pastor who was in charge of the church at Tutbury.

Fig. 13: Ebenezer Congregational Church, Tutbury

---

[191] *Report of the Staffordshire Congregational Union, 1915* P. 28
[192] Staffordshire Congregational Union: *Scheme for the Federation of Churches in the Northern Division of the County of Stafford* P. 1. Inside the Executive Committee Minute Book

Moore, was, like Mark Bairstow, a former Methodist, though from the Primitive Methodist Church rather than the UMFC. A native of Lincolnshire, he was born in the village of Quadring in 1882. As a young man he spent some time working in London with his older brother, who was in the publishing trade. A man of definite Christian convictions, he returned to his native county to work as a lay agent for the Primitive Methodists, an evangelist who worked in Holbeach and March. He seems not to have restricted his work to the Primitive Methodists, and in 1902 the Congregational Church at Chatteris called him to be their pastor. Moore, as a lay agent, felt able to move denominations, and so became a Congregational pastor. In 1907 he was called to Ebenezer Congregational Church, Tutbury, where, his obituary in 1939 recorded, "he is still remembered with gratitude for the excellence and faithfulness of his pastoral work."[193] In 1914 he was called to take the joint-pastorate of Hope and Silverdale.

Silverdale was also a struggling cause, and had been so for some years. In 1902 a report to the Union Assembly stated, "The Church at Silverdale has for some time been a matter of great anxiety to the Executive Committee."[194] Between 1900 and 1901 attendance at the main Sunday service had fallen from 160 to 67, the membership from 50 to 37, and the number of Sunday school students from 300 to 175. Despite various attempts to revive the work, it continued to flag.

Moore came to the Potteries in 1914. He lived at 23, Eaton Street, Hanley, a comfortable end-terrace house close to the home of the Church secretary in Festing Street and within easy walking-distance of the chapel. It is obvious from this that Hope was considered to be the senior partner of the two churches. Reflecting on the first months of his work, the Staffordshire Union recorded, "We believe that now [the Hope Diaconate's] courage may be met with some reward. The grouping of the Church with Silverdale under Mr. T.L. Moore's ministry has already been beneficial... we believe the right thing has been done to help the Church. We hope for a brighter future."

---

[193] *CYB 1939* P. 720. Visiting Tutbury Congregational Church in January of 2012 I found that the name was still recognised some of the members after the best part of a century
[194] *Report* P. 28

The promise of March of 1914 was short-lived; the outbreak of war on 28th July was at first hardly noticed. It was widely thought that it would be "all over by Christmas", and at the 1915 Assembly there was an optimistic report that while the church had lost eleven members (one wonders how many were young men killed in action), the church debt had been reduced by £370 from £918 to £548. The war was however to have devastating effects on the Churches.

That the shooting of the heir to the throne of the Austro-Hungarian Empire should have triggered the slaughter of the Western Front was the result of a series of international treaties that fell like dominoes as the great powers decided to use the war as a pretext for settling old scores. Britain's entry into the war was caused by the German invasion of Belgium and the conduct of the invading German forces, often exaggerated by the press who practically demonised the very nation whose theologians had been the teachers of many of the leading British theologians. The Germans, who had been regarded as our natural allies a few years before were now "the Hun", the brutal enemies of all that was good and noble; never mind the rather awkward relationship between the Kaiser and the British royal family. Ministers who had been devoted disciples of German theology for decades could suddenly be found saying that they had always been suspicious of the Germans.

Dr. Norman Goodall recalled, "The shock of the invasion of Belgium with its high-lighting as *the* great moral issue of the day resulted in an 'overnight' conversion of the vast majority of Free Churchmen to the necessity to fight. Long before Conscription the youth of the Free Churches flocked voluntarily to Kitchener's Army. Large numbers of our (Congregational) central city churches were denuded, within a few months, of their 'young men's classes' (often with memberships running into one or two hundred)."[195] Leading Free Church theologians such as the Scottish George Adam Smith became enthusiastic recruiting-sergeants for the armed forces, encouraging idealistic young men to join "the war to end war."

At Silverdale, and presumably at Hope as well, Longcaster Moore initially found the war a "nuisance", as the 1916 County Union

---

[195] In F.W. Dillistone, *C.H. Dodd: Interpreter of the New Testament* (London, 1977) P. 84

report puts it; "Some of the best officers and workers are now 'lads in khaki'. The loss of these young men – temporarily – means much to a church like Silverdale."[196] We of course know that many of those losses were not temporary at all, and those "lads in khaki" lie in the war cemeteries in Flanders' Fields, their names recorded on Silverdale's war memorial. Those who did return were rarely the same, and many never renewed their connection with the churches. The evidence of membership alone shows that in Hanley at least it was the War that struck the fatal blow to the Congregational Churches.

By the 1916 Assembly in Stafford, the true nature of the conflict had begun to be apparent. Another 17 members had been lost at Hope, no doubt among them young men cut down in Flanders' fields. The report to the Assembly said, "Like many others, the Hope Street Church has been badly hit by the war, and considerable difficulty has been encountered. Mr. Moore is, however, well supported by his officers and his services are undoubtedly appreciated. The Church is well holding its own." In fact it was struggling financially. The deficit of income over expenditure was a little over £61, and the income was £150.9/10d.

Moore had the difficult task of trying to keep the church together during the war, and ministering to families who lost sons, fathers, husbands, brothers in the terrible carnage of the "War to end War". He saw congregations go down, and week by week there was news that members, former Sunday school pupils and the young men who were the future of the chapel had been killed in the slaughter of the Western Front. Though numbers fell slightly from the high point of 195 at the end of Bairstow's pastorate in 1912 to 181 in 1914, no doubt owing in part to the pastoral vacancy, it was the loss of the young men of the church that caused the membership to drop to 156 in the following year and to 126 by 1917. It must all have been highly discouraging.

Moore left Staffordshire in 1916 to return to Holbeach, taking the pulpit of the Congregational Union Chapel in the town where he had laboured as a Primitive Methodist. He remained there until 1922, when he moved to Worpelston Congregational Church in Surrey. He retired from the ministry in 1933 and settled in the Norfolk village of Heacham,

---
[196] P. 28

where he attended the Methodist Church on Station Road. He died on January 8th 1938. The author of his obituary wrote: "He had been granted a life of long and varied service, in which he preached with vigour and enthusiasm the unsearchable riches of Christ. He was a man of very definite opinion, evangelical, whose whole attitude is summed up in the words, 'Christ for me.'"[197]

1918 saw the churches looking forward to the peace that was to come after the senseless slaughter of many of the most promising young men who had been their members. The report from the Federated Churches is worth quoting at length: "The central committee of the federated churches has carried on its work this year under special difficulties. Attendances have not been as good as formerly, but that may be due to the comparatively smooth working of affairs. The vacancy in the Hope Street, Hanley, and Silverdale group has been filled by a system of short temporary pastorates which have served a useful purpose in securing that pastoral as well as prophetic work has been done. But we hope that the vacant pastorate will soon be filled. The officials of the committee especially hope so."[198]

These temporary pastors are likely to have been of a variety of types, both retired pastors and students during the summer vacation. We know the name of only one, Rev. Alfred Holling, who had a temporary pastorate of five months in 1918-19. Trained under Rev. John Brown Paton at the Nottingham Congregational Institute, Holling had been pastor at Sedgley Congregational Church from 1876 until 1911, when he retired. He was a stalwart of the County Union, serving as its secretary for some years. The building at Sedgley, now called St. Andrews, was constructed during his pastorate. Born in 1843 in Barnsley, Holling continued to live in Sedgely after his retirement. As well as doing pastoral work and preaching at Hope, Holling helped with fund-raising activities; helping to organise a bazaar that raised £300. The fact that the church had to depend on such special events to raise necessary funds for running the chapel shows how bad its condition was. In fact, even with the £300 from the bazaar, the church had a 6d. deficit for 1918-19. Membership continued to decline, with the loss of 11 members over the

---

[197] *CYB 1939* P. 720
[198] *Report* P. 19

year. The committee might put on a brave face, but the fact was that Hope was in a very bad way, and the decline was continuing.

In retrospect we can see that the First World War severely weakened Congregationalism. Hope began the war with 181 members and finished it with 126; the Tabernacle began with 390 members and ended the war with 358. Neither church rose above the figure again; both entered a period of decline. For the wealthier, larger Church at the Tabernacle, this was not such an immediate cause for concern; they did not know that membership would continue to fall, and had lost, both numerically and proportionally, a smaller part of the membership. The loss of 32 members out of 390 would have been felt less in the daily life of the Church than the loss of 55 out of 181, especially when the losses devastated the PSA and the young men's group. Hope had already been in trouble, and the loss of some of the Church's best workers in the War sent the fellowship into a steep decline.

Henry Thomas Hood

1919 saw the Hope and Silverdale Churches get a new pastor of their own in the person of Rev. Henry Thomas Hood. Born in 1872, he was, like Hollings, a former student at the Congregational Institute in Nottingham.

The Congregational Institute (later Paton College), Forest Road, Nottingham, was established in 1863 to train for the ministry men from non-traditional backgrounds; these were generally what we today would call mature students, many had little formal education. It began with the work of Rev. Joseph Parker during his pastorate at Cavendish Congregational Church in Manchester. Parker came from a working background himself, and had entered the ministry without any formal training at all. During the 19th century, as the average level of education of the population improved, the entry requirements for theological colleges also became stricter. This did not mean that many who were gifted for ministerial work were disappointed, but rather that the numbers who went into the Congregational ministry without formal theological training increased. Parker realised that there were men who were entering the ministry under-prepared and under-equipped, but the existing colleges did not cater for them.

Parker believed that the solution was to start a new kind of college where the training would be largely in preaching and pastoral work, and mostly in English. Parker began this as a project of Cavendish Church, almost as an experiment to see if there was really any call for such a college. Cavendish had, like many large city churches of the period, substantial halls and school rooms, ample accommodation for a non-residential training course. The new project was christened "Cavendish Theological College", and within a year it had 20 students. Parker taught homiletics and invited two other Congregational pastors to assisting him in the work. The first of these was John Brown Paton, pastor of Wicker, Sheffield, who taught theology, apologetics, Philosophy and Old Testament. Rev. J. Radford Thompson of Heywood, Lancashire, taught English, Greek New Testament, and Church History.

The project was adopted by the Congregational Union, but as there was already a college in Manchester it was decided to move the new college to Nottingham, where it was re-named the Congregational Institute and housed in purpose-built accommodation in Forest Road. Paton was the first principal, and established the ethos of the new college.[199]

The Congregational Institute was created largely to train men for evangelistic work and to enable them to transition from being lay preachers to full-time evangelists and pastors. It differed in particular from the older colleges in that it did not teach the ancient languages, but taught men theology and preaching skills. It was not a residential college, and so the students 'boarded out' during their course. The principal during Hood's time as a student was Dr. David Lakie Ritchie, who served from 1904 until 1919, when he moved to Canada to teach at the Congregational College of British North America. Ritchie was himself an earnest and passionate preacher, described by the young D.H. Lawrence as possessing a "dramatic fascination."[200]. As a pastor in Dunfermline, Ritchie had helped to revive a flagging town congregation at Canmore Congregational Church, "His vigorous preaching, his organising abilities and his attractive personality drew not only his own

---

[199] See Kaye, *For The Work of Ministry*
[200] *The Selected Letters of D.H. Lawrence* (Cambridge, 2000) P. 7, letter dated 3rd December 1907

members to him, but also many then unconnected with any church"[201] Later he wrote a number of books on the 'youth question'.

After completing his course at the Nottingham Institute, Hood was called in 1911 to the pastorate of the Congregational Church at Silloth, Cumbria, where he served for four years. He also served four years at his next pastorate, Shaw, Oldham, Manchester. In 1919 he took over the joint pastorate of Hanley and Silverdale. The membership at Hope did not recover from the effects of World War I, and it is likely that the Spanish Flu pandemic further damaged the congregation. In 1919 the membership was at 115, and by 1920 it had fallen still further to 113. Students from the Institute were often called to undertake work in challenging circumstances, and Hood understood that he was not going to have an easy time. He quickly set to work with great enthusiasm in an effort to reverse the decline.

In 1921 it was reported to the Staffordshire Union that, "The pastorate of the Rev. H.T. Hood has been much blessed in both churches. The interior of Hope Street has been renovated. A debt extinction effort to wipe out all liabilities has been launched and is being carried forward energetically. A short mission was held by the Rev. F. Ives Cator of Burslem. A young people's society, started by Mr. Hood, is doing well."[202] The aim of the young people's society would have been to retain those young people who were now so often lost to the Churches on reaching adulthood. Neither the young people's society nor the debt extension effort, in the event, seem to have done anything to pull the Church out of decline.

Elsewhere, in the suburbs, Congregationalism was doing better. In 1922 the new Wolstanton chapel was opened by Rev. R.F. Horton of Hampstead, one of the chief men in Congregationalism at the time. In the urban areas it was a different story; the Churches at Stoke and Hanley Park were small and poor, and Hope was still struggling financially. Though there had been some enthusiasm when the debt extinction scheme began, with the annual income rising to £417.0/3d, the following year it fell back down to normal levels and the Church

---

[201] *http://dunfermline.urc.org.uk/?page_id=191* Accessed 1/8/2012
[202] *Report* P. 20

received £187.7/4d, meaning that the deficit for 1921-22 was £78.3/9d. Yet the annual report read: "The congregations at Hope Street have increased and the financial position has been well maintained. £50 has been repaid of the debt due to the Union. The young people's work is in a flourishing condition, and, while the times have been felt to be difficult, the Pastor has given a bold lead which has been well supported. A Church Council, comprised of Pastor and Deacons and two representatives from each organisation, has been formed and promises to be a real inspiration to the Church."[203] There is a stark contradiction between these hopeful reports and the real state of affairs, as if the Secretary of the Union was still trying to put a brave face on it all.

The following year promised better. Though the church had a debt of £300, it ended the year 1922-3 with a surplus of 5d. Membership dropped slightly, probably owing to the deaths of a few older members of the church. Still, it could be said by those on the ground that things were actually looking up. By 1924 the County Union could report, "The visitors had an encouraging meeting with the minister and deacons in December 1923. Though no extraordinary progress could be reported, there was ample evidence of sound and steady work being done."[204] Here was perhaps the greatest frustration for the Church; it was not that they were '"settled on their lees" and doing nothing, they were doing a great deal; but none of it seemed to be having very much impact. There was one bright point; Hope still had a flourishing Sunday school, where attendances were usually over 250. This was not as encouraging as it would have been in the pre-war years, however. The transition between Sunday school and church was increasingly uncertain; many who studied at the Sunday school behind the chapel simply ceased to have any connection at all with organised Christianity when they became adults. The Church was also in the difficult condition of subsidising the Sunday school with money it did not have. Though the teachers were volunteers, there were costs such as books, work materials for the children, and of course prizes and certificates.

The optimism was short-lived; the progress that the earlier reports had mentioned so enthusiastically came to nothing. The 1925

---

[203] *Report* P. 23
[204] *Report* P. 22

Assembly at Burslem heard that the church had "suffered some severe losses in 1924."[205] Church finances were only maintained by a bazaar, a form of fund-raising that had become increasingly important for the struggling cause. In an attempt to secure the men of the Church, Hood established a men's class in the Church, evidence that the PSA that had been so successful under Gascoine had ceased, probably another casualty of the war. The following year Hood left to take up a pastorate at Ellesmere Port, perhaps discouraged by the lack of progress he had seen in Hanley.

Like his predecessor, Hood lived in Hanley and gave the bulk of his time to the urban church rather than to Silverdale. He lived close to the chapel, at 440, Waterloo Road, on Cobridge Bank; a relatively large, middle-class terraced house. Also like Moore, he tried very hard to turn around the slow but steady decline of the Church, and like Pastor Moore he found the burden was too much for him, and moved on without seeing any real progress for all the effort he put into the work.

Following his ministry at Hanley and Silverdale, Hood served for six years at Ellesmere Port. In 1932 he moved to a joint-pastorate at Pontefract and Brotherton in Yorkshire. His obituary says, "Thus his experience was varied, and he undertook some pastorates which presented great difficulties, and offered little to encourage. Mr. Hood, however, was a man of buoyant spirit; not easily daunted, and he served in all his pastorates with a zeal and devotion that earned him the high esteem and affection of his people."[206] His health began to fail in the 1940s, and in 1946 he was forced to retire. He died in July, 1949, having ministered through both World Wars. His obituary noted that, "His faithful ministry, his cheerful personality, his kindly and gracious spirit and his readiness to serve endeared him to all his people."

---

[205] *Report P. 21*
[206] *CYB 1950* P. 514

Chapter 11: Trials and Revival

After Hood

Henry Thomas Hood was the last joint-pastor of Hope and Silverdale. In 1927 the North Staffordshire Federation broke up by the mutual consent of the federated Churches, and Hope was left to find its own way again. Unable to support a pastor of its own, the Church approached the struggling cause at Hanley Park and proposed that the two smaller Hanley Churches should have a joint pastorate. While this made geographical sense, it was financially difficult; both had serious financial issues and falling membership rolls. Despite this, the two churches began to consider the logistics of a joint pastorate.

Urgent and expensive repairs to the Park building in 1926-7 forced a delay in the establishment of the joint pastorate with Hope. By early 1927 the work was finished and the two churches began to consult on calling a minister who was acceptable to both. Though the County Union frowned on Churches in financial trouble calling a pastor, efforts were made to secure a lay-pastor without the help of the Union. Their choice fell on a Mr. T.O. Sander of Stone. We know very little about Mr. Sander apart from this, because he was never recognised as a full Congregational pastor by the Union. One intriguing possibility is that he is the same as Mr. J.O. Sander, who was a Wesleyan Methodist lay agent in the Stafford circuit from 1913 to 1928.[207] It would not have been at all unusual for Mr. Sander to have followed the same path as Pastor Moore and accepted a call to service in a Congregational Church. J.O. Sander had served briefly in the trenches, but within a year was discharged as 'unfit for further service', and so he had functioned as a *de facto* minister during the latter part of the War.[208] Respected and loved in the Wesleyan Churches, J.O. Sander left his work in the Stafford circuit on 14th March 1928, about the time that the mysterious T.O. Sander took up the work in Hanley. The evidence is not conclusive, but it is compelling. He

---

[207] D.G. Kirby, *Living Stones: A History of Methodists in Eccleshall* (London, 2003). The letters 'J' and 'T' can be very similar to one another. It would not be unknown for the *Congregational Year Book* to include a spelling error. Eccleshall and Stone are of course very close to each other.

[208] Kirby, P. 51

remained resident at Stone throughout his Hanley ministry, which hampered his work in the Potteries; the Committee of the Staffordshire Union, which was responsible for the two churches, cautioned that the financial situation of the two churches was so bad that the best they could do was support Mr. Sander as a temporary minister.

The financial situation at Hope was terrible. On June 10th 1929 the Executive Committee of the Staffordshire Union heard that, "The Church is heavily overdrawn at the bank, which refuses to advance any more money. After hearing from the treasurer the result of his own investigations and his interviews with the Hope Deacons, it was resolved that a loan not exceeding £250 be granted to allow the church to liquidate its debts, subject to the trustees first of all agreeing to transfer the trust of the property to the Union." In response to this report, "Mr. Hartley moved and Mr. Shaw seconded that the Hope Church be informed that in view of the unsatisfactory state of its finances and the unlikelihood under present conditions of any substantial improvement the executive committee cannot see its way to make any further loan, and that a special meeting of the Northern Committee together with the Hope diaconate be arranged, if possible."[209] The motion was carried, and the Church at Hope limped on, even more heavily indebted to the County Union. Of course, none of this appeared in the annual report of the Union.

Because of these financial difficulties on the eve of the Great Depression (the Wall Street Crash would take place in October 1929), Mr. Sander's support was impossible, realistically speaking. In the event the Union continued the pastorate for some 18 months, but could not continue the arrangement beyond March 31st 1930. Hope and Park were without ministers or money, at a time when money was in short supply for everyone. Today the most likely outcome of such a situation would have been to merge Hope with either Park or the Tabernacle, but in 1930 the Congregationalists were still determined to keep every Church open if at all possible. So, in January 1930 it was reported to the Executive Committee that, "A fresh arrangement whereby a List A [ordained] minister might be invited to take charge of Hope and Silverdale"[210] was

---

[209] *Minutes of the Executive Committee of the Staffordshire Congregational Union* June 10th 1929
[210] *Executive Committee Minutes*

being considered. Looking back on the whole Park and Hope joint pastorate, the Committee reflected, "The arrangement between the Hope and Park Churches, Hanley, had not been a success, and... the joint pastorate was terminated on March 31st." It is a salutary lesson that something that makes sense on paper may not actually work in the real world.

Though negotiations continued to try to set up a joint pastorate with Hope and Silverdale once again, in the event both Hope and Park would cease to be Congregational Churches as a more attractive proposition was to be brought to them both from a rather unexpected source.

Under a New Banner
Park was on the verge of closure; the Church that had begun the new century with such optimism had lasted only about three decades, and the last decade had seen steep decline. Hope was practically bankrupt, a membership of 77, mostly poor, struggling to keep a historic building going in the centre of Hanley. The only real asset was a large and thriving Sunday school, which did not translate into income. The joint pastorate experiment had only proved how weak the Churches were, and had ended in humiliation. They looked to the County Union for help, but knew from years of experience that the Union could not guarantee anything. They needed something more than the County Union could provide, and must have spent much time in prayer seeking divine assistance. Help came, quite unexpectedly, and from a source that no-one could have anticipated. Suddenly, at the end of 1930, the *Sentinel* was filled with reports of enthusiastic mass meetings in the city's largest halls, divine healings, thousands coming forward to seek salvation, and singing in the streets. All of it was connected with a man called Edward Jeffreys; and then this charismatic evangelist approached the leadership of Hope and Park with a suggestion that would end their financial difficulties, but which would also radically change both churches; they could join his new Bethel Evangelistic Society, gaining both his support and an influx of new and enthusiastic converts from the great meetings he was holding. The offer was too good to refuse.

Edward Jeffreys

So who was this Edward Jeffreys who had set the Potteries in a blaze of evangelistic fervour not seen since the heyday of Primitive Methodism? The soft-spoken yet assured young Welshman who came offering salvation to the dying Churches was part of an inter-war religious revolution that changed the face of British Christianity.

The older churches struggled to adapt to the new world that emerged after the First World War. While there had been those in the Churches who, as pacifists, had opposed a war that came to be seen as a largely pointless waste of life and resources, during the war the majority of denominational leaders enthusiastically supported the conflict and characterised the war as a righteous crusade against Prussian militarism, too often identifying Christianity with a jingoistic patriotism that sent young men off to die in the Trenches. In a post-war world of cynicism and what has been described as "confident agnosticism"[211], the traditional denominations struggled. At the same time the period saw the rise of new groups. Some of these, like the Jehovah's Witnesses and the Christian Scientists, were definitely outside the pale of Christian orthodoxy, but there were others that were more orthodox in their teaching. Among these were the Pentecostal Churches. Edward Jeffreys was brought up in the midst of this new tradition, and belonged to a family that had a formative influence on the young Pentecostal movement.

Edward Jeffreys was born in 1889 in Nantyffyllon, a part of the Welsh mining town of Maesteg, in the South Wales valleys.[212] His father, Stephen Jeffreys, was a miner and a member of the Welsh Independent Church at Duffryn Chapel, though when the family moved house they also transferred to another Independent Chapel, Siloh, closer to their new home. The family was poor but respectable. Stephen himself was born in 1876, and his main recreation, according to his son, was playing in a flute band belonging to the church.[213] Thomas Jeffreys, the father of Stephen and George, was a coal miner in one of the many collieries that

---

[211] Adrian Hastings, quoted in Kaye, *Mansfield College*, P. 170
[212] I am indebted to Keith Malcolmson for a copy of the chapter of his book *Pentecostal Pioneers Remembered* that deals with Edward Jeffreys
[213] The standard biography of Stephen Jeffreys is Edward Jeffreys, *Stephen Jeffreys – the Beloved Evangelist* (London, 1946)

were the chief reason for a town existing high in the Llynffi valley. He was a victim of "chronic bronchitis", probably actually Miner's Lung, and died in 1895 at the age of only forty-seven.[214] He left Stephen, his eldest son, as the chief breadwinner of the family. Stephen Jeffreys had begun his work in the mine at the age of 12. It was hard, long and unhealthy work, work which many Welsh mothers wished to keep their children from. But the pits were the main employers, and so the son so often took up the same work that had killed his father. It was said that in the winter the only time a miner saw the sun was after 2PM on Saturday, which was a half-day, and on Sunday. A miner could expect to start on two shillings a day (a little under six pounds in modern money) and work long days. It was with some relief that Kezia Jeffreys was able to get her younger and frailer son George a position in the Co-Operative store. Such posts were highly sought-after, because shop assistants were regarded as a cut above colliers; this could lead to an unpleasant snobbery at times, but it is pleasant to be able to report that nothing of the kind ever disturbed the Jeffreys family.

Fig. 14: Siloh, Nantyffyllon, today. Picture by Dr. Gerard Charmley

---

[214] Desmond Cartwright: *The Great Evangelists* (London, 1986) P. 14

The chapel was the centre of both cultural and religious life in Wales in the period. D.R. Davies, a contemporary of Stephen Jeffreys in Maesteg, writes, "Let me point out that the Welsh Nonconformity in which I was reared did not make for narrowness and fanaticism of mind as so many of the frustrated, embittered critics of my generation have maintained. Today [writing in 1958] we are living upon the capital of those same 'tin Bethels', and when that gives out (as it is now doing) the futility and leanness of our contemporary life will become more obvious and disastrous."[215] Siloh, Nantyffyllon, was a Welsh-language chapel; the majority of the inhabitants of Maesteg were Welsh speakers. Its building was designed by the celebrated Welsh chapel architect and minister Thomas Thomas, Glandwr, and opened in 1876. Today it has been converted into flats.

Along with the huge influence of 'Chapel', the Bible was a daily fact of life; Davis writes, "Bible reading was an institution of Welsh family life. People knew their Bible. It was a layman's book."[216] The miner home from the pit settled down in his easy chair by the fire after his bath to read the Bible. D.R. Davies described his mother as "The greatest Bible student I have ever known."[217] A child might well be promised extra pocket-money for reading the Bible through in a year,[218] or for memorising sections of the book. Davies' parents were by no means unusual; Davies was not a son of the manse, but like Stephen Jeffreys, the son of a coal miner, and a miner himself for a brief period.

Davies describes Maesteg as "One of the pleasantest coal-valleys in Glamorgan. It is a wide valley, and the collieries are situated away in the mountains, so that the town hardly wears the aspect of a colliery district, as do the Rhondda, the Garw and the Monmouthshire valleys. It is surrounded by delightful scenery and within eight miles of the sea."[219] This was where Edward Jeffreys spent his early years, and while the pits have all gone, the landscape remains much as it was a century ago.

---

[215] D.R. Davies: *In Search of Myself* (London, 1961) P. 29
[216] Davies, P. 29
[217] Davies P. 30
[218] Davies gratefully recalls his parents doing this
[219] Davies, P. 34

Stephen Jeffreys was one of those awakened to the reality of God in the 1904-5 revival but who was not openly ungodly before that. His need was to see that his own righteousness was never enough for God to accept him, and that he needed the righteousness of another. Being a respectable church-goer, he attended one of the special services held during the revival and was convicted of his sin. The liberty he sought came in a meeting at Siloh Independent Chapel, Nantyffyllon, addressed by the earnest evangelical minister of the Church, Rev. William Glasnant Jones, on November 17th 1904. There Stephen embraced Christ as his saviour. He soon joined the church at Siloh and took an active part in the activities of the church, including preaching in the streets with other men from the Church, and with Pastor Glasnant Jones.

Pentecostalism came to the United Kingdom from the United States of America, via Norway[220], whatever 'forerunners' there may have been, such as Edward Irving and the Catholic Apostolic Church in the Victorian era. It grew out of the Wesleyan tradition; while other evangelicals identified only one crisis-point, that of conversion, in the Christian experience, John Wesley taught that there was the possibility of a second experience, that of "Perfect Love." He laid a heavy emphasis on this teaching at some points in his ministry, something that added to the tension between him and the Calvinist wing of the Evangelical Revival.

The later Holiness movement, led by such figures as Asa Mahan and Charles G. Finney, drew on Wesley to create a distinctive view of the Christian life with these two crisis points. Mahan and Finney were neither of them Wesleyans, or Methodists; Mahan (1799-1889) was a New England Congregationalist, and Finney (1821-1875) a Presbyterian who later identified himself with Mahan's Congregationalism. Finney was one of the leading revivalists of his day, but depended very heavily on what he called 'New Measures' to create an emotionally-charged atmosphere. He was criticised by older evangelical leaders including Asahel Nettleton and Charles Hodge for this approach, and for teaching a theology that disregarded the doctrine of original sin and taught that revival, understood by the earlier tradition as "A surprising work of

---

[220] See: *http://pentecostalpioneers.org/pioneerslist.html*

God" was in fact the assured result of the proper use of means.[221] After a career as an itinerant revivalist, Finney tried to settle as a minister in New York in 1836. The attempt was not a success; methods adapted for creating excitement in a community for a few weeks of evangelism were not appropriate or effective in a settled congregation. From New York, Finney went to teach at Asa Mahan's Oberlin College, Ohio. He continued to keep in touch with the scenes of his labours as an itinerant evangelist, and became increasingly concerned at how many of his converts were falling away and returning to their old lives. Rather than concluding that they were never really converted, Finney decided that they had needed a second experience to confirm them in the Christian life; he and Mahan began to study the literature of Perfectionism, and came to the Wesleyan teaching of a 'second blessing'. Finney's teaching was more radical and more thought-out than Wesley's, but in common with Wesley he came to believe that there was a 'higher Christian life' available to believers. Just as he taught that revival was the result of the right use of means, so he taught that one could reach this higher life by the ascent of a number of steps.[222]

Others followed where Finney led; by the end of the 19th century there were conventions in the United States and the United Kingdom teaching variations on the 'Higher Life' doctrine of Finney; in the United kingdom such teaching was identified with the Annual Keswick Convention, which began in 1875. Abandoning Wesley's terminology, the Holiness movement called the second crisis point in the Christian life "The Baptism of the Holy Spirit." The difficulty that faced them was identifying marks of whether or not a person had undergone this experience.

The Pentecostal movement emerged from the Holiness movement, gave a definite answer to the question as to how to recognise the Baptism of the Holy Spirit. Modern Pentecostalism began in the United States at Charles Parham's Bible school in Topeka, Kansas, where ecstatic speech, identified with the Biblical 'speaking in other tongues', was recognised as the distinguishing characteristic of the Baptism of the

---

[221] For Finney, see Charles E. Hambrick-Stowe, *Charles G. Finney and the Spirit of American Evangelicalism* (Grand Rapids, 1996)
[222] Hambrick-Stowe, Pp.181-2

Holy Spirit. Students from Parham's school were invited to various local churches and took his teaching with them. Parham himself held meetings in many towns where he announced that people were baptised with the Holy Spirit, sanctified and healed of diseases. One of his pupils, a black preacher called W.J. Seymour, was invited to Los Angeles to preach at a small African-American Holiness church. Though he had not himself received the 'Baptism', Seymour preached it, declaring that, "Anyone who does not speak in tongues is not baptised with the Holy Spirit."[223] He was immediately excluded by older members who disagreed with this new teaching. Some members of the Church remained with him, and they started the Azusa Street Mission, regarded by Pentecostals as the birthplace of the Pentecostal movement. From that old Methodist chapel in Azusa Street Parham's teachings went out to the world, though they were often modified in the transmission.

The historian Walter Hollenweger described early British Pentecostalism as "A blending of aristocratic Anglicanism and Welsh revivalism."[224] The Anglican element came through two men, Rev. Alexander A. Boddy and Mr. Cecil Polhill-Turner. A.A. Boddy, the first British Pentecostal, was the Anglican vicar of All Saints', Sunderland, who received his Pentecostal experience through Rev. T.B. Barrett in Oslo in 1907. Boddy had the experience that Pentecostalism characterises as the 'Baptism in the Holy Spirit' and 'speaking in tongues'. Returning to England, he began to teach Pentecostalism in his Church. The parish hall of All Saints' became a centre for English Pentecostalism. Boddy remained within the Church of England to the end of his life and regarded Pentecostalism as a revival within the Church. He and other like-minded men in the Church of England joined in the formation of the Pentecostal Missionary Union in 1909 as a co-ordinating body for Anglican Pentecostals.[225] Cecil Polhill-Turner, Squire of Howbury Hall, was an evangelical Anglican who had served as a missionary in China and Tibet. One of the 'Cambridge Seven', promising and aristocratic undergraduates who went to China in 1885 with Hudson Taylor's China Inland Mission, Polhill-Turner had considerable private wealth as well as standing among Evangelicals.

---

[223] Walter J. Hollenweger, *The Pentecostals* (London, 1969) P. 22
[224] Hollenweger P. 176
[225] Hollenweger, P. 185

In 1910 reports of events in Sunderland reached the converts of 1904-5 in Maesteg. Special meetings were arranged at Maesteg, and among those who embraced the Pentecostal message were the Jeffreys brothers. In fact Edward was the first of the family to have the experience understood by Pentecostals as "the Baptism of the Holy Spirit"; he went on a holiday, presumably with a number of other young people from the Churches, to Crosshands, near Ammanford, and at a meeting "began to speak in other tongues."[226] This led to his father and uncle changing their minds about the Pentecostal movement, which they had hitherto been suspicious of, and the whole family became Pentecostal.

Congregational Churches baptise the infants of believers, but even by 1910 many Pentecostals were embracing Baptist principles; therefore Edward Jeffreys and his father were baptised by immersion on profession of faith in the open air on March 26th 1911.[227] This baptism was a break from the older Churches and an identification with the new Pentecostal movement; the baptism was conducted by Mr. Price Davies, a local Pentecostal.

Stephen Jeffreys not only preached in the open air but spoke of his faith to his fellows in the coal-mine. This did not adversely affect his work; he attacked a coal-seam with as much earnestness as he preached. Several of his fellow-miners professed faith through his work, and he began to consider his future. His decision may well have been affected by the premature death of his father from the effects of work down the pit. Discerning a call to the ministry, Stephen Jeffreys became a missioner, at first in his spare time, travelling around south Wales to preach at special services. By this time his son Edward was old enough to go with him. As Edward had an excellent singing voice, he acted as his father's singer, giving solo performances of popular Gospel songs. The success of this ministry meant that Stephen was soon able to give up his work as a miner. He began his work in Cwmtwrch, near Swansea, and was then asked by a Quaker to come to Pen-Y-Bont in Radnorshire, not far from Llandrindod Wells, to conduct a campaign based at the historic Pales Meeting House.

---

[226] Cartwright, P. 24
[227] Cartwright P. 26

Fig. 15: The Pales Friends' Meeting House

While his brother George entered a Pentecostal Bible School in Preston, Stephen never received any formal theological education. His first pastorate was at a mission-hall in Llanelli called Island Place Mission, where he came in 1914. The building was a small structure that seated about 200 and had previously been used by the Mormons. The church grew rapidly under Stephen Jeffreys' leadership, and Edward Jeffreys was wonderfully happy there. His father was away often on evangelistic work in the week, and in the holidays he was in great demand as a convention speaker. Despite this, Edward Jeffreys was close to his father and remained so as long as Stephen Jeffreys lived.

Pentecostalism is characterised as a restorationist movement, with its emphasis on the miraculous and its attempt to get back to the First Century. In the uncertainties of inter-war Britain such ideas were attractive to many, and while the older denominations were struggling in the 1920s, the Pentecostal movement was growing and attracting many converts with its bright singing, powerful preaching and emphasis on holiness and consecration. This was why Stephen Jeffreys was in great demand, even taking a campaign in the West End at what is now Kensington Temple, but was then the Horbury Chapel Congregational Church. Cecil Polhill-Turner had approached the Church at Horbury Chapel, which was small and struggling, seeking to help. The result was

Stephen Jeffreys coming to preach in Kensington. The Mission was a great success, many were converted, and there were many who were miraculously healed. The Pentecostal emphasis on miracles soon ended the mission; the pastor did not want Pentecostalism in a Congregational Church![228] This mission would set the pattern for Edward's own campaigns; the rejection of the Pentecostal movement by the Congregational pastor further cemented the division between the old and the new.

The other thing that characterised early Pentecostalism was its emphasis on *experience*. It may indeed not be too much to say that the experience came before the theology; that is to say that the manifestation of what came to be called "speaking in tongues" came before any theological basis was worked out. The emphasis on the direct experience of God was no doubt attractive; liberals and Pentecostals alike were *mystics*, placing great emphasis on experience. After the raw emotional suffering of "the war to end wars", people were looking for emotional healing, and that is what the Pentecostal outpouring of emotion offered.

The movement as a whole was astonishingly historically illiterate; it sought in some ways to leap directly from Pentecost and the Book of Acts to the 20th century as if what happened between was of little significance. There was a certain attraction about this; people would forget all the difficult issues in the past history of Christianity, not least the role Anglican and Nonconformist ministers alike had played in drumming up enthusiasm for the War. The unfortunate result of this was an impatience with the existing Churches and a naïve acceptance of traditional interpretations of Biblical texts as though they were self-evident and not in fact based more on experience than upon the text itself. A prime example of this, and in many ways one of the defining characteristics of Pentecostalism, is what is called "Speaking in tongues"; despite the Biblical evidence that the 'Tongues' of the Day of Pentecost were human languages (languages that are even named in the text in Acts 2), the random vocalizations of the Pentecostal converts were treated as if they were the Biblical phenomenon. The same phenomenon was declared to be *the* evidence of "the Baptism of the Holy Spirit", and an experience that every Christian should have,

---

[228] Jack Hywel-Davies, *KT: The Kensington Temple Story* (London, 1998) Pp. 33-4

regardless of the fact that the Bible says none of this. Divine healing was regarded as available for all believers, despite the fact that the New Testament teaches nothing of the sort; the movement was not primarily driven by Biblical teaching but by the experience of its leaders. The possibility of direct revelation from God in some cases meant that supposed "divine insights", often really the mistaken interpretations of men who were ignorant of the Biblical languages and misled by archaic phraseology in the Authorised Version of the Bible ('tongues', an archaic word meaning in context 'languages' being again a good example), could in practice trump the plain meaning of the text itself.

On the other hand, Stephen and George Jeffreys were first and foremost preachers rather than miracle-workers, and in that they stood firmly in the Nonconformist tradition, in some ways consciously. The men who most influenced Stephen Jeffreys were Welsh preachers in the great tradition of evangelicalism, from John Elias[229] (1774-1841), one of the most popular of all Welsh preachers, to R.B. Jones of Porth[230] (1869-1933), one of the great men of the 1904-5 revival and a stalwart of Welsh Evangelicalism. Unlike the Jeffreys brothers, Jones was not a Pentecostal, but still Edward wrote that Stephen's "hero as a preacher was the Rev. R.B. Jones, of Porth. Whenever we discussed great preachers my father would always bring in his name as the greatest preacher he had ever heard: he would walk many miles to hear this mighty man of God." This acted as a corrective to Pentecostal restorationism; they learned from the past and saw much that was good there.

The Jeffreys brothers, with their emphasis on mass evangelism, were also a corrective to the elitism of some of the early Pentecostals, who regarded their main work as "ripening the Church for the rapture"[231], gathering in the elite of the Church. This approach, rather similar to excesses of some of the early Brethren, meant that the Pentecostal assemblies targeted those who were already evangelical Christians, rather than the masses outside the Churches. The Jeffreys brothers would have none of this; they took as their models the great

---

[229] See Edward Morgan, *John Elias: Life and Letters* (Edinburgh, 1973)
[230] See Noel Gibbard: *R.B. Jones: Gospel Ministry in Turbulent Times* (Bridgend, 2009)
[231] Boulton, *George Jeffreys* P. 22

evangelists who sought to bring the Gospel to those who were perishing, though they had their own disagreements and misunderstandings with the existing Churches. Rather than making use of gimmicks and sensational tricks, the Jeffreys brothers were pre-eminently preachers in the Welsh tradition who relied on their addresses to win the audience. Stephen's sermons were, "Packed with meaning, straight to the point and spiced with humour", and George, "captured his audience by his musical voice..." and "the logical clarity of his always brief but powerful sermons."[232]

Many new Pentecostal churches had their beginnings in the 1920s through the evangelistic campaigns of Stephen and George Jeffreys. One of these was the Southend Christian Tabernacle, which came out of a campaign held by Stephen in Southend-on-Sea in May 1926. Edward Jeffreys was asked to take the oversight of the work, and so he became pastor of a large Pentecostal Church. The church continued to grow under his leadership, with many being added by conversion. The building was a simple wooden structure, but it was packed every Sunday, in contrast to many grander buildings in the town. No wonder that Dr. W.E. Orchard, minister of the King's Weigh House Congregational Church and soon to become a Roman Catholic, was reported to have said that "The future of religion in Britain would be in the hands of the Roman Catholics on the one hand, and on the other side with the Fundamentalists."[233]

In 1928 Stephen Jeffreys went to Bristol to pioneer a work. It was by now his pattern to form his converts into a church, and he asked Mr. Heard, a friend of his son's who was seeking a pastorate, to take charge. Seeing the scale of the work at Bristol, Mr. Heard was overcome and declared that there was no way he could take the oversight of the work at Bristol. Disappointed, Stephen called on his son, the man he knew would not let him down. "Well, Eddie, you must come here for three weeks until I can find a suitable man."[234]

---

[232] Hollenweger, P. 197
[233] Cartwright, P. 112
[234] Edward Jeffreys, *Stephen Jeffreys* P. 76

At first Edward Jeffreys came for only a three-week period. To his amazement some 250 people came forward after his first sermon in Bristol, "It is impossible to describe my feelings on that memorable night," he wrote later. "I have never experienced anything just so wonderful as happened then. But I would give almost anything to go through that same thrill and experience again."[235] He was won for Bristol by that experience, and soon the church bought a large former United Methodist chapel in Milk Street and re-named it 'Bethel Temple'. It was to be the first of many. Looking back on the work, Edward reflected, "They were to me days of heaven upon earth. God was preparing me quietly, and all unknowingly, for campaigns similar to my father's."[236]

In 1929 Edward used Bristol as a base of operations for a series of campaigns in other parts of the country. The plan was simple: Edward Jeffreys would arrive in a town, book the largest public halls available, and begin a series of evangelistic and healing meetings. These meetings would continue for some weeks, and the end result would be a new Bethel Temple, and in the case of a city of any size, more than one new Temple. He worked steadily northwards, and by the end of 1930 he reached the Potteries.

The Bethel Evangelistic Society had a simple set of Articles of Faith, which were:
1. The Trinity of the Godhead; Father, Son and Holy Spirit.
2. The Fall of Man. Total Depravity.
3. The Divinely Inspired Word of God and its Infallibility.
4. The virgin birth of Jesus by the Virgin Mary.
5. The Deity and humanity of Jesus Christ.
6. The atoning sacrifice as the only means whereby man may have the guilt of sin removed.
7. Divine healing for the body.
8. The baptism of the Holy Ghost as the spiritual heritage for every believer.
9. The personal, literal return of Jesus Christ for his own.
10. The kingdoms of this world ultimately becoming the

---
[235] *Stephen Jeffreys* P. 77
[236] *Stephen Jeffreys* P. 77

kingdoms of our Lord and Christ. He shall reign until all powers are subject to him.[237]

The Pentecostal Desmond Cartwright, in his biography of George and Stephen Jeffreys, says of the Bethel Churches that, "It is not proper to consider them as being fully Pentecostal."[238] Nevertheless, in emphasising healing and teaching "the baptism of the Holy Ghost" as a particular experience subsequent to conversion that all Christians should seek, they were certainly very close to Pentecostalism. The pre-millennial emphasis is also typical for the newer denominations of the period.

Edward Jeffreys arrived in the Potteries in September of 1930 and engaged the Victoria Hall in Hanley for his first meetings. The hall was soon packed out, and he began to hold meetings in the King's Hall in Stoke as well. The centre of the campaigns was Gospel-preaching, not supposed manifestations of the Holy Spirit, contrasting favourably with many modern imitations where the Word is hardly preached at all. One of his hearers commented, "Such preaching as that of Pastor Edward Jeffreys I have seldom, if ever, heard. To me it is remarkable because of its purity and simplicity, its richness in Scripture quotation, its avoidance of emotional anecdote, and its irresistible power."[239] Anglican clergyman P.D. Haddock commented, "I was struck by the atmosphere of reverence that prevailed."[240] Richard Kayes, converted under his ministry in Bootle, writes, "I have heard, met and accompanied many well known healing evangelists from both sides of the Atlantic but none impressed as did Edward Jeffreys. He was quiet, compassionate, undemonstrative; so unlike his uncle George who founded the Elim Movement. There was not the disturbing dichotomy between what is promised and what is performed that you find in so many healing missions."[241]

The many testimonies of divine healing from the Potteries campaign were remarkable, but of course they caused a great deal of controversy, as according to a report in a medical journal, "Splints and

---

[237] Cited in Anon. *A Man Sent From God*
[238] Cartwright, P. 99
[239] Quoted in *A Man Sent From God*
[240] *A Man Sent From God*
[241] *A Man Sent From God*, Pp. 59-60

surgical appliances were, it was stated, removed from crippled children."[242] This led to the Corporation, understandably concerned that some of the children might well not in fact be healed and therefore adversely affected by the removal of the devices, to cancel all of Edward Jeffreys' bookings of municipal halls. This briefly brought the campaign to a grinding halt, but Edward Jeffreys was never an unreasonable man. Recognising that the town Corporation had legitimate concerns, Jeffreys promised that no appliances would be removed from children, and after a brief correspondence the matter was resolved, and the meetings were allowed to continue. Edward Jeffreys put far more emphasis on the Gospel than he did on healing.

Many reading about the thousands who were saved through Edward Jeffreys' work will ask, what was his secret? Speaking to one of the converts from the Liverpool campaigns, he said, "What happened at Bootle had little to do with me, it was the work of God and to Him belongs the glory."[243] Jeffreys believed that it was not him at all, but that God graciously worked through him, and that we cannot force God to bless our work.

Thousands came to hear Edward Jeffreys. As he had begun as his father's soloist, so he continued to emphasise singing in his campaigns; quite understandably for a musical Welshman. Groups would walk home through the streets of the city singing the "Bethel Rallying Song."

> *We are marching in the ranks of Bethel,*
> *Keep the Bethel Banner waving high,*
> *Tell the old, old story*
> *Of the One who came to die,*
> *That we all might have Salvation*
> *And the power to conquer every foe,*
> *Keep the Bethel Banner waving*
> *Wheresoever we may go.*[244]

---

[242] *The Lancet, 1930, 2: 1130*
[243] Richard Kayes: *One Man and His God* (Milton Keynes, 2007) P. 59
[244] Quoted in *A Man Sent from God*

Edward Jeffreys understood the need of pastoral care for the new converts, and he made sure that each Bethel had a minister, ideally of its own, but where that was not possible there would be shared pastorates. Among the men who served in the other Bethels in the Potteries was Mr. A. Heard, the young man whose diffidence and reluctance to take up the work at Bristol had led to the foundation of the movement; he became pastor of the Longton Bethel.

As a result of the revival that accompanied the campaigns at least eight fellowships were founded in the Potteries and the surrounding districts. These included churches at Hanley, Shelton, Longton, Burslem, Silverdale, Milton, Talke, and Congleton in Cheshire. These fellowships needed buildings in which to meet; most of these were entirely new fellowships, and new buildings, simple and plain in style, were built for them. New Temples were built at Silverdale, Longton and Milton; in the case of Milton the church (now Breathe City Church) has moved to Abbey Hulton, but at Silverdale and Longton the simple 1930s Temples remain, though the Silverdale Temple is now used by the Methodists.

In Hanley, however, Edward Jeffreys somehow came to hear of two small Congregational churches that were struggling but which had strategically located buildings. He approached the leaders of both Park and Hope with a proposal that the Bethel Evangelistic Society should take over the churches, which would then become Bethel Temples. Large numbers of converts from the campaign would be added to the churches, and the Bethel Society would supply pastors. Both churches agreed to the proposal, and a new era began at Hope Street.

Chapter 12: Under New Management

The Hanley Bethel Temple had a new name on the board outside, but in a very real sense it was the same church, if we understand the church Biblically as the people rather than an organisation. While the records for Hope have disappeared, a letter from Mr. Thomas Hartley concerning the events at Park has been preserved inside the minute book of the Executive Committee of the Staffordshire Congregational Union. The letter documents how the Church at Park loaned their building to the Bethel Society and were so impressed by Edward Jeffreys and his chosen minister, Pastor George Albert Hibbert, that they decided to merge themselves with the Bethel Society. The County Union agreed, "with some reluctance... it being manifest that we were acting in accordance with the wishes of the former Church members. Most of the supporters of the place still attended, though some – including at least one of the former officers – left about this time."[245] This letter only survives because it was fixed inside a minute-book, and was only written because by 1933 the Park Church was seeking re-admission to the Congregational Union. It is an incredibly valuable insight into what happened at Park, and there is no reason to think that matters at Hope were any different. Based on this letter and the fact that the Sunday school at Hope was maintained after the church joined the Bethel Association, we can safely say that the Bethel Evangelical Free Church of today is the direct descendant of the Hope Chapel of 1812, renewed rather than replaced in 1931.

In the early years of the Bethel period, all 500 seats in the old chapel were full, and in the building was often packed. A letter to the *Sentinel* in 2007 records that "As children we sat on the pulpit steps to make more room for adults. In those days the church was packed every night it was open."[246] It must have been a welcome change for those who had attended before the Church entered the Bethel Society.

---

[245] T. Hartley, letter dated Basford, July 2nd 1933
[246] Letter from Harry and Mary Bettaney, Rhyl, *Staffordshire Sentinel* June 9th 2007. The Bettaneys attended Bethel from 1931 until 1940

The first pastor at the Bethel Temple, Hanley, was Pastor W.J. Jones, a fiery Welshman who was in many ways Pastor Jeffreys' right-hand man. He did not stay long, being called to take over the work in Preston in 1932. He was succeeded by Pastor Alfred Anderson Brown, who remained at Hanley until 1934.

Pastor Anderson Brown, as he was known, came from Essex, and had been converted through Edward Jeffreys' ministry in Southend in July of 1926. Anderson Brown had a good Church-of-England background; he had been a choirboy and a boy-scout. A respectable young man, he nevertheless had something missing from his life. Looking back in 1937, he wrote, "Some conversions are sudden, demonstrative, like a flash of lightning; others are like the rising of the sun, gradual, silent, but illuminating. My conversion was of the latter order."[247]

Pastor Brown's conversion testimony is found on a page with several other ministers' testimonies, and the variety is striking. Some of them were very worldly before their conversions, Anderson Brown was not, "The Lord preserved me," he says. What led to his final conversion was the conversion of the other members of his family at one of Edward Jeffreys' meetings at Southend. Anderson Brown returned home for a week-end to attend services, and his father bought him a season-ticket so that he could more easily attend services. The services first led to deep conviction; he saw that his religion was not deep enough, that it lacked something that the others had. As is often the case, he at first tried to escape from the feeling of conviction, but found it impossible as he was going to Edward Jeffreys' meetings every week. He recalls, "For two weeks I had no rest night or day, the Spirit of God was striving with me." So he decided to stop going, and to take a walk on the promenade instead of going to Church. But one cannot escape God's pursuit that easily; first of all he missed the friends he was trying to meet up with, and then dark clouds began to gather above, and people ran for cover. He tried the bandstand, but that was already full, and as it happened, the only shelter for him from the storm was the Tabernacle where Edward Jeffreys was preaching. Pastor Jeffreys was preaching from John 3:14, "As Moses

---

[247] *Bethel Messenger 1937, P. 56*

lifted up the serpent in the wilderness; even so must the Son of Man be lifted up." As he proclaimed life for a look at the crucified one, Anderson Brown recalls, "I could not resist the appeal by the earnest evangelist, and later in the enquiry room sought and found a true refuge from the storms of life in Jesus, the Rock of Ages."

His conversion gave Pastor Anderson Brown a deep desire to tell others of Christ, which in due course led to his joining Edward Jeffreys in the ministry. He preached Christ wherever he could, and closes his testimony, "I trust God will give me sufficient grace and strength to witness for Him until the day dawns and the shadows for ever flee away." The prayer was answered; Anderson Brown remained in the ministry for many years and died in faith.

Fig. 16: Pastor Anderson Brown leads the 'invasion' of Hanley by Bethel Crusaders from Bootle.

Though the work at Hope Street went on without much trouble, the wider Bethel movement began to show some strain; Edward Jeffreys was an autocratic leader, despite the Society's Advisory board, and concern about this, a perceived lack of financial accountability and Edward Jeffreys' doctrine led to twelve out of the movement's sixty churches leaving in 1932. The following year Pastor Jeffreys' reconsideration of the baptism of the Holy Spirit and the position that speaking in tongues was the sign of it led to further secessions. The Church at Park had already left the Society, and was on its way back to Congregationalism, due to disagreements between Pastor Jeffreys and Pastor Hibbert over financial accountability. The Hope Street Church, however, was firmly Bethel.

Edward Jeffreys had adopted Pentecostal theology as a child because of his experience at Crosshands as a boy; he had not come to the theology by study, and when he was driven to examine that theology in the light of the Bible, to his alarm he found the theology wanting. The Bible simply did not teach what he had thought that it did. In particular he found that the Pentecostal view of the Baptism of the Holy Spirit was not actually supported by the Biblical texts that were appealed to. While he had been teaching, with the rest of the Pentecostal movement, that tongues-speaking was *the* mark of the baptism of the Holy Spirit, and therefore all Christians should speak in tongues, the Bible taught quite plainly that not every Christian speaks in tongues. As for the Baptism of the Holy Spirit, he had taught that it was a "second blessing" after conversion, but the Bible indicated that it was something that was once-for-all, and a part of salvation itself. This was a disquieting experience for him, but he continued with his studies.

Edward Jeffreys began to re-shape his theology as he studied the Bible more closely. He was certainly courageous; the easy thing to do would have been to put the Bible down and keep on teaching what was popular, but he could not honestly do that. At the same time he came to see more fully that the Holy Spirit is a person, and that the Pentecostal emphasis on the gifts of the Spirit had tended to obscure this, even though Pentecostals saw themselves as particularly people of the Spirit. Healing, he came to see, was not to be understood simplistically; God works through medical means as well as immediately, something that the early Pentecostal teaching had, again, tended to obscure, sometimes with tragic results.

As a result of his maturing understanding of theology, especially the work of the Holy Spirit, Edward Jeffreys re-wrote the Articles of Faith, which the Hanley Bethel duly accepted. The re-written articles were as follows:

1. The Trinity of the Godhead; Father, Son and Holy Spirit.
2.. The Deity and humanity of Jesus Christ.
3. Divinely Inspired Word of God and its Infallibility.
4. The Fall of Man. Dead in trespasses and sins. Rom. 3:23: For all have sinned and come short of the glory of God. Sin also means moral defilement.
5. Atoning sacrifice of Jesus Christ.
Romans 8:1: There is therefore now no condemnation to them that are in Christ Jesus.
The only possible way to have the condemnation removed is through the cross of Christ. Man through sin suffers moral defilement, but 1 John 1:7: The blood of Jesus Christ, God's Son, cleanseth us from all sin.
6. Virgin birth of Jesus by the Virgin Mary.
7. Resurrection of Jesus Christ from the dead with a glorified body
8. Personality of the Holy Spirit and the Fullness of the Holy Spirit.
a). We believe that the Holy Spirit is a Person. Being a Spirit He can give new life and indwell our personalities to form Christ within. (We dogmatically affirm that when a man or woman is born again, such a miracle is the direct work of the Holy Spirit)
b). All believers have been baptized into one body by the Spirit (1 Cor. 12:13). We also teach that there is a blessing subsequent to Salvation; the only Scriptural term for this is the fullness of the Spirit. To be born again and filled with the Spirit are quite different experiences. There is no Scriptural teaching that 'tongues' or any other physical manifestations must accompany this as a sign.
9. Divine healing for the body
a). Subject always to the Sovereign Will of God
b). By natural means and by supernatural means, miraculously.
10. Second Coming of Jesus Christ.
We believe in a personal, literal, bodily return of Christ.

11. Kingdoms of this world ultimately becoming the kingdoms of our Lord and Christ. He shall reign until all powers are subject to him

12. Eternal bliss of the believer and the eternal doom of the unbeliever.[248]

This was a significantly more Biblical and balanced confession; it was now a studied theology, not a traditional one, and encompassed all the ground covered by the historic creeds apart from the doctrine of the Church and the Sacraments, both of which were commonly weak points in Evangelicalism in the period, and often remain so to this day.

During Pastor Anderson Brown's ministry the Church received several visits from Edward Jeffreys. Pastor Jeffreys returned to Hanley at Easter 1932, when he conducted a series of meetings in the Victoria Hall and at the Bethel Temple. A full two years after the great campaign he made a full return visit to the Potteries. On Monday, January 30th 1933 Edward Jeffreys returned to Hanley to a welcome from 2500 Bethelites, and conducted a week-long tour of all the Temples in the Potteries, and the nearby Bethel Temple in Congleton. It was quite an event, and demonstrated that the various Bethels in the Potteries were quite closely linked at the time.

The climax of "The Founder's" visit to the Potteries was in the Bethel Temple in Hanley on 5th February, where Pastor Jeffreys began the day's meetings with "a Great Breaking of Bread service." The building was packed with people, and the report in the Bethel Messenger records, "This was a unique service in the history of the Hanley Bethel Temple. As the great throng gathered round the Lord's Table all were deeply impressed and reluctantly left the building at the close of the service."

Six PM saw a "Full Gospel Service" at the Hanley Bethel conducted by Pastor Anderson Brown, and then a procession from Hope Street to the Victoria Hall where a great United Rally of all the Temples in the Potteries was held, led of course by Pastor Jeffreys. All of the local pastors were on the platform with him, including a man who would have

---

[248] These were printed in every issue of the *Bethel Messenger*.

a very significant influence on the Hanley Bethel, the newly-ordained Pastor A.W. Mead of Bethel Temple, Congleton.

The united rally was a display of the Bethel Society at its height, a massed choir made up of members of the Bethel Crusaders young people's society, all in white, a solo by the Founder himself, all leading to a sermon delivered by Edward Jeffreys on the healing of the woman who touched the hem of Jesus' garment, and an appeal to come to Jesus. The meeting concluded with the singing of the hymn 'Blessed be the Ties that Bind'.

As long as the Bethel Society existed, the churches that were members of it were closely linked, especially locally. Members and ministers would attend each other's services, and all the local ministers would often attend installation services for new pastors. On Tuesday April 14th 1934 Pastor H. Orme, who had been over the Talke Assembly, was ordained over the Silverdale Church.[249] Pastor Anderson Brown conducted the service, and Pastor Davidson of Longton delivered the sermon, from 1 Timothy 1.12. Pastor H. Griffiths of Milton "Delighted everyone with his rendering of the Gospel in song." The small Talke group was placed under the oversight of Pastor Mead of Congleton.

Anderson Brown was greatly involved in the work of the 'Bethel Crusaders', and remained so when he moved to Bootle in 1934, becoming the overall superintendent of the Crusaders. In 1935 he came back to Hanley for a day-mission with the Bootle Bethel Crusaders. The report in the *Bethel Messenger* is headed, "Bootle Crusaders 'invade' Hanley in Bethel Special."[250] The actual meetings were mostly singing, with short sermonettes from Pastor Brown. The report records that "In his own zealous style [he] thrilled everyone by his illustrative exhortations and challenges."

Brown's theology was Christ-centred; its heart is revealed in a piece he wrote for the *Bethel Messenger* in 1937 entitled 'The Master's Presence'. He begins with the trials of the times, "In these days when the world is so crowded with sorrows and sufferings, trials and temptations,

---
[249] The language is that used in the report in the Bethel Messenger
[250] P. 207

regrets and remorses, poverty and pain, griefs and graves, one may well ask who will comfort those who mourn, who will feed the multitudes, who will lift the masses from the pit of poverty, who will prevent them from sinking into the abyss of sin and shame, who will show them the way to God and home. It seems to me that the only true solace and comfort for men who are burdened with the cankering cares of life is to be found in the Master's Presence."[251]

He begins by speaking of the presence of Christ in the Old Testament, and God's fellowship with his people, but devotes most of the space to speaking of Christ's presence with us today, and explains, "A careful study of the Scriptures reveals the blessed fact that it is possible for all who are saved by grace to enjoy the Master's Presence." He gives seven aspects of Christ's presence with his people. Christ is: Above us to help, beneath us to support, before us to guide, Behind us to guard, around us to protect us, within us to strengthen, and within us to satisfy.

This is the typical theology of the Bethel Churches; a conversionist, revivalist evangelicalism. The emphasis is firmly on Jesus, and there is an explicit declaration that, "This transformation does not come about by self-effort. All self-mastery towards regeneration is futile." It only leads to failure, despair and hopelessness. "But when the Son of God, by His Spirit, comes into the heart, He sets sin's captive free and gives joy for sorrow and for gloom He gives glory."

Pastor Vernon

Appointed in 1934, Ernest John Vernon (Usually referred to as John) was a Bethel man through and through. He was born in Cwbran, South Wales, in 1903. Like Edward Jeffreys and Anderson Brown, he wore a clerical collar and was generally referred to as either 'Pastor' or 'Reverend'. He was a frequent contributor to the magazine of the Bethel movement, and his wife wrote at least one article for it.[252]

These contributions reveal the theology that was taught at the Church during Pastor Vernon's long period as pastor. Of particular interest is an article called 'The Remembrance of Christ's Love' which

---

[251] *The Bethel Messenger* 1937 P. 129
[252] On 'Enthusiastic Rebekah' in the December 1937 issue

171

reads like a condensed version of a sermon. Pastor Vernon's text is taken from the Song of Solomon 1:4, "We will remember Thy love more than wine." Taking the time-honoured interpretation of the text as an allegory of the love between Christ and the Church, Pastor Vernon writes that the passage, "Reveals a beautiful word-picture of the Lord Jesus as the Bridegroom who manifested such love that He gave His life a ransom."[253]

Fig. 17: Pastor E. J. Vernon

"There is something in the salvation Jesus offers that causes us to run after him, the Lover of Souls," he goes on. "What love He had that He could leave the Ivory Palaces to come into this sin-cursed world to find a Bride. I am sure that we marvel at such condescension, but there it is, a blessed reality. 'He loved me and gave Himself for me.'" Pastor Vernon goes on to speak of the incarnation as the humiliation of Christ, referring to John 13:4 and Jesus washing the feet of the disciples, and to the *Carmen Christi* of Philippians 2:7. This then leads on to the humility that is fitting for the Christian, and the things that people must lay aside to come to Jesus and experience that love for themselves. The emphasis is typical of Evangelicalism in the period, and decidedly devotional rather than doctrinal.

---

[253] *Bethel Messenger* 1938 P. 67

The 1930s proved a time of growth and blessing for the Bethels in the Potteries. Though we have no Church records from that period, we can gain some idea of the life of the Church from reports in the Bethel Messenger. In April 1937 we read "We greatly rejoice at the wonderful way God is working in the saving of souls." Special missions were a feature of Bethel Churches and continued to be at Hanley long after the Bethel Society was wound up. In March of 1936 the church welcomed William Jeffreys to Hanley to lead an evangelistic campaign that lasted from 21st to 31st of the month, during which twenty people professed faith in Christ. Pastor Vernon was responsible for organising these events, and seems to have done so very well.

In addition to the special meetings there was a monthly series of week-end 'demonstrations' during which the various departments of the Church held services. There were four such departments, the Sunbeams, or children's work, the Sisterhood, the Brotherhood, and the Crusaders. Apart from the sisterhood meeting, where the preacher was Mrs. Davies, Warrington, all the meetings were addressed by Bethel pastors. Clearly the Church was thriving at this time.

The December of 1937 saw the last visit of Pastor Edward Jeffreys to Hanley, and Pastor Vernon supplied a report of the events to the Bethel Messenger for February. The Founder led a series of services from 12th-14th December that saw continued blessing. It began with a Sunday morning devotional meeting where "The founder gave a homely talk on prayer and many said that we did not want him to finish."[254] It was followed by a communion service, the normal pattern in Bethel Assemblies at that time. On the Sunday evening 700 people packed into the building despite the cold and the snow, filling every available space. No doubt the Temple was quite warm enough inside! Pastor Jeffreys preached from the text "Christ died for our sins according to the scriptures", a typical text for the devoted evangelist. Eleven people made professions of faith at the end of the service. "Everyone went away rejoicing", Pastor Vernon records. Monday saw "A divine healing service," but even then the Gospel message was preached clearly, Edward Jeffreys took as his text "For me to live is Christ and to die is gain", and four more people professed faith in Christ. A final meeting

---

[254] *The Bethel Messenger* 1938 P. 37

was held on the Tuesday night, when the Bethelites from Longton joined the Hanley congregation. Edward Jeffreys was supported in this meeting by Pastor Heard of Longton, and also Pastor Haines and Pastor George Jeffreys. The message was on "The facts about saintship." In his parting counsel he "urged the importance of Bible study and of a steady tramp with God, the result being a Church still going on under the faithful and devoted ministry of our Pastor J. Vernon."

In Pastor Vernon's report we have other news of the Church as well. He reports that "God is blessing the Sisterhood." Earlier in 1937 the Sisterhood had a major event during which special pieces were presented, and the preacher was Mrs. Back, a member of the Salvation Army. Mrs. Vernon, who led the sisterhood, was presented with "a handsome dinner service." The Crusaders were raising up the next generation of Church leaders, for it is in this report that the name of long-serving future Church secretary, Mr. Fred Goldstraw, appears as one of two Crusaders who presented a Bible to Pastor Vernon "as a symbol of his work in our church not only as a Pastor, but also as a brother and a friend."

Pastor Vernon would need those helpers; in 1939 Edward Jeffreys unexpectedly wound up the Bethel Evangelistic Society, setting the many Bethels loose as independent Churches to find their own way in the world.

George Jeffreys had been experiencing problems with Elim, the denomination that he had founded. In the opinion of Elim, they had been experiencing problems with George Jeffreys. George was fundamentally a pragmatist in his view of Church government; he went with what worked. The problem was that what worked in one place did not work so well in another. According to Elim historian Desmond Cartwright, "The basic problem was not his views on prophetic interpretation, but his constant change of mind."[255] He also became deeply worried about Elim's financial position and attempted to restructure the denomination to deal with both issues. Though he had been instrumental in founding Elim, the reforms and restructuring George Jeffreys suggested were too much for the Board, and they resisted, resulting in George Jeffreys

---

[255] Cartwright, P. 139

leaving Elim to establish a new work called the Bible-Pattern Fellowship, which was formally established at a meeting in Nottingham on November 28th and 29th 1940.

Among other problems that had been affecting the Churches, not only in Pentecostal circles, at the time was British-Israelism. This is the teaching that the British, in some way, are the so-called "lost tribes of Israel". Based on bad exegesis and worse theology, it nevertheless had a broad appeal in England in the period between the wars. No less a figure than Dinsdale T. Young, renowned Methodist evangelical and minister at Westminster Central Hall from 1914 until his death in 1938, supported the work of the British Israel Word Federation[256]. Its great attraction lay in the fact that it seemed to provide "a philosophy of the present unparalleled power and influence of the British Empire."[257] It made Britain into God's elect nation, Israel reborn in the north.

It need hardly be said that the idea is wrong, but in the 1930s it was very attractive; it declared that Britain's imperial splendour was no mere accident of history, but God's hand of blessing. It also made Great Britain into God's covenant nation, God's channel for blessing the nations. It gave a convenient theological basis for the desire to bring Britain back to God, and allowed a rather simplistic application of Bible texts referring to Old Testament Israel to Britain as a nation. On a less savoury side, it could lead to an attitude of racial superiority that justified the subjugation of other 'lesser races', and in an extreme form denied that the Jews were really Jewish at all. H.L. Gouge, Regius Professor of Divinity in the University of Oxford, felt it was so important that he wrote a book against the teaching, *The British Israel Theory*, published in 1933[258]. In it he stated that the theory, "Though it may be in itself harmless, is not harmless in its consequences. It fosters a nationalism which is profoundly un-Christian, and a pride and self-complacency which come only too easily to us English people; it is associated with a mode of interpreting Scripture which conceals its true meaning from us, and like all baseless theories, it wastes our powers of attention."[259]

---

[256] Harold Murray, *Dinsdale Young* (London, 1938) P. 105f
[257] Dinsdale Young, quoted in Murray, P. 106
[258] H.L. Gouge, *The British Israel Theory* (London and Oxford, 1933)
[259] Gouge, *British Israel Theory* P. iii

Pentecostalism in particular was forced to struggle with this strange teaching; Charles Parham, in whose Bible school the movement began, was an ardent advocate of British-Israel teaching, and the theory was one of the outstanding characteristics of the early American Pentecostal movement.[260] George Jeffreys embraced the British Israel theory in 1920[261], and in 1932 at the Northern District Conference of the Elim Church he proposed that it should be made an article of faith for the Denomination. Thankfully this was defeated at the main Conference, where it was decided that Elim pulpits should on the whole be silent on the matter, neither attacking nor propagating the idea. This did not of course end the issue, as there were many who thought that it was a truth of vital importance that should be preached as often as possible. While the majority of the Elim leadership clearly just wanted silence on the matter, George Jeffreys continued to raise it, wanting there to be liberty for all Elim ministers to proclaim the identity of Great Britain with Old Testament Israel.[262] His dogmatism on the issue was eventually one of the factors that contributed to his breach with Elim.

British Israel teaching led to trouble in the Potteries as well. The Rev. George Hibbert, minister of Park, was an advocate of British Israel teaching and would end his career as a travelling lecturer and Area Commissioner for the British Israel World Federation. His departure from Park in 1939 may have been linked with this teaching; certainly his last years at the Church saw a drop in the membership, from 80 in 1938 to 50 in 1939 and only 30 after his departure in 1940. A British Israel World Federation group rented rooms on the second floor of 61 Stafford Street in Hanley for worship in 1934. In the absence of data, we can only speculate that they may have been former worshippers at the Hope Street Bethel dissatisfied with the Church's refusal to sanction their favourite teaching. The end of the British Empire has largely eliminated the attractiveness of British Israel teaching, though there are still some places where it can be found.

At the time that George Jeffreys parted company with Elim, Edward Jeffreys was seeking his own way in the Church. At first he

---

[260] Hollenweger, P. 23
[261] Cartwright, P. 120
[262] Cartwright, Pp. 120-126

joined his uncle George in establishing the Bible-Pattern Church, but in 1946 they parted company, probably because Edward found his uncle as hard to work with as the Elim leadership had. His connection with the Pentecostal stream over, Edward sold the Southend Church to Elim, and entered St. Aidan's College in Birkenhead to train for the Anglican ministry.

St. Aidan's was in 1846 founded as a Protestant and Evangelical college to counter the Anglo-Catholic teaching in many of the Diocesan colleges and colleges associated with the universities. While he became an Anglican, Edward Jeffreys remained an Evangelical for the rest of his life. After his course in Birkenhead he was ordained and inducted as Priest-in-Charge at St. Elizabeth, Buckhurst Hill, London. He was not very successful there, and moved to the small church of All Saints, Higham Park, not far away. He came to a run-down building with a small congregation, and by the time he left 12 years later the building was refurbished and the congregation strong. Richard Kayes records that Jeffreys told him as he showed him around All Saints, "Isn't it lovely? I am so happy here."[263] He retired to Bournemouth in 1965, where he died in 1974 after a long and varied life of Christian service.

Though the Bethel Society was wound up in 1939, most of the churches continued to exist, although some foundered without the support of the central organisation. In the Potteries there are today three old Bethels, Hanley, Longton and the former Milton Bethel, now Breathe City Church in Abbey Hulton. And the same is true up and down the country. Not all are still called Bethel, though many are, many, like Hanley, have adopted the name Bethel Evangelical Free Church. Old Bethels can be found in Liverpool, Warrington, Preston, Bolton, Oldham, and many other places.

The Second War and After

World War II was as much of a challenge to the Church as World War I was, though in the Second World War the question of good and evil was clearer in one sense; Hitler was a dictator and an aggressor. On the other hand, the Allies included Soviet Russia, under the equally

---

[263] Kayes, P. 59

ruthless and repressive dictator Joseph Stalin. Hitler was a threat to England in a way that the Kaiser had never been, threatening invasion as well as engaging in aerial bombardment of civilian areas. Yet at the same time British aircraft were also involved in large-scale bombing of civilian targets in Germany, often with horrific loss of life.

As in World War I, many joined up before Conscription was introduced. Among them was Pastor Archibald W. Mead, who was over the small Bethel congregations in Congleton and Talke. As a pastor he could not be drafted, but he offered himself for military service in the army.

The Second World War affected the Hope Street Church just as the first had. The break-up of the Bethel Society meant, however, that there was no denomination to fall back on; the Church had to rely on its own resources under God. Many of the men in the church were called up, and finances became difficult once again.

In 1944 the Congregational Union, who had been the trustees since the 1920s, and from whom the church had previously been renting the building, sold the property to the Church in December. This purchase put the Church in debt again, but the alternative was the loss of their home, which might lead to closure. To safeguard the property, it was put in trust, the trustees being blacksmith John Dibden of Keelings Road, garage mechanic William George Jackson, retired coal merchant Thomas Copestake, fireman Arthur Pinches and miner George Millwood., all members of the Church.[264] Their occupations give a good idea of the working class membership of the Church; of these leading men of the congregation, only one, Thomas Copestake, would have been regarded as middle-class. Here at least there could be no accusation that the Church was out of touch with the working man. The trust deed reveals that Bethel was run by a committee at the time, but a later document reveals that the committee rarely met, and for all practical purposes the daily business of the Church, including its financial affairs, was in the sole hands of Pastor Vernon. The deed also reveals that by 1944 Pastor Vernon lived at 'Glenroy', 309 High Lane, Burslem, a house very similar to the current manse.

---

[264] Trust Deed dated 29th December 1944.

The end of the war in 1945 did not mean the end of the Church's difficulties any more than peace in 1918 had; numbers were still depleted, and the end of the Bethel denomination had caused something of a loss of direction. After the break-up of the Bethel Evangelistic Society Bethel Temple Hanley was an independent Church by default rather than by choice or conviction. It was also a church that had a thoroughly unbiblical leadership structure, a true one-man operation. To use a business analogy, it was a branch office which had been forced to become an independent operation by the sudden closure of the head office. Increasing financial trouble meant that the Sunday School hall, already disused, had to be sold to keep up payments to the Congregational Union. A local garage initially bought the building for storage; they sold it to the New Hall Pottery, who wanted to have access to Hope Street from the factory and did not use the building at all, leaving it to slide into dereliction.

Pastor Vernon struggled on, taking on the burden of the church personally, and conducting all its business affairs as well as its spiritual work himself.[265] He suffered personal tragedy in the death of his young daughter, and his marriage was affected; in the last years of his life he lived with Mr. Millward, the Church caretaker, and his wife, often spending several days at a time in the vestry at the back of the Church. It was there that he died, sitting in his chair. He left the Millwards' on the morning of Tuesday 20th January, 1953, after breakfast. Later in the morning Mrs. Millward, the last person to speak to him, went to the Church to give him a message, which she called through the window of the vestry. He replied quite normally, but that night he did not come home. When she went to the chapel on Wednesday morning, Mrs. Millward found the light in the vestry was still on, and Mr. Vernon did not reply when she called for him. The vestry door was locked, but still she did not think there was anything wrong. However, when she arrived for the prayer-meeting at 6 PM the door was still locked, the light on, and there was no answer to her calls. The police were contacted, and entering the room they found the pastor, seated in his chair, the gas fire on, the wireless turned on, looking very peaceful, and dead. He had been the pastor in Hanley for almost 20 years.

---

[265] Undated letter to a Mr. Bale in the Church archives

Chapter 13: Pastor A.W. Mead

Pastor Vernon's sudden death caused a crisis in the Church; what had been by default a benevolent autocracy was suddenly required to become a church with a corporate leadership, a situation complicated by the fact that there was no formal membership; the congregation were *de facto* the members of the Church.

A body of leaders, presumably those men in the congregation who were most capable and most involved in the work, were appointed and named trustees, though legally only Mr. Pinches, the sole surviving trustee under the 1944 trust, had such status. According to the first minute-book we have, at a meeting held after the evening service on 25th January 1953 the Congregation elected Mr. Fred Mountford Goldstraw, one-time Bethel Crusader, "President and Secretary of the Hanley Bethel Temple", while six members, Mr. Len Churton, Mr. P. Frost, Mr. A. Pinches, Mr. T.N. Bannister, Mr. A.M. Bannister and Mr. F.A. Thorley as trustees "to tend to the working of the Church, and to all monies given to the work of God." The following Sunday we have it recorded that, "We, the undersigned, do, on behalf of the Hanley Bethel Temple, appoint this day February 1st 1953 Mr. Fred Mountford Goldstraw to be the President and Secretary of the aforementioned Church." The minute is signed by the six "trustees".

The "trustees" acted much as the elders and deacons of the Church do today. Len Churton was the first treasurer, a job that must have been made harder by the heavy debt on the building. Mr. Goldstraw's Presidency did not last long, as the next entry in the minute book, on Sunday 31st May 1953, we read that the trustees offered Mr. A.W. Mead the pastorate of the Church, and he agreed to take the pastorate from September of that year. Mr. Goldstraw still retained the past of secretary. There are no minutes recorded between February and May of 1953, but it is clear that the pulpit was served by visiting preachers for a time.

Fig. 18: Pastor and Mrs. Mead

Born in Bristol in 1907, Pastor Archibald ('Archie') Walter Mead had been converted under Edward Jeffreys' ministry and ordained as the minister of the Congleton Bethel Temple on 3rd February 1933 by Edward Jeffreys. The Bethel Messenger records that it was a crowded meeting and "A time of wonderful blessing ensued." Ten people came forward at the meeting. The Congleton Bethel did not, however, "flourish" as was hoped; and it was united with the small Assembly at Talke Pits, with Pastor Mead living in Congleton and alternating Sundays between the two churches. It was this that led to his meeting Miss Ethel Tabinor, the daughter of a couple at Talke who entertained the Pastor for meals. A friendship formed between the two, and on August 1st 1936 Pastor Mead and Miss Tabinor were married at Christ Church, Kidsgrove. Their son David was born on 2nd August 1937, and he was followed by two sisters, Beryl and Valerie. As the war was the catalyst that led to the Bethel Society being wound up, so it affected Pastor Mead; he joined the army in 1939.

With the Bethel Society no longer in existence on his demobilisation, Pastor Mead settled in Kidsgrove and took secular employment as an insurance agent for the Liverpool Victoria Friendly Society. As an agent, his work was not onerous and enabled him to carry on a Bible-teaching ministry in local churches while working. With the churches where he had pastored no longer in existence, he attended a Brethren Assembly in Butt Lane. He often assisted Stoke on Trent Youth for Christ in their follow-up rallies.[266] While he attended a Brethren Assembly, and it is clear that his thinking in terms of Church government was developing; he had not embraced the Brethren view of the Church. A call to take the pastorate of the Bethel in Hanley was swiftly accepted, though it did not mean a return to full-time ministry because of the heavy debts and precarious financial position of the Church.

The first pastor called to Hanley after the break-up of the Bethel Society was from that same Bethel tradition, and the identity of the Church in 1953 was still that of the Bethel Temple, Hanley. Yet Pastor Mead was to lead the Church to a new identity while retaining continuity with the past. Evangelicalism was picking up again; in the spring of 1954 an American Baptist preacher would pack out the Harringay Arena with his 'Greater London Crusade'. His name of course was Billy Graham, and he would come to represent a resurgent evangelicalism.

Following the invitation to Mr. Mead it was agreed to hold "A general meeting of the members of the Church, and place before them the findings of our meeting." This meeting was for Monday June 22nd, where it was agreed that Pastor Mead "be accepted as part time Pastor, for a period of 12 months trial, and he is to start the first Sunday in September."

At some point it was decided to hold a "rededication service" for Pastor Mead on Monday evening 7th September 1953, as he took up the work of a pastor once again. On Sunday July 5th it was decided to invite Rev. Matthew Francis "to attend to the rededication service of Pastor A.W. Mead." This minute also indicates that at the time Bethel still owed the Congregational Union 800 pounds, which it was hoped to be able to pay off in instalments of one hundred pounds. The meeting also discussed buying "labour saving device (namely vacuum cleaner) and lino for the upper room."

---

[266] *E-mail from David Mead, Pastor Mead's son, 23rd January 2012*

Pastor Mead's first recorded public service at the Church after his call was the dedication of the infant Susan Ann Roberts on Sunday morning July 12th, when the minute-book records that hymn 683, 'Mothers of Salem' was sung.

Pastor Mead's first recorded trustees' meeting was on September 6th, when they discussed the programme for the following day's induction. It was agreed to pay him five pounds a week, to be paid on the first Sunday of each month. An evangelistic campaign followed from 18th-28th September followed the induction; this was the age of the Crusade meeting, when not only Billy Graham, but a host of lesser luminaries, brought the claims of Christ to post-war Britain.

There is then a gap in the records of nearly a year, though intriguingly the date of Jan 3rd 1954 has been written in and crossed out. Pastor Mead proved acceptable, as on August 29th 1954 he was invited to become "lay pastor", this meant that he was to be working a secular job as well as the pastorate, "for an indefinite period of time", while the hope was expressed that in the future he would be able to take up the work full-time. The financial condition of the fellowship was however not thought sound enough for Pastor Mead to be asked to take up the work full-time in 1954, and the position would be reviewed periodically. The trustees agreed that, if Pastor Mead should have to give up his secular employment, they rather than the Church would take the responsibility of providing for his financial needs. Thankfully this eventuality never came to pass.

In this minute it is stated that, "If, in the future, the trustees feel that the Pastor has, or is preaching, any other gospel, we can ask him to vacate his ministry." Happily the contingency never arose. They also agreed that if he was to receive a call from another Church, they would consider it.

The following year saw another milestone in the history of Bethel; on February 1st 1955 the trustees agreed to affiliate to the Fellowship of Independent Evangelical Churches. This meant another change in the way the Church was governed, as the FIEC seem to have required the Church to have a membership roll; in any case it was agreed to compile a list of Church members.

The Fellowship of Independent Evangelical Churches was founded in 1922 as "The Fellowship of Undenominational and Unattached Churches and Missions" under the leadership of Rev. E.J. Poole-Connor of the Talbot Tabernacle, Bayswater, London.[267] Its aim was to bring together the large number of completely independent evangelical congregations that existed in Britain at the time; the FIEC was never intended to be a new denomination, but a means of fellowship for the nondenominational. While some of these churches, such as Surrey Chapel in Norwich, were very large and prosperous, others were small and struggling. Their ministers were not always recognised as accredited "ministers of religion", and some were hardly aware that other similar churches even existed. The Fellowship was envisaged as a body for mutual support, a fellowship of independent churches. The name was eventually changed to reflect a more positive view of the churches; rather than describing them by what they were not, it described them by what they were. Membership of the Fellowship required the acceptance of a brief but decidedly conservative theological basis. Joining the FIEC gave Bethel links with other like-minded churches. At the time there was a thriving West Midlands Auxiliary of the Fellowship, and it meant an end to the isolation that the end of the Bethel Society had brought.

Trustees meetings were at first on Sunday evenings, but from 1955 they were held on other days of the week. The minutes become fuller, and the structure of the leadership meeting assumes the form it has retained to this day, with opening devotions followed by a discussion of business. In those days the devotion included a short address, while today there is only Bible reading and prayer.

1955 saw another change to the Church; it was agreed on August 27th "that the Sunday evening services start at 6:30 PM on a 3 month trial." We still have a 6:30 evening service every Sunday, a return to the arrangement that prevailed in the days when William Lansdell was pastor.

---

[267] *David G. Fountain, E.J. Poole-Connor* (Worthing, 1966), P. 124

In 1956 another change was introduced into the way the Church leadership meetings were conducted; Mrs. Muriel Rowland was asked to become assistant secretary with the responsibility of taking the minutes. Other important issues in 1956 were the chapel ceiling, the gate in Hope Street, which was shared with the New Hall Pottery owned by Mr. Ridgeway, and the cellar, which had an unsatisfactory access located in the ladies' toilets, regarded as "a danger to the ladies and children." There was also a question as to who owned the gents' toilet, the church or Mr. Ridgeway! This is not as strange as it sounds; the gents' was in the old Sunday School building behind the chapel, and the ownership of the building was apparently uncertain (though in fact the building had been sold to Mr. Ridgeway). One piece of excitement that year was the demolition of part of a churchyard wall by a pottery lorry belonging to Johnson Bros. It was not all business, though; there was a Christmas Festival discussed at which gifts were to be given to "the old people."

On 8th September 1956 Mrs. Rowland took over the minutes; the change is immediately apparent with her neat hand. In the event she did not serve long, her last minutes are in May 1957. The Church was re-opened in October 1956 after repairs, and a rededication service was held as one of a number of special meetings. On Saturday 13th October a rally was held, and then the rededication at the Communion the following day. Advertising was key for special services then; there was just a poster for the Harvest Festival, but the re-opening warranted an advertisement in the Sentinel, for which a photograph of the interior was wanted. Window-bills were printed, and "a poster board propped up outside the Church was suggested for our 'Radiant Life' Rally." The regular monthly family services saw a special 'guest night' once in three months, no doubt a special evangelistic effort. These services involved Sunday School scholars contributing "items", and in 1957 it was felt that the services had become too long, and so the number of these contributions would have to be curtailed! Monthly family services were, by April 1957, being taken by departments of the Church. In April the service was taken by the "Good News Club", and May was to be taken by the Old Age Pensioners.

Musically, things also picked up, by 1957 the Church had a choir and a quartette, the latter of which which led to some sort of difficulty, for on 6th April 1957 we find there was "a general discussion about the quartette problem", and Mr. Goldstraw, who was then choirmaster, was absent from Church too often, as he was also asked to preach in other churches in the area. It was agreed that choirmasters should be present three out of four Sundays a month. The "quartette problem" was finally solved by the decision that if there was to be any community singing before the evening service "pastor should lead it himself."

The great annual event in these days was the Church anniversary, when a guest speaker was brought in and a temporary stage set up in the chapel. Other special events were the Harvest Festival and the Flower service. The Church observed a basic form of Christian Year, with special services at Whitsun as well as Christmas and Easter. These services were widely advertised and were seen as opportunities to bring new people in. Christmas was celebrated in style; There was an Old Age Pensioners' party at which small gifts were given. The service was taken by "visitors" with items from the Sunday school led by Miss E. Pointon. A Christmas tree was brought and set up in the Church, and a good time no doubt had by all.

September 1956 saw the wedding of a former Sunday school scholar in the building, leading to a discussion about fees for weddings, agreed at one pound and one shilling. Youth for Christ sought the use of the Church for three months for their rallies in December, January and February, and obtained the building for a fee of three pounds. They were also allowed to use the Church's crockery, "provided they replace any breakages," always a risk with groups of young people.

By their nature, Church records tend to deal with the outward affairs of the Church rather than spiritual things, it is only the odd reference to 'mourners' at the end of a service that betrays the spiritual reality that there were people coming the Christ through Pastor Mead's ministry, the Church was growing by conversion. Finances seem to have been doing well, since by this point Pastor Mead was receiving nine pounds a week, a great increase since his arrival, when he was receiving a mere five pounds a month.

The Church magazine from September 1958 shows more of that growth. Sadly we have only a few magazines from this period, but they paint a picture that is supported by the testimony of older members. The magazine was issued quarterly, and so gives a slice of congregational life. We find that in this quarter two people came into fellowship with the Church, there were five weddings (it does cover the period including June!), one infant dedication, and seven people baptised at a service on July 7th. The Sisterhood reported an increase in numbers, and Mr. Ron Rowland was training at the Birmingham Bible Institute in preparation for missionary work. There was a Monday evening Bible School for those wanting to go deeper in the Word, and the picture is of a thriving, happy congregation. The Bible study in the magazine was on "The Centrality of the Cross."

The second 'snapshot' is from June 1961, where one infant dedication is recorded. The news of the Young People's Fellowship is encouraging; youth evangelism had resulted in a number of teenagers professing faith in Christ. With the coming of summer there also came open-air work in the town centre. By this point Ron and Muriel Rowland were training with Wycliffe Bible Translators for overseas mission work.

The town centre site, while in some way strategic, also created problems of its own; in April 1957 we find that there had been damage caused to the graveyard, presumably by the usual combination of children at play and juvenile delinquents. May 1961 saw a break-in on the premises through the back door into the vestries, highlighting the difficulties of the town-centre site in an area of decline. Another sign of changing times is that the May Trustees' meeting sent "a very strong protest letter on behalf of the Church" on the subject of Sunday opening of cinemas.

Pastor Mead was invited to become full-time in September 1957, showing that the Church's finances had improved considerably since his coming in 1953; in the event he declined and remained part-time so that the remaining debt on the building could be settled more quickly. He was asked to become full-time again from April 1959, when he accepted.

Youth for Christ were common visitors to the church building in the 1950s, a note in November 1958 indicating that perhaps they were a little lackadaisical in their approach, since it is stated "Y.F.C. to give at least a week's notice before a meeting." Evidently they were in the habit of suddenly announcing a meeting just a few days in advance! Youth for Christ used the Upper Room in the old chapel for many years on Sunday nights for an after-church rally. Youth for Christ were not the only ones holding events in the Chapel. Church special events continued, 1958 saw the usual Church Christmas party, and in 1959 Mr. Arthur Bannister brought "his Messiah records to play in the Church."

Pastor Mead lived in his own house in Third Avenue, Kidsgrove throughout his ministry in Hanley, sometimes making the journey from there to Hanley by bicycle; he was not alone in cycling; enough members came to church on bicycles in the period for a special cycle shed to be built at the back of the chapel in 1961. Prone to asthma, Pastor Mead often travelled by bus to Hanley, and in the days when smoking was widespread and allowed on the upper deck of double-decker buses, he often arrived at the Church hardly able to breathe and had to sit in the vestry for some time before being able to preach. It is therefore not surprising that when Church finances began to assume a more healthy condition there were discussions about purchasing a manse closer to the Church so that, when Pastor Mead was able to take up the pastorate full-time, he would not have such a long journey. Accordingly, in November of 1958 it was proposed that a manse be purchased. The debt owed to the Congregational Union was finally paid off in 1959, at which time "the Baptism tank" became a priority. Since becoming a Bethel, the Church had practised the baptism of believers on profession of faith by immersion, but the chapel had been built for a congregation who baptised infants by sprinkling, and consequently had no baptistery for immersion. To supply the need, a large collapsible canvas tank had been purchased, and was now starting to show signs of its age. It would either have to be replaced by a new tank, or by a baptistery installed in the building.

The name of the church was changed in 1958 from 'Bethel Temple' to the present 'Bethel Evangelical Free Church', often shortened to either 'Bethel Evangelical Church', or simply 'The Bethel'.

Nevertheless 'Bethel Temple' continued to be used for some years on some pieces of stationery, probably because there was a reluctance to replace old printing-blocks. While the Church magazine for September 1958 uses the new name, the hymn-sheet for the anniversary services in 1961 is still headed 'Bethel Temple', but by 1963 the sheet has 'Bethel Evangelical Free Church' on it.

At the Trustees' meeting on Feb 27th 1960 Pastor Mead "spoke from Isaiah 54.2, Lengthen thy cords and strengthen thy stakes, a challenge for us, to hold the fort in Hanley." A number of evangelists used the building during the 1950s and 60s for crusade meetings. In 1960 the evangelist Eric Hutchings held meetings on Saturday April 30th and 1st April at Bethel, when the Church received a fee of two and a half guineas for the use of the building. The same meeting also sees the first mention of a man who would be Pastor Mead's successor, "Evangelist Desmond Evans." Special meetings were still going strong, with a social evening as well as the usual meetings. The Church's commitment to crusade evangelism is seen in that when Billy Graham came to Manchester in 1961, Bethel reserved 100 seats for Friday June 2nd and 150 for Saturday June 10th.

A revealing statement in the minutes reads, "We discussed prayer and the prayer meeting, and were concerned about it. Prayer is the key to all our problems." There was obviously concern for the spiritual condition of the Church, as well as soul-searching about the future. The choir was struggling a bit by 1961, for we find that there were appeals to the young people to become choristers. Sunday evening services were also slipping a bit, since it was resolved to try to get the services going by 6:30 prompt!

As many things had changed at Bethel since his appointment, Pastor Mead felt that there ought to be a new constitution that stated what the Church stood for in the Gospel, and how the Church was governed, setting everything on a proper basis. As part of this re-organisation deacons were introduced into the organisation of the Church once again. The Trustees were all made deacons, while three other men, not trustees, were recommended as deacons. These men were Peter Peaskett, Colin Goodman and Andre Clowes. This meant that there would be both trustees' meetings and deacons' meetings for a while. The Constitution also introduced an annual general members' meeting, something we still have, although from 1963[268] members' meetings have been held quarterly. At the first AGM on November 4th 1961 there were 112 people in membership.

With the Congregation once again taking a major part in the government of the Church, it became necessary to clarify the position of the young people in membership. In the event it was decided that they would not take a part in the government of the Church, though Deacon Andre Clowes would represent their interests. Their names were entered in a separate junior Church roll. Membership became much more formal at this period, and great effort was put into making sure that only those who actually came to the Church were on the membership roll. It is at this point that applications for membership begin to be listed in the minutes.

The resurgence of evangelicalism in the 1950s also meant a resurgence of evangelical missions; older societies like the China Inland Mission (now the Overseas Missionary Fellowship) were strengthened and new organisations, often founded in the United States, gained support in Churches like Bethel. In 1961 Ron and Muriel Rowland were accepted to work with Wycliffe Bible translators. The Church has supported them over the years in the various work that they have done, both on the field and at Wycliffe Headquarters. Ron served as Pastor Mead's assistant for a time in the early 1960s while he and Muriel prepared for overseas work. In all about ten missionaries went out from the Church during Pastor Mead's pastorate. The ten years of the Mead era were truly a new beginning for the Church.

Pastor Mead remained at Bethel for almost exactly a decade. On Monday 24th May 1963 Pastor Mead received in the morning post a letter from the Evangelical Church at Feltham in Middlesex. It contained a unanimous call for him to take up the post of Pastor there full-time, if at all possible by the end of September. This was a new work, and Pastor Mead immediately accepted the call and wrote to Mr. Goldstraw informing him of the fact. His farewell service was on Sunday

---

[268] Church Meetings Minute Book 1961-1975. Minute dated January 31st 1963

September 29th 1963; he had been serving the Church as pastor for a little over a decade. Pastor Mead was inducted at Feltham on Saturday 5th October, when Mr. Goldstraw and the Bethel choir travelled down to Feltham to take part in the service. Pastor Mead is still fondly remembered by some in the fellowship, and his son David, a missionary in Italy, remains a member of Bethel; his annual visits are a welcome part of the Church calendar.

Archie Mead's pastorate had seen many changes at Bethel; the name of the Church had changed to Bethel Evangelical Free Church; there was a committee of leaders, originally called trustees, but now called deacons, and there was a membership roll. The church had joined the FIEC, and had a new constitution. In many ways the Church was now more like it had been in the Congregational era; though it had changed, the change had been conservative, restoring the government of the Church to the membership rather than leaving it in entirely the hands of an executive.

Pastor Mead retained a link with the Church at Bethel for the rest of his life. He served at Feltham for another ten years, but his last sermon was delivered in December of 1973 at Bethel on the text "Sir, we would see Jesus." The following day he had a heart attack and, as his son David puts it, "Three days later he saw Jesus!" Fittingly, given how important the ten years of his ministry at Hanley had been, both to him and the Church, the funeral was held at Bethel on December 27th 1973. The final hymn sung at the service was 'Jesus, the very thought of Thee.'[269] It was a fitting final hymn; Pastor Mead's ministry was marked by that note of Christ-centred confidence.

---

[269] Hymn-sheet in History File

Fig. 19: The chapel in the 1950s

Chapter 14: Desmond Evans: 1963-1965

Following Pastor Mead's acceptance of the call to Feltham the Church began the process of seeking a successor. To that end the Church sought various avenues, contacting the FIEC for help. The FIEC provided a list, and candidates for the pastorate were invited to come and preach during the period following Pastor Mead's departure. In the meantime the Deacons ran the Church, led it seems by Mr. Goldstraw. Visiting speakers were paid expenses and then another payment "according to merit" decided after the service! Visiting speakers boarded with Mr. and Mrs. Thorley, who received a pound a week for providing this service, apart from when the speakers were missionaries, whom they put up free of charge. Miss A. Buckley undertook visitation of the sick in the absence of a pastor. No speaker was told that he was under consideration for the pastorate, even if this was the case.

Various men were suggested for the pastorate and invited to preach. These included Rev. F.G. Money of Park Hill Church in Brighton, Rev. C. Medhurst of Redhill, Surrey and Rev. P.D. Barlow of Teddington. The FIEC also suggested men with training who were seeking a first pastorate. These included Mr. Brian Freer and Mr. D. Stephens, in the case of Mr. Stephens he was still a student at the London Bible College. Of interest to the present pastor is a letter in the files indicating that Rev. Bernard E. Lambert, at that time of Cullompton, Devon, preached at Bethel in January of 1964. Pastor Lambert went on to be the Pastor of Hethersett Baptist Church in Norfolk, home Church of the present pastor for many years.

Until the Church found a successor to Pastor Mead, it was felt desirable to obtain a stand-in to take weddings, funerals and infant dedications, and unusually the Rev. P.C.L. Smith, a local Anglican vicar, was approached. The Bishop of Lichfield wrote back that there were certain legal difficulties involved, and so Mr. Smith ought not to conduct weddings or dedications, though he was happy to take funerals if needed.

Under Pastor Mead *The Believers Hymn Book*[270] was used on Sunday mornings, but it was certainly not the only book the Church used, they also had Redemption Songs, Sankey's and Alexander's. The visiting speakers tended to choose the hymn-book according to their own preference, leading to some dissension as a result. This led to an announcement informing the congregation that the choice of books was with the visitors, not the deacons.

On 7th December 1963 Fred Goldstraw received a letter that brought to his attention a name we have already come across in this history, the name of Desmond Evans, who first visited the Church as an Evangelist in 1960. Mr. Evans had been in business, but his business had just failed, leaving him at a crossroads in his life. The letter is signed 'Harry S.' and clearly comes from a man well-known to the church and a member at Bethel Evangelical Free Church in Wigston, Leicester, where Mr. Evans was also in membership. In the letter Harry S. suggests Mr. Evans as a possible pastor for Bethel. "I did wonder if you had ever give thought or associated our brother with the work in Hanley. He has ministered in your church and in the area generally quite regularly over recent years. If we view Bethel as a preaching centre and this it surely is, then his name might be worthy of your consideration. You probably know too of his background in the exclusive brethren where he was truly nurtured in the doctrines of grace. He has also exercised a fruitful ministry in the Fleckney Baptist Church for a period of three years. You are well acquainted with his ability in the realm of preaching and teaching as I am. We have shared in the official life of the church a deep concern for him over recent months, and this is another factor prompting me to write in the way I have."[271] Mr. Evans was a Welshman, though he lived in England. Like many Welshmen he was a good singer, and involved with the choir at the Bethel in Wigston; he lived at 27 Repton Road, Wigston, which is literally just around the corner from the church. Desmond Evans was a valued member at Wigston, though his evangelistic work meant that he was not as involved with the work of the congregation as he might have been. He did much of his evangelism under the auspices of the National Young Life Campaign.[272]

---

[270] Subtitled, "A collection of Scriptural Hymns for use at all assemblings of the Lord's People", this is a Brethren book
[271] Letter in the Correspondence File Vol. 1
[272] Information supplied by Mr. Alan Cunnington at the Wigston Bethel

Mr. Goldstraw took note of the letter, and on 18th December 1963 a letter was sent to Mr. Evans inviting him to speak at the Church. As was normal, there was no intimation in the letter that he was being considered as a possible candidate for the pastorate; this was done to avoid difficulties should the candidate not be called. Mr Evans replied on 27th December offering to come on 12th January. In the letter he alludes to the trials connected with the failure of his business, "The Lord has taken us through experiences we never thought possible. Dark days and difficult ways when the Lord appeared to be actually working against us. Now, however, it is clear that He was, in His wonderful way, preparing us for the work He has for us… For the time being, suffice it to say that the leading of the Lord and the openings in our life are so significant that we know beyond doubt that He will guide both you and us with regard to the future."[273]

His visit to Bethel went well, and seems to have resulted in an informal call being given there and then. This was confirmed in writing on 17th February. The call draws attention to the fact that Mr. Evans would be expected to devote most of his time and effort to Bethel; emphasising the difference between his former work as a lay-evangelist and his future work as a Pastor. "We do not intend to prevent you from taking an active interest in other evangelical work in the city, but rather to ensure that through other work you are not exhausted when it comes to tending your own flock."[274] In his reply Mr. Evans reassured the Church, "I can readily understand your fears with regard to my wider ministry while I am your pastor. All I can say is that it is my whole intention at the present time to give myself under God to the ministry of the Church over which He has made me shepherd."[275] He was to begin his preaching duties on Good Friday of the same year.

A manse was obtained in 1964, just as the church called the new pastor. It is a standard 1930s suburban semi-detached house, and at the time had front and back gardens. Pastor Evans was the first pastor to live there, and as well as providing a house for him, the Church got it connected to the telephone with the number Stoke on Trent 21300.

---

[273] Letter in Correspondence File vol. 1
[274] Letter in Correspondence File vol. 1
[275] Letter in Correspondence File Vol. 1 dated 25th February 1964

Desmond Evans was ordained to the Pastorate at Bethel on Saturday 25th April 1964.[276] The service was followed by a tea at the Scout Hall in Brunswick Street. A team of young people from Leicester came over for his ordination, and this team returned a couple of times during his pastorate to help with outreach work.[277]

At the deacons' meeting on 5th May 1964, Pastor Evans was asked to outline his 'vision for the Church'. The first matter he referred to was "his missionary vision", the importance of supporting overseas workers. Ron and Muriel Rowland were already on the foreign field in Peru, and David Mead was about to go out to Italy, while two more members of the Church were applying to Bible Colleges, namely the Birmingham Bible Institute and Moorlands College. One of these, Miss Cherry Christie, later went to Brazil. Pastor Evans' next concern was evangelism; he laid out the plan that the morning services should concentrate on praise, while evening services would be evangelistic in emphasis. The custom of hymn-singing preceding the evening services would continue. The service was to be preceded by twenty minutes of prayer among the Church leaders in the vestry. Mr. Evans took over the Young Peoples Fellowship himself and planned a literature ministry.

Pastor Evans introduced a new Church logo, a cross atop a semi-circle intended to represent the empty tomb of Christ, with the Biblical text, "He is risen" as the motto below. This was introduced in the Church magazine, *The Pathfinder* for April 1965. "The empty tomb surmounted by the empty cross. Both are now Christless! Their powerful message to men is that Christ's saving work is an effective and finished work."[278]

The missionary concern led to two actions. First of all it was decided to hold a Missionary Convention at the Church in the autumn of 1965 at which various missionaries would speak to increase interest in missions. Secondly it was decided to target missionary giving to six agencies; UFM, ESVA, Wycliffe Bible Translators, EMF, the Leprosy

---

[276] There are a pair of letters in the Correspondence File Vol. 1 that give the date as Saturday 25th April 1963, but they are clearly in error, as Pastor Mead did not announce his intention to accept the call to Feltham until 24th May 1963. Also, 25th April 1963 was a Thursday.
[277] E-mail correspondence with Alan Cunnington of Wigston Bethel, January 2012
[278] *The Pathfinder* April 1965 P. 2

Mission and SIM. Reports from the mission field enliven the minute book at this time; Richard Rowland brought before the meeting a need that had developed in the village where Ron and Muriel were located; the village pump had broken down, forcing the villagers to drink local river water that was contaminated. The church looked into buying a pump and shipping it out to them.

Already the Church had begun to make tape-recordings of sermons. Pastor Evans saw a great potential in this technology that was still relatively new, and set up the "Bethel Christian Sound and Vision Team" in the Church. This was announced in the *Pathfinder* with great anticipation. "Slowly but surely, a technical team and equipment are joining forces at the Church" reads the report. "Number one target of the team is the production of a variety of evangelistic tapes. Differing in content and length, these tapes will be suitable for anything from a works C.U. gathering to a full hour's meeting. Workers will take the tape-recorders into hospitals and homes in the city and the country. In fact wherever prayer opens a door, through it the 'Plastic Preachers' will go." Though the ambition of this work may have exceeded the ability to perform, the recording and distribution of sermons and addresses at the Church goes on to this day. Magnetic tapes have given way to CDs, and now, thanks to the Internet, sermons from Bethel are being heard all over the world on the same day that they are preached in Hanley. From Sweden to Brazil, Malaysia to Poland, the ministry touches lives around the globe.

The older method of distributing literature was also taken. Pastor Evans approached the Christian Literature Crusade (CLC) seeking their assistance in starting a serious literature ministry. By this point the Banner of Truth Trust had begun to reprint the classics of the past, and the *Pathfinder* for April 1965 contains two recommendations for books, both by J.C. Ryle. The first is *Five English Reformers*, the second *Holiness*. The reviewer states, "The name J.C. Ryle on a book is an unreserved guarantee of its content value."[279]

Church activities continued as before. In addition to the Sunday services, the Sisterhood was held at 3 PM on Monday, and the Bible

---

[279] *The Pathfinder* April 1965 P. 16

School, the congregational Bible study, at 7:45 PM. On Wednesday night at 7:45 PM there was a prayer-meeting, and on Friday night there was a Youth Club meeting. There was of course also a Sunday school.

Pastor Evans had been deeply involved in the National Young Life Campaign while at Leicester, and this may have been one of the contributing factors which put him on a collision Course with the rival group Youth for Christ in the Potteries. By 1964 the usual meeting place for the Youth for Christ Sunday evening Rendezvous meeting was the Upper Room at the back of the Chapel. The Bethel young people had fallen out with Youth for Christ and, having threatened to withdraw from the YFC Rendezvous meetings, had actually carried out the threat in October, holding their own meeting instead. Pastor Evans encouraged this, and organised a Bethel Rendezvous from November. This was just one sign of growing tensions between Bethel and YFC, which came to a head in 1965.

Pastor Evans committed himself to break off most of his activities outside the Church when he came to take the pastorate; that is only to be expected of a man just beginning his pastorate; a pastor's ministry should be chiefly in the Church over which he has been ordained. The problem was that he also began to expect and to demand that all Church members made the work of Bethel primary in their lives and ministry; while most were not involved in work outside the Church, it happened that one of the members, Mr. Reg Allman, was also the leader of Stoke-on-Trent Youth for Christ. There seems to have been something of a personality clash between Mr. Allman and Pastor Evans, a clash which soon came to a head as Mr. Allman was referred to the Diaconate, probably by Pastor Evans. First of all it was complained that his visits to the church were "very sporadic" and that his level of involvement in the Church was not what was expected of a member. Secondly, it was alleged that he had impugned Pastor Evans' doctrinal views, a charge he vigorously denied.

Despite his denial of the accusation of slander, Mr. Allman found that his infrequent visits to the church were actually the main reason for Mr. Evans' decision that he should meet the leadership. Not surprisingly Mr. Allman objected to being told that he was expected to choose between Youth for Christ and Bethel. His ministry, he pointed out, was primarily in the para-church youth organisation, but he valued the support that came from being grounded in the local Church. Pastor Evans persevered in his insistence that Mr. Allman should attend Bethel more often. For his part, Mr. Allman felt that Pastor Evans and others were questioning his spiritual position, and wrote, "I am happy to tell you that the Lord is my constant joy and peace – and everything else."[280] A meeting was arranged, but it did not produce the desired result from Pastor Evans' point of view; Mr. Allman "intimated that he lacked confidence in the elders and deacons." He resigned his membership, and sent a sarcastic letter to the leadership confirming it. "Having no wishes to be excommunicated with all (?) other members who do not give of all their time and tithes I should be glad if my name were removed from the membership list."[281] The church accepted his resignation, but with concern over the tone of the letter. It is apparent the Pastor Evans took the lead in putting Mr. Allman under discipline. The action was not called for; Mr. Allman was not challenging Pastor Evans, nor was he teaching false doctrine; he was a senior officer in a para-church organisation with his own responsibilities. Pastor Evans seems to have forgotten that Mr Allman was just doing what he had done himself while a member at Wigston

This was just one sign of the fact that Pastor Evans had placed himself under an enormous strain and was beginning to crack under it, resulting in erratic and irrational behaviour. Pastor Evans was a hard worker, but he was no longer a young man, and his work-load was too much for him to handle. The falling-out with Mr. Allman seems part of a pattern that should have acted as a warning-sign that all was not well with the pastor. In March of 1965 the diaconate advised him to take a holiday, but he "forcefully refused" to do so; was he becoming overly controlling? It was plain that he was not well; the diaconate continued to insist he take a holiday as his condition deteriorated. He became increasingly erratic, and the question of whether or not he would be taking meetings became all but impossible to answer. On more than one occasion speakers who had been engaged by the Church Secretary were cancelled by Mr. Evans but had to be re-engaged when he decided not to

---

[280] Typed letter on YFC headed paper, dated 3rd March 1965 in Correspondence File Vol. 1
[281] Handwritten letter on blue letter paper dated March 8th 1965 in Correspondence File 1

speak after all. On one occasion this was literally within minutes of the meeting![282] This was unacceptable; he was finally sent on holiday at the end of April. On his return he was admitted to hospital. The Church suspended him from all duties on full stipend for three months to aid his recovery and expressed every hope that he would soon be restored. He had evidently never fully recovered from the shock of the collapse of his business, and the strain of the pastorate on his already-weakened constitution led to a further decline.

Pastor Evans' health problem seems to have been clinical depression. Mr. Plaskett, the Church secretary at the time, contacted the Clinical Theology Centre seeking help, and described Mr. Evans as "Suffering progressively more severe depressive attacks." They wrote back saying that Mr. Evans, whose name had not been given by Mr. Plaskett, "Does seem to be severely depressed."[283]

Then, without any warning, Pastor Evans suddenly discharged himself from the hospital and took a train to Cardiff; after this he simply disappeared, telling no-one, not even his wife, where he was or what was going on. Then Mr. Plaskett received a letter dated 7th July from Mr. Evans in Aberdare resigning the Pastorate. It is short and to the point. "I would appreciate it if this resignation were accepted without any attempt to refuse it, because I have nothing to say, either by way of explanation or justification." This was the first that had been heard from Pastor Evans since his departure, and it is ominous in what it does not say. As is usually the case, there is nothing explicit said, but a letter from Margaret Evans, Pastor Evans' wife, indicates how serious events were. Dated 15th July 1965 it shows that what had happened had seriously affected her. By going to Wales and telling no-one where he was (even the letter is simply addressed from 'Aberdare', without any further address) he had in effect abandoned not just the Church, but his family. Under the circumstances the only thing that could be done was to accept Pastor Evans' resignation, and the letter of resignation also relieved the Deacons of the responsibility of investigating Pastor Evans' actions any further. Further evidence that Pastor Evans was not well was the letter he

---

[282] Typewritten document in Correspondence File vol. 1 marked in pen "Read at Special Church Meeting"
[283] Letter from Brian Lake of the Clinical Theology Centre, 25th May 1964.

sent in response to the Church's acceptance of his resignation. While in the resignation letter he had made it quite clear that he simply wanted the Church to accept it without any explanation on his part, in an aggressively-worded letter dated 23rd July he complained that the Church should not have accepted his resignation without any explanation – the very thing he had asked the Church to do.

Pastor Evans' letter of resignation had come as a welcome way out of what was threatening to become a very serious situation. In a letter to the FIEC Mr. Plaskett writes "Mr. Evans had been ill with nervous debility, but this was not the reason for his resignation... I would prefer not to go into details."[284] Another letter refers to "household problems and illness."[285] They had no desire for a long and drawn-out process, and wanted to be kind to Mr. Evans by allowing him to leave gracefully and quietly. He had served the Church for a little over one year, and his departure was regarded with sorrow by the congregation. In August 1965 the Church wrote to the FIEC asking for a list of prospective pastors.

Mr. Evans continued a correspondence with the Church, and his third letter was thankfully far more conciliatory in tone, begging forgiveness and stating, "The Lord has made it clear to me that I must apologise to the fellowship at Bethel."[286] It is apparent that the Church wisely did not respond to his previous, aggressively-worded letter.

Pastor Evans eventually returned from south Wales; he was not well, and his actions were not rational or considered. He and the Church finally parted on reasonably good terms, a matter of relief to all involved. While he had been a gifted evangelist, he had proved quite unsuited to the very different work of a pastor. While every pastor should to some extent be able to "do the work of an evangelist", not every evangelist is able to do the work of a pastor.

---

[284] Letter dated 24th July 1965 in Correspondence File Vol. 1

[285] Letter to Mr. R. Chester dated 17th September 1965 in Correspondence File Vol. 2. This is a version of the standard letter sent out to all those invited to take the pulpit and copies are preserved addressed to all the men suggested by the FIEC

[286] Letter, from the Manse, dated 12th September 1965 in Correspondence File Vol. 1

Church Government

When the Hope Street Church was Congregational, government was quite clear; the Church was run by the membership who elected a Pastor and Deacons to guide them. The final decision in all matters was down to the Church Meeting. While the early Congregationalists usually had several elders in any one Church, by 1812 the usual pattern was for a single pastor with several deacons. The Deacons, being selected from the membership and usually being respected members of the local community, shouldered a great deal of responsibility. In the difficult later years, when the Church was aided by the County Union, Rev. Henry Thomas Hood instituted a Church Council in 1922 to give the leaders of the Sunday School and other organisations in the fellowship a larger role in the work, but this was short-lived.

With the Church coming under Edward Jeffreys' Bethel Movement, things changed again; Jeffreys was a benevolent autocrat, and his churches had no formal membership, or officers beyond the pastor. In effect there was just a pastor who was in charge and who answered to Bethel Headquarters. With the dissolution of the organisation in 1939 all that was left was one man in charge at Hanley, Pastor Vernon. Though notionally there was a committee in charge, it rarely met.

After Pastor Vernon's death there was a board of trustees with a president, and under Pastor Mead's leadership this became a board of Deacons led by the Pastor. With a formal Church membership re-instituted, the Church once again adopted a Congregational form of government on the traditional English Nonconformist model. In the Bible, however, the New Testament documents that touch on Church government clearly envisage a situation where the Church has a plurality of elders. While the Puritans had both elders and deacons in their Churches, the former concerned with the spiritual welfare of the people and the latter with material concerns such as poor relief and the administration of the Church funds, this distinction was lost in the eighteenth century, and Deacons took on the role of elders as well.

A formal Church constitution was adopted in 1963, based on a draft that had been worked out by the Pastor and Deacons. In order to fully discuss this the second quarterly Church meeting, held on April 27th 1963, was extended to a full afternoon and evening, when the constitution was discussed paragraph by paragraph. Paragraph one, which was adopted as unalterable, reads:

> The Church shall be known as Bethel Evangelical Free Church and shall be dedicated to the glory of God and for the following main objectives: - (a) to preach Christ as the only Saviour of men; (b) to strengthen and encourage believers; and (c) to contend for the faith once delivered to the saints. It shall always maintain the fundamental truths of the Word of God, the Bible always being its final court of appeal in all matters of doctrine and practice.[287]

The records show that there was a full discussion of every paragraph of the draft constitution; even with afternoon and evening sessions it was necessary to hold an additional meeting to finish discussing the whole constitution. It was finally adopted at a meeting on June 10th 1963, called because Pastor Mead had announced his intention of accepting the call to Feltham.

The 1963 AGM decided that deacons were to serve for a fixed term of years rather than being in the position for life, though deacons could be re-elected; this remains in place to this day. During the interregnum after Pastor Mead the custom of the deacons meeting with the speaker in the vestry for prayer began. Today it is the elders who do so, but the custom began as a result of a vote in the Deacons' meeting on 7th January 1964.

The twentieth century in particular has seen a recovery of the plural eldership in the local Church, and Bethel has participated in this. At the Deacons meeting on 8th October 1964 Pastor Evans spoke on Biblical Church government and showed that the early Church had elders and deacons, and that the deacons were the ones who looked after the business side of the Church while the elders were concerned with the spiritual welfare of the fellowship. He emphasised that these were offices

---

[287] *Draft Constitution* in the Church archives

to which God called men, and the Church was to recognise the gifts God has given and call God's men. He sought to introduce the office of Elder into the Church, noting on 26th October 1964 that the diaconate as it then stood could be divided pretty neatly into half elders and half deacons. Pastor Evans' departure prevented this from being properly implemented; it was not until the first decade of the 21st century, by which time Desmond Evans' attempt had been forgotten, that a Biblical plural eldership was instituted. In another proposed change to the way the Church was run, Pastor Evans wanted the AGM to be a meeting for praise and fellowship rather than a business meeting; this was never done. The balance of the spiritual and the business side of these meetings is always difficult. A note in the minutes of 26th October 1964 brings a smile when it says that the removal of the business matters would make the AGM "a meeting that the Lord's people would look forward to." In the event he departed before any of the proposed reforms could be carried into effect.

A plural eldership was finally instituted at Bethel in the 21st Century following the departure of Pastor Phil Roberts. Under this system, which is based on the teaching of the Apostle Paul and the evidence in the book of Acts in particular, the Church is led by a team of elders rather than a single pastor. All elders are equal, including the pastor, and they differ in their roles rather than anything else.

Chapter 15: Seeking a Successor

The first matter that confronted Bethel on Pastor Evans' departure was arranging for the pulpit to be supplied. Men known to the Church, including Pastor A.W. Mead, were contacted for the short-term, and the FIEC sent a list of four names as possible candidates. These were Rev. C.S. Medhurst of Redhill, who had first been considered after Pastor Mead's departure, Rev. George McLeod of Street, Somerset, Pastor M.A. Collins of Brixton Hill and Mr. B. Chester of London. Mr. Collins had been serving a Shaftesbury Society work, namely the Shaftesbury Welcome Mission in Battersea, and therefore was not eligible for Ministerial Recognition, which is why he was called "Pastor". Mr. Chester was a recent graduate of the London Bible College and had not yet been ordained.

Other contacts were approached, including Selwyn Morgan of Holywell, who was asked to supply the names of men that he thought might be suitable for the pulpit. Rev. David Smith, vice-principal of the Birmingham Bible Institute wrote asking the Church to consider Rev. H.E. Lewis, a friend of his and a pastor at that time without charge, as a pulpit supply.

The men being considered as candidates were of course also preaching at other Churches as well as Bethel. Richard Chester accepted a call to Cranleigh Baptist Church in Surrey, and so on 15th October 1965 he wrote to cancel his engagement at Bethel, at the same time suggesting a friend from College, Mr. P. Smutts, as a possible replacement.

The first two men mentioned specifically in connection with the Pastorate are Rev. George Macleod, who came to preach on October 25th and Pastor Collins, who came in January 1966. Other names were received from Rev. Omri Jenkins by December 1966. These were Rev. Paul Brown, assistant Pastor at Spring Road Evangelical Church, Southampton, Rev. M. Munday of the Evangelical Movement of Wales and Rev. Neil Richards of London. They were also asked to preach.

The commitment to the mission field continued, even in the period without a pastor; Mr. Brian Adams was accepted by UFM for work in Brazil. In order to do the work he not only took a language course with Wycliffe Bible Translators, but he also took a course in diesel engineering. The missionaries already in the field continued to receive not only prayer support but also financial and practical assistance. Ron and Muriel Rowland received a new Volkswagen estate car for their work in Ghana. The secretary's report for 1965 gives six missionary items. As well as Mr. Adams and Mr. and Mrs. Rowland the missionaries or future missionaries were Miss Cherry Christie in Brazil, Mr. David Mead, studying Italian at the University of Perugia, Mr. and Mrs. J. Addison who had been accepted by EMF for work in Portugal, and Miss P. Middling, who had just begun her studies at the Birmingham Bible Institute in preparation for missionary work.

The departure of Pastor Evans led to a rebuilding of the Church's relationship with Youth for Christ, and they returned to Bethel for meetings in 1965 and continued to meet at Bethel at least to 1966 (the minute-book between March 4th 1966 and 1st May 1970 is missing). Reg Allman was invited back into membership and the diaconate apologised for the misapplication of Church discipline in his case. For his part, Mr. Allman graciously accepted the apology and stated that he had no hard feelings despite the fact that he had been wronged.

Although Bethel was never strictly a Pentecostal Church, and Edward Jeffreys had a rather complicated relationship with the Pentecostal movement that his father and uncle had been so instrumental in establishing, there were still some connections with the Pentecostal movement. Pastor Evans took an Easter meeting at the Longton Elim Church in 1965, and in 1966 Mr. Potts, who led the Young People's fellowship, expressed an interest in Pentecostalism and helping at a local Assemblies of God Church. The Church is not named, and there are several fellowships in the Potteries associated with the AOG. It seems that Mr. Potts became fully Pentecostal, and he finally left Bethel and joined the AOG. The parting of the ways seems to have been thankfully cordial.

A Church without a pastor can suffer from the lack of systematic teaching; after Pastor Evans' departure various proposals were made to ensure a continuity of teaching in the Monday evening Bible study. It was generally agreed that the Church could and should set out a series of subjects to be treated in the study, and that the visiting speakers would have a subject (but presumably not a text) assigned to them.

Having invited the ministers who had been suggested for a visit each, it was then decided to invite some of these for a second visit. It seems that some men rather indiscreetly asked one of the other men if he had been invited for a second visit when he had not.[288] Apparently unhappy in the rural pastorate he held at the time, it seems that he had pinned his hopes on being called to Hanley. He seems to have taken umbrage at this, and wrote a letter in which he forcefully put himself forward as the right man for the job.[289]

Dear Mr. Clowes,

This afternoon I was asked, by Rev. L. Evans, if I had been invited back to Hanley. Similarly a few weeks ago Rev. Oliver Sainsbury enquired had I 'been to Hanley a second time'. As I have never discussed the matter with the they must have been given the impression, perhaps at Hanley, that such a matter was being, or had been, considered.

This has led me to write to you because I have been surprised that matters went not further than my first visit. It was my impression when I last left Hanley that we should meet again – indeed, the deacons said this. My subsequent thoughts were that I could probably do an effective work there because your type of work and people are nearest to my own heart.

---

[288] Letter dated 7th May 1966
[289] Correspondence with the Church in question has confirmed this, but I have withheld names and places in order to protect the people involved. The Church today admits that the young man was placed under a lot of pressure and not given the support that he should have received.

Could I suggest that, if you have not yet come to any conclusions about your pastorate, we should meet again for a frank and open talk? I well recall your own apprehensions and feel that these have become related to myself. If your deacons would care to meet me for frank discussion I would be willing to meet half the expense of travel. Will you please put this before your Diaconate?

Praying the Lord's blessing upon you all,
Yours in Jesus' love…

One feels deeply for the young man in question, who was obviously deeply unhappy in the struggling rural Church where he was, but the letter is a textbook example of how not to behave in such a situation, and it is no surprise that he was not asked back.

The financial situation of the Church at the time seems to have suffered somewhat; a loan had been taken out, and there were some difficulties experienced in repayment. Though Christian work is not about money, it still needs money to run, and a Church without a pastor is in a difficult position, as people seek spiritual help elsewhere. The depopulation of the area immediately around the building also contributed to a decline in membership. However, the pastoral vacancy was not to last long, for the minutes of a deacons' meeting held on Tuesday 12th April 1966 indicate that the church's consideration had already fallen on one young man who had supplied the Pulpit.

Chapter 16: Paul Brown: Early Years

Paul Brown was the son of a Baptist minister; he studied under Ernest Kevan at the London Bible College (now the London School of Theology) between 1957 and 1960. He was assistant Pastor at Spring Road Evangelical Church in Southampton at the time that he became known to Bethel, and with his family growing, he was seeking a pastorate of his own. Ernest Kevan, first principal of the London Bible College, was a student of the Puritans and an enthusiastic believer in the Reformed or Calvinist theology that the Puritans held to. He communicated this enthusiasm to many of his students, including Paul Brown.[290]

Paul Brown first came to Bethel for the 6th/7th February 1966. In the letter inviting him back we read "We much appreciated your ministry, in particular the Bible Study on Monday evening."[291] In the minutes for March 4th 1966 we find that Paul Brown was one of two visiting speakers asked back a second time, the other being Rev. N. Richards, and by the meeting held on 12th April it is quite clear that he was under serious consideration. On an 'additional sheet' with a pencil outline of the Church building on the top right corner, we read under the heading "Questions for Pastor", "It was decided to ask Paul Brown and all possible candidates for the Pastorate to subscribe to the FIEC declaration of faith and also to give answers to the following questions:
1. What are your views on evangelism?
2. What are your views on Believers' Baptism?
3. What are your views on Divorce?
4. What would be your missionary vision?"

On 5th June a deacons' meeting at Bethel met to consider the choice of the new pastor. The field had narrowed in their minds to two men, Paul Brown and Neil Richards. It was a difficult choice; the two men were very similar; both were gifted and godly ministers. But

---
[290] Paul E. Brown, *Ernest Kevan* (Edinburgh, 2012)
[291] Letter dated 11th February in the Correspondence File Vol. 2

ultimately the matter came down to the Church's FIEC membership and Paul Brown's "position with the FIEC."[292] Because of this it was eventually decided unanimously to extend a call to Mr. Brown to take up the pastorate of the Church, and to recommend to the Church meeting on 18th June that he be accepted as Pastor.[293] The deacons recognised that the timetable proposed was rather compressed, and in the letter wrote, "Please forgive us if we now appear to be hurrying, but having prayed much about this and made our decision, we are now only too anxious to see the right man in the right place."[294] Neil Richards went on to become, in 1981, the pastor of the historic Wheelock Heath Baptist Church, less than fifteen miles from Bethel.

Mr. Brown replied in a letter dated 10th June 1966 accepting the Pastorate and giving some indication of how he came to accept it.

> "I have of course been praying about the Lord's will, believing it was time to move from Southampton, and since visiting Hanley, this has naturally been in my prayers. My feeling generally was that the Lord might be leading me amongst you. The invitation from the deacons I regard very seriously indeed, for following the Scriptural principle seen, for example, in Acts 13:1-4 such a call, if truly initiated by the Holy Spirit, is from God Himself and, therefore, cannot be refused. Subsequent prayer and consideration of all the relevant factors of which I am aware, strengthened my conviction that it is right to reply as I have. I would like to add that my wife shares my feelings in this."[295]

One of the "relevant factors" was that Mary Brown, Paul Brown's wife, was pregnant, and a quick move to Stoke was desirable in order to be settled in by the time it came for her to give birth.

---

[292] Letter to Neil Richards dated 13th June in the Correspondence File Vol. 2. The relevant minute book is missing
[293] Draft letter in Correspondence File Vol. 2
[294] Draft letter in Correspondence File Vol. 2. What is interesting is that this is the original draft, not a copy of the letter sent, and shows the process of formulating a call letter. Originally the words 'prayed much about this' were not included, but clearly it was suggested that without them the letter might give the impression that the decision was primarily of man.
[295] Correspondence File Vol. 2

Letters were sent out to those candidates for the pastorate who had not been called, including to the man who had written the unfortunate letter. In this letter Mr. Clowes assured him that the two men who had asked whether he had been asked back were not privy to any special information regarding the call to the pastorate. "Our present concern is that we might not have offended you in any way, though I well remember your last words to me, being, that if you heard no more you would not be offended."

Thankfully he was not offended, and replied with a gracious letter in which he wrote, "Personally I had become convinced that I could usefully serve at Bethel. However the Lord has led you otherwise and I am glad that, having met the man of His and your own choice, you have not hesitated to call him."[296]

Fig. 20: Pastor Paul Brown

---

[296] Letter dated 21st June 1966 in Correspondence File Vol. 2

Once again preparations began for the arrival of a new pastor. Before Paul Brown could bring his family up to Stoke to meet the Church, Richard Rowland and other Church members, on holiday in Bournemouth, made their way to Southampton one Sunday evening to surprise Pastor Brown. They were at once invited back to the family's residence to meet Mrs. Brown, who was at home with the children.[297]

Moving house is always a difficult job, and planning for the Brown family to move into the manse began in July, with a date of 8th September planned for arrival. The firm used was Pickfords, founded in nearby Buxton.[298]

It is traditional for the incoming pastor to arrange speakers for the induction service, and in the case of Paul Brown these were Rev. Keith Tanner and Mr. David Fountain, the senior pastor at Southampton.[299]

Links with Pastor Mead at Feltham were kept up; August saw the arrival of a letter from Pastor Mead inviting "all our friends at Hope Street, including your new pastor" to the Autumn Convention at Manor Lane.[300] In the course of the letter he wrote, "May I take this opportunity to convey to you our congratulations on the settlement of Rev. Paul Brown and his family among you."

As usual letters were sent out to the various local churches inviting their members and ministers to the induction services, and indeed letters went to Churches further afield. Replies in the Church archives show just how varied these relationships were, with letters from the Fenton Church of the Nazarene in Smithpool Road, from Rev. Douglas Millar of Arnold Road Baptist Church in Nottingham, from the Hanley Assembly of God Pentecostal Church in St. John Street, and from Rev. David Price of St. Chad's, Bagnall. In hindsight it may not have been a good idea to have the service replace the Wednesday night prayer meeting, as Wednesday night is a popular night for weeknight meetings.

---

[297] Letter from Paul Brown dated 28th June in Correspondence File Vol. 2
[298] Letter from Paul Brown dated 22nd July in Correspondence File Vol. 2
[299] Letter from Paul Brown dated 26th July in Correspondence File Vol. 2
[300] Letter dated 26th August 1966 in Correspondence File Vol. 2

As a result of this, Rev. David Price from Bagnall and Rev. W.B. Kelly of Fenton Church of the Nazarene were unable to attend due to meetings at their own churches.

The induction service was on the evening of Wednesday 14th September 1966; it was presided over by Rev. D.R. Kerwood of Lawnswood Evangelical Church, Handsworth, Birmingham. Rev. K.B. Tanner of Beechdale Evangelical Church, Walsall, gave the charge to the pastor, and Rev. David Fountain of Southampton gave the charge to the Church. Greetings and letters were read from a number of churches and institutions, including a telegram from H. Brash Bonsall of the Birmingham Bible Institute that read simply, "Warm greetings God bless pastor and flock Acts 20:32."[301]

Pastor Brown arrived at a church that was suffering from financial problems; there was a bank loan that had been taken out to but the manse, and the 150-year-old chapel (strangely referred to as "approximately 100 years old" in a letter of the period[302]) was showing its age. Its large size meant that heating costs were high, and for various reasons the sale of the site which had seemed to be quite certain when the loan was taken out was now highly unlikely. Payments of fifty pounds a month to the bank, a pastor's salary of forty-four pounds a month and missionary giving of thirty pounds a month left sixteen pounds out of the average 140 pound a month giving – by no means enough to pay for the upkeep of the building. At the same time the church roof sprang a leak, which meant two hundred pounds had to be spent on repairs. The only solution to the financial trouble that the FIEC was able to suggest was to take out a mortgage on the manse; to this end the Church approached the Temperance Permanent Building Society in July of 1967. All through the Paul Brown era church finances were a struggle, and yet the Church has by the grace of God continued. There were times when the church did not have enough money on hand to pay bills, one occasion where there was the money, but a postal strike prevented payment. God provides, but he often provides one day at a time.

---

[301] In the archives, in Correspondence File Vol. 2
[302] Letter from Mr. Clowes to Rev. D. Mingard of the FIEC dated 12th January 1967 in Correspondence File Vol. 2

The manse is a small semi-detached house of 1930s date with two bedrooms and a box-room. Downstairs it has a kitchen, a front room and a back room. With Pastor Brown's growing family, it was hard for him to get peace and quiet to study in the house, and so he hit on the idea of obtaining a touring caravan, which was parked on the property and fitted out as a study. This allowed him to 'go to work' in the morning, and to have peace and quiet in the caravan while he worked. This proved to be a very successful idea, although the caravan was quite cold in the winter.

Outreach work continued; 1968 saw a new venture in which the Church approached the Bible Text Publicity Mission seeking to place a Bible text poster and a poster advertising the Bethel at Stoke railway station. This was successful, and in due course the poster appeared. There was however some difficulty surrounding its initial display, as when a representative of the Church went down to check on the poster, it was discovered, to the dismay of everyone, that the contractor had put up the wrong poster! The Bible Text Publicity Mission was quickly informed of the error, which was corrected.[303] Other evangelistic efforts in the 1970s included several mission weeks in which there were a variety of activities from formal meetings to discussion groups in which questions about the cults and science were raised and the showing of films in the church. These films were not all of the same type; of those which we know were shown one was the biographical historical drama *Luther*, the other, *The Stones Cry Out,* was a documentary film about the archaeological background of the Bible. The showing of films was abandoned because of poor attendance which did not justify the cost of the events.[304]

Support continued for missionaries, although the financial difficulties that faced the Church made giving a strain at times. But the Church had sent missionaries out into the field, and had an obligation to contribute towards their support.

---

[303] Correspondence in Correspondence File Vol. 2
[304] Minutes of Deacons Meeting 5th April 1973

The literature work of the Church had been confined to a stall in the chapel since Pastor Evans began it, but in 1969 Paul Brown proposed that it should be expanded, and a stall set up outside the church for the sale of Christian literature, another stage in the development of the present Church bookshop. This meant that the church had to go to the city council, and the council decided that planning permission would be required for the stall. Permission was granted.

Relations with other Churches of similar convictions were fostered in various ways. One of these, founded in 1967, was the North Staffs. Evangelical Fellowship. Among its activities were an annual convention and a ministers' fraternal. It had something of a 'Keswick' and Billy Graham ethos, and does not seem to have continued very long.[305] While Youth for Christ had moved their regular meetings to Trinity Presbyterian Church, probably at least in part as a result of the disagreements between Pastor Evans and Mr. Allman, in 1970 another young people's organisation, the National Young Life Campaign, began to use the Upper Room for their Tuesday morning prayer-meetings.

A Church library was started in 1972. The core of it consisted of books already on the premises in a bookcase in the vestry. The rest was made up of books donated by Church members.[306] It has never been large, and at times has been more or less neglected, but it is still in the Church today, and contains many useful and helpful books. The bookcase for the library was purchased in 1981 as a memorial to Mrs. Cotterill.[307]

Sunday trading has been an issue that the Church has had to deal with for a number of reasons over the years. The most serious issue with Sunday trading took place in the early 1970s. At the time the building across Newhall Street from the church was used as a DIY warehouse by Rotocroft Ltd., and in 1973 it began to open on Sunday mornings. At the time those who drove to Church relied on the ability to park on the street, something that the opening of the store on Sundays threatened.[308] Under

---

[305] A copy of its constitution and a letter relating to the 1969 AGM are preserved in the Church archives.
[306] Minutes of Church Meeting 22nd January 1972
[307] Minutes of Deacons Meeting 15th January 1981
[308] Minutes of Deacons Meeting 22nd February 1973

the Shops Act 1950, shops were normally required to be closed on a Sunday, though partial exemptions could be granted under certain circumstances.[309] The fact that the DIY warehouse was opening on a Sunday therefore led to some surprise at Bethel, and it was decided to investigate the provision of the law. The result was that it seemed the company might actually be flouting the law on Sunday trading, but it turned out that the owners of the store were Jewish, and registered as such under the 1950 Act. They were therefore within the law,[310] and the Church had to turn part of the site into a car park.

One amusing incident in the history of the Church took place in 1973. The question of Communion wine came up in discussions. The Church had been using blackcurrant cordial at Communion for some years, at least since Pastor Mead's time, and Paul Brown felt that this was taking the actual Communion too far from what was instituted by Christ. The matter was brought before the Church Meeting, and Paul Brown suggested that it would be better to use non-alcoholic wine, "the true fruit of the vine."[311] What followed was a period of discussion on the topic. As always there was someone who wanted to keep the status quo, who remarked that, "It was just a symbol." Mr. Richard Rowland replied that "What we used was a symbol of a symbol." It was finally decided that something made of grape juice should be used.[312]

The central site of the Church has often led to requests for it to be used by other Churches and organisations for special events. Where these are in general agreement with Bethel doctrinally, the requests have usually been granted unless there is a good reason not to, for example, the Church wanting to use the building at the time requested. Youth for Christ and the National Young Life Campaign were frequent visitors in the 1970s; the Stoke on Trent Young Life branch used the Church for annual carol services. On April 5th 1975, at the request of Mr. David Saltwell, the building played host to the Spring Rally of the North Staffordshire Christian Endeavour Society; the speaker was Rev Dr. Arthur Skevington Wood of Cliff College, Calver.

---

[309] *http://www.legislation.gov.uk/ukpga/Geo6/14/28/enacted* Accessed 30/07/2012
[310] Minutes of Deacons Meeting 17th May 1973
[311] Minutes of Church Meeting 24th November 1973
[312] This also has the advantage of being impossible to dilute to the point where it is little more than coloured water.

A baptistery had been installed to replace the cumbersome and awkward portable canvas tank of earlier years, and this meant that the Church also received requests from other churches which did not possess such facilities to use the building for baptismal services. Among these was Park United Church, who used the building on 21st July 1973. Bethel took advantage of this and held a baptismal service in the evening after the Park baptismal service.[313] It is to be hoped that Park left the water relatively clean.

The building itself, and the Church's location on the corner of Newhall Street and Hope Street, had been in question for over a decade by this point. There were real questions as to whether there would be a Free Church in the centre of Hanley for much longer.

---

[313] Minutes of Deacons Meeting 21st June 1973

Chapter 17: Urban Regeneration

The period following World War 2 saw an unprecedented transformation of Britain's urban landscape. In part this was forced by the Luftwaffe's bombing of the nation's industrial cities, and in part by the short-lived optimism of a "new Elizabethan" age. Whole districts of cities were swept away, streets of terraced houses gave way to multi-storey blocks of flats, and vast urban shopping centres replaced old streets of shops. Hanley, where pot-banks had stood cheek-by-jowl with terraces as the town grew in a pattern that was dictated only by availability of land, was ripe for redevelopment.

The redevelopment of Hanley affected Bethel directly. The greatest reminder of it today is the huge blank wall of the Potteries Shopping Centre which looms over the Church building like some huge fortress. The scheme was intended to lead to the redevelopment of most of the town centre. A continual theme in the minutes through this period is the question of sale of the site. It seems that some unknown party was interested in the site in 1962, but the Church refused to sell because it was suspected that the prospective buyer might want to build licensed premises on the site. One good effect of this was that the Church constitution was finally put on a legal basis rather than being a mere 'gentlemen's agreement'. The discussion of selling up and building a new church also gives us a glimpse of the sort of congregations expected at the time; it was felt that they would need a building capable of seating 350 with provision for a Sunday school and car parking. Consideration was giving to moving to the new development in Bucknall New Road; in 1962 there was even a serious proposal to buy the Tabernacle building.

The Tabernacle had never recovered from the effects of the First World War and the subsequent move of the wealthier classes from which it drew many members to the suburbs. In 1919 the membership had stood at 350[314]; ten years later in 1929 it was a mere 225, and by 1930 it had fallen to 215. Under pastor Arthur Oates, who came to the Church in

---

[314] All statistics are from the *Congregational Year Book* for the relevant year.

1931, the membership recovered slightly; by 1942 it was back to 236. The Second World War had a catastrophic effect on the Church; by 1946 the membership was down to 183, and it continued to fall. In 1952 Oates moved to the pastorate of a brand-new Church at Clayton, a leafy suburb of Newcastle. Membership at the Tabernacle immediately dropped from 177 to 135, as those members who could do so followed the pastor to the suburbs. The new church was smaller than the huge Victorian Gothic sanctuary on Town Road, and more suited to the postwar era. Those still in Hanley struggled on without a minister for a little over a decade; by 1962 they were in talks to merge with the Presbyterian Church at Trinity on the Trinity site; a smaller building was more suited to the changing religious landscape of the Potteries. There were only 77 members at the Tabernacle by the time of the union. This union between the Congregational and Presbyterian Churches in Hanley reflected the national movement that would issue in the formation of the United Reformed Church in 1972. The redevelopment and accompanying depopulation of the town centre contributed to the demise of the mother-Church of North Staffordshire Congregationalism; there were simply fewer people living in the area by 1962.

In 1962, then, the Tabernacle Church were seeking to sell the huge church with its spire and hall so that they would be able to enter into a union with the Trinity Church; so the approach from Bethel would have made sense to some degree. The Secretary of the Tabernacle was approached with the proposal, but nothing came of it. In retrospect the plan was over-ambitious in the extreme; with the estimates of the seating capacity a new building would have needed being about 350, the purchase of a vast Victorian Nonconformist cathedral seating over 1000 would have been buying a huge white elephant. Nevertheless, the proposals to redevelop Hope Street continued. The sale of the Hope building was agreed in principle by the trustees in June 1962, and by the membership at an extraordinary meeting on July 5th of the same year. Despite the sale very nearly going through in 1962, in the event the sticking point was the question of the sale of intoxicating liquor on the site; the would-be purchasers did not want a site with a restrictive covenant on it, so the sale fell through. This was still the heyday of urban redevelopment, so the question of the future home of the Church was still very much open. The redevelopment question was one of two matters discussed at the first quarterly meeting of the Church membership on January 31st 1963; it was insisted that any new site would have to be "Somewhere in the vicinity of our present Church."

On two occasions planning permission was sought for the Church site to be redeveloped and shops and offices to be built on the site, but on both occasions it was denied. The reason given was that the site was not in the main shopping area of the town, and therefore such a development would be inappropriate.[315] The Church seems not to have known this at the time.

With the redevelopment of Hope Street very much in the cards the Church seriously considered moving. The two options open were either finding an existing church building suitable for the needs of the Church or securing a site on which to build a new chapel. The Tabernacle was an unrealistic option, but there was another former Church building in the area; the former Tabernacle Town Mission in Union Street. This seated about 300 people, and as an old Mission Church was a more flexible building than the old chapel. Once again, however, nothing came of the scheme. The building is still standing, and is used by the New Testament Church of God. While building a new chapel on another site was a more attractive option, as it would allow the Church to build for their specific needs, there seemed to be no suitable site available. As a comment in the minutes for 1963 reads, "Endeavour had been made to find a suitable site, and it seemed that each way was a closed door."[316] One of the reasons for this was that the Church was determined to remain in Hanley, where vacant sites were still rare and expensive.

Another suggestion came from the Welsh Congregational Church in Meyer Street, who in 1963 offered to sell their building to Bethel on the condition that Bethel built a smaller Church in Hanley for the diminishing Welsh Church. Although the site of the Welsh Church was a good one, the proposal came up against the problem of finding any new site at all in Hanley. Another possibility of acquiring an existing building

---

[315] *Report of the Director of Environmental Services to the Development and Building Regulations Sub Committee* dated 8th January 1976, in Church archives

[316] Minutes of Church Meeting August 22nd 1963

came in 1970, when the Providence Methodist Chapel in Upper Hanley closed, and it was suggested that the Church might buy it.[317] Again, nothing came of the proposal, for reasons that have not been recorded, though possibly related to issues with selling the Hope Street site.

As Hope Street hung in the balance, shops closed and were not re-opened. With the street all but derelict, crime and vandalism increased. This is shown most vividly in the minutes from 8th October 1964, where, "it was pointed out that the lead pipes had been stolen from the ladies toilets." This act of metal theft led to the dusting off of old plans for moving the toilets inside the building. The old Sunday school building was in a parlous state by this point, and it is reported that it was "slowly being demolished by local children" and "in a dangerous condition." The building was the property of the New Hall Pottery, a fact that seems not to have been understood by either the pottery or the church at the time! The council wrote to the Church in the summer of 1965 asking who they should contact over the fact that, after decades of neglect, the roof of the building had finally fallen in. The ruins were demolished soon afterwards.

At some point Pastor Desmond Evans prepared his own sketches of a possible new Church building. These have disappeared, probably taken by Pastor Evans when he left the Church. Andre Clowes, the Church secretary, who was an architect, seems to have considered these sketches to have been unsatisfactory and prepared sketches of his own. Though he moved to Leicester for work reasons, he remained closely connected with Bethel and acted as the Church architect.

In 1966 it was suggested that the church might sell the Hope Chapel property and move into a temporary building, but research indicated such a building would be impractical, the outlay on the temporary structure would be at least six thousand pounds, but its sale would realise at most one thousand; any move should be to a permanent new home. Mr. Clowes informed the diaconate he had done a thesis on Nonconformist church building, he was asked to prepare plans for a possible new church building, but these were never used.

---

[317] Minutes of Church Meeting 21st February 1970

By April 1967, Pastor Paul Brown had made it clear that a new building should include a bookshop.[318] The continuing failure to find a new site led thoughts to turn to redeveloping the existing site, as mine workings under the chapel were starting to cause minor subsidence. The National Coal Board refused to accept liability, and the Church was not prepared to pursue the question.

As car ownership increased, cities built for pedestrians, trams and buses felt the strain. While today there are strenuous efforts being made to draw people back to public transport, in the 1950s, 60s and 70s the emphasis was on changing cities for the car, creating new roads, especially large ring-roads around city centres. A number of proposals for a Hanley ring-road were brought forward; one would have required the demolition of the chapel. It almost went ahead, but changes in policy, and probably lobbying from local businesses, caused a change of mind, and instead the current route of Potteries Way was decided upon in 1971. The council was therefore no longer interested in the Hope Street site.[319]

The early 1970s saw a further development in the long-running saga of the Chapel site; the realisation on the part of the council that there was a burial ground containing some 200 burials beside the chapel. The Disused Burial Grounds Act of 1884 made it illegal to build on a disused burial ground for any reason other than to enlarge a place of worship, and so if the site was to be redeveloped the burials would have to be exhumed and removed. This could require the permission of living relatives of those buried there, but the Church had little idea who these people were. The official burial list had disappeared after being lent to a Mr. Cope-Cartilidge, making the finding of relatives extremely difficult. It was considered by some in the Church that the graveyard was being made an excuse for the council either to give the Church an unacceptably low price for the building and land, or to just slow down proceedings.[320] There was some discussion of moving the graves, but this never happened. The question of price also became a sticking point; having been offered sixty thousand pounds once, the Church was not prepared to accept any less.

---

[318] Minutes of Church Extraordinary General Meeting on 15th April 1967
[319] Minutes of Church Meeting 23rd January 1971
[320] Minutes of Church Meeting 26th September 1970

Bovis approached the Church in 1972 expressing an interest in redeveloping the site. This was accepted by the Church as a possible way forward, and there were suggestions made about re-purchasing the old Sunday school site so as to make the whole site more attractive to any possible purchaser.[321] However Bovis then replied that they were not interested after all, probably because the planning permission they sought for the site had been refused. Hammersons, who owned the old Sunday school site, replied that they already had a purchaser for all their land in Hanley.[322]

With the receipt of this news it was finally agreed that God was leading the Church to remain where it was in Hanley, putting an end to a decade of uncertainty. Minimal maintenance had been done on the building in the last decade, and it was by now too large and inflexible for the needs of the congregation. The loss of the schoolroom meant that there was no hall for Sunday school and things like teas and youth meetings. Various proposals to remedy this were discussed, including the insertion of a floor at gallery level to provide a hall above the church. In the short-term, the old building was thoroughly renovated and its graveyard, which had become quite overgrown, cleared up. It was finally proposed to build a new hall next to the building, maybe using a prefabricated structure, and perhaps to buy back the land on which the old school hall had stood.[323]

Other proposals made to renovate the building included the installation of toughened glass panels in the main doors to make the building look more inviting and more obviously open. One of the problems with older church buildings has been the solid doors; when they are closed they shut out, and can give the impression that the church is unwelcoming – they have even, joined with a building marked by the smoke of hundreds of bottle-ovens, given the impression that the building is closed, one response to visitation in the area had been surprise on the part of some local residents on learning that the building was actually still open. On the other hand glass doors, or doors with

---

[321] Minutes of Church Meeting 30th September 1972
[322] Minutes of Church Meeting 16th December 1972
[323] Minutes of Deacons Meeting 21st September 1972

glass panels, give a view into the interior of the building and help to invite people in to participate in what they see going on inside. The loss of the railings outside the building during World War 2 was a blessing in disguise here, helping to give an open and inviting appearance to the building and removing a possible psychological barrier to outsiders.

The decision to stay coincided with "Operation Eyesore", an initiative by the council to clean up buildings blackened with soot from industry and landscape what green spaces there were. The Church was therefore able to obtain a 75% grant for external renovation work on the building and its surroundings.[324] This still left the Church having to find 25% of the cost, £440.80 out of £1,276.50, and costs for internal work; no easy task given that the Church membership were not wealthy. The Church's contractor, Mr. J. Robinson, offered to employ the men of the Church as labourers to reduce the cost to only about £300. The question, Pastor Brown told the Church, was whether or not they were willing to work to Mr. Robinson's requirements, and prepared to find the £300. The answer given was a resounding "Yes."[325]

The Church was still looking at a new building as its long-term goal. At the Church Meeting on 14th December 1974, "The Secretary expressed the thoughts of the diaconate on the question of a new Church building, saying that the time had come when we should take positive steps to obtain a new church. Emphasising the point the Pastor said that the time had come for us to commit ourselves to a building programme. He suggested that we should obtain plans and costs as an initial move. All were in agreement with this."[326] Mrs. Sumnall merely added that first of all something needed to be done about the toilets, which were in a shocking condition. Any new building would after all be some time in the future. It would be sooner than anyone thought.

---

[324] Minutes of Church Meeting 16th December 1972
[325] Minutes of Church Meeting 18th March 1973
[326] Minutes of Church Meeting 14th December 1974

Chapter 18: Tesco

Following the closure of the New Hall Pottery, which had stood next to the chapel since its construction, Tesco Stores obtained the site for a new supermarket, the largest that the company had built to date. The developers, G.P. Trentham, approached the Church with a variety of options, and an extraordinary Church Meeting was called to discuss them. Trentham's presented the Church with two suggestions; the first, and probably that preferred by the developers, was that Trentham's would buy the Church site and allow the Church to continue worshipping there until the development took place. The old chapel would then be demolished, and the development would include a new church above the store. This is seen in other urban redevelopment schemes of the period; the Methodist Church at Wrexham in North Wales, built in 1971, is a classic example, being located on the upper floor of a shopping centre on Regent Street that includes the site of an earlier chapel, and gives a good idea of what G.P. Trentham intended for the Newhall Street site. If Bethel had agreed to this offer, it would of course have given Trenthams the largest possible site area to work with, but a chapel above the store would have led to problems of access, and questions about the future of the Church if the store should close and the building change hands. Andre Clowes, the Church architect, was not happy with the proposal.[327] The Church Meeting agreed the proposal was unsatisfactory.

The second proposal was that Trenthams would buy the site during the "danger period" of about a year while construction took place, leaving the Church with the option of buying the site back after the danger period was past or using the money to buy a new site elsewhere. This was also deemed unsatisfactory by the Church.[328] Instead the Church made a counter-proposal; Trenthams should provide adequate accommodation on the lawn beside the church (i.e. the former graveyard), give adequate compensation for any damage, and if possible restore the church to its previous condition if minor damage occurred, minor damage being defined as any damage which did not require the

---
[327] Minutes of Deacons meeting 24th March 1975
[328] Minutes of Church Meeting 29th March 1975

demolition of the building. Should major damage occur, Trenthams would have to construct a replacement building. This was agreed verbally, and Mr. Dalzell of Trenthams also offered to build a church hall at a cost of £6000 as compensation for inconvenience caused. Meanwhile the leadership of the Church went to the planning department to get permission to build a temporary hut on the old graveyard. This was granted.

The plans for the new store required the excavation of an underground car park very close to the chapel. It soon became apparent that this was too close; some seven foot down the workmen disturbed the burial of Pastor Vernon's young daughter. A call to Richard Rowland, who at that time worked for the local Coroner's office, summoned him to the site, where he found a group of workmen gathered around the tiny coffin, looking in shock at what they had done. The excavation had been just inches away from the side of the grave cut, so there had been no disturbance visible in the soil, but when they came below the level of the burial itself, the still-intact coffin had broken through the side of the excavation. The coffin was carefully replaced and the side shored up.[329] Later, the incident led to a superstition that the store was haunted; when Tesco left the old store in 2010 there were suggestions that the present minister of Bethel should perform an exorcism. Thankfully (in the opinion of the minister) nothing came of this.

After a time cracks began to develop in the building, first of all in the vestry at the back, and then in the sanctuary itself; pictures were taken, Trenthams and Tesco were informed. A piece of land from the car park, located between the chapel and the Tesco site, slipped into the excavation. It was decided to place 'tell-tales' over the larger cracks to make sure that there was no further movement. The rear buildings, the vestry and Upper Room, were declared unsafe. At the end of April a site hut was loaned to the Church by Messrs. Bossons and Deakin for the Sunday school and other activities which had taken place in the rooms at the rear of the Church. In the opinion of Mr. Clowes "We had 'reached the end of the road' with our rear buildings... and we should make every effort to raise money and prepare plans for a new building."[330]

---

[329] Conversation with Mr. Rowland in 2010
[330] Minutes of Deacons' Meeting 18th April 1975

Sunday 20th April 1975 was very difficult. The preacher that morning was a visiting missionary; it was already known that the rear of the Church was unsafe, but it had been proposed to use the main sanctuary for the Sunday school. Doubts arose in the minds of some of the members; what if the rest of the building were unsafe? Was it right for children whose parents did not know what was going on to be brought into a building that might be unsafe? It was finally decided that it was not, and the Sunday school was cancelled that day, though the evening service went ahead.[331]

Things got worse. The next Friday cracks began to appear in the main building. Paul Brown described Sunday 27th April 1975 as "one of the most miserable in my whole ministry. The building was not yet considered unsafe but everyone could see – and did see – a black half-inch wide crack above one of the gallery windows, and the plaster which had fallen from a crack between the gallery and the wall meant that three or four pews could not be used as the plaster had to be left as evidence." Standing in the high pulpit looking out on the chapel and its congregation, Paul Brown was tormented with fears about what would happen should the building suddenly shift during the service; the injuries and perhaps even fatalities that might result.[332] The evening service brought the same anxiety with it; Pastor Brown was very relieved when it was over and the building was empty once again, the congregation safe for another week at least.

The cracks continued to grow, and on the following Friday, 2nd May, Mr. Clowes declared that in his expert opinion the building was no longer safe for worship. The fall of a coping-stone from one of the windows from the side of the chapel confirmed this verdict. A special meeting was called for the following Saturday, and arrangements were made for Sunday 4th May to hold worship in the small hut that had been built on the site in the morning, and at Twyford Hall, the Scout and Guide centre in Brunswick Street, in the evening; it must have been quite a relief for Pastor Brown. Other meeting places suggested were the Samson Street School and the Welsh Chapel, with the possibility of a

---

[331] Typescript by Paul Brown in the Church archives.
[332] Typescript by Paul Brown in the Church archives.

larger hut on the site suggested as a future possibility.[333] Rebuilding was now not just an option, it was a necessity. Already Andre Clowes had drawn up rough plans for a new building; he had probably been drawing up such plans for years, but finally one would be used.

The Church took legal advice and were advised to obtain an injunction to stop the work to prevent further subsidence. Tesco, were at first unwilling to accept liability, and the solicitor advised that a high court injunction should be obtained. A *Sentinel* report of 8th May had suggested that the Church had already been suffering from subsidence due to coal-mining, and Tesco seems to have viewed this as a possible way of escaping the obvious conclusion that the severe subsidence leading to the damage to the building was due to their excavations. A Tesco spokesman said, "We naturally regret this situation, whatever the cause."[334]

By 17th May, G.P. Trentham seemed ready to accept responsibility for what had happened, and had voluntarily ceased work along the Church boundary.[335] Tesco, however, refused to admit liability, and so it was necessary to pursue an injunction to stop work and establish liability.[336]

Ecclesiastical neighbours were swift to offer support. The closest chapel to Bethel was Trinity United Reformed Church, and they offered to help in any way that they could. The Welsh Chapel in Northwood offered its building as a possible temporary home, but they also had a 6:30 evening service, and it was felt that, in the circumstances, it would be better for Bethel to use the temporary building on the church car-park in the morning. Bourne Methodist Church in Sneyd Green offered to lend 103 chairs for the temporary building, with an option to buy.[337] All of these churches are now gone, not only have the churches closed, but their very buildings have been swept away, leaving nothing to suggest that the sites were ever used for the worship of God.

---

[333] Minutes of Church Meeting 3rd May 1975
[334] *The Sentinel* 12th May 1975
[335] Minutes of Church Meeting 17th May 1975
[336] Minutes of Deacons' Meeting 14th August 1975
[337] Minutes of Deacons' Meeting 26th May 1975

With Tesco unwilling to accept liability, the Church had to move forward with the legal option, and seek an injunction against Tesco. It was a difficult decision; the outcome of the case was not certain, but it was decided that it was the right thing to do. A company as large as Tesco was even in 1975 had far greater legal resources available than a small local congregation, and may have thought that the cost and inconvenience of a legal action would dissuade the Church from taking matters further. If so, they were wrong. The Church leaders were determined that those responsible for the damage to the building would acknowledge their responsibility and make amends. To this end an injunction was sought restraining the removal of any further support from the land where the Church stood unless equivalent support was provided. The deacons pledged to mortgage their homes to pay legal expenses if necessary.

The case was heard in the High Court on Tuesday 17th June, 1975 before Mr. Justice Walton; a transcript of the judgement is preserved in the Church archives. Mr. Justice Walton found in favour of the Church, noting the deep excavation on the common boundary between the Church and the Tesco site. "One has only to mention that fact to make it abundantly obvious to the layman, as well as to the experts in the construction industry, that there were likely to be problems of subsidence and support for the next door Evangelical Free Church," he stated.[338] Because of the hazard to the Free Church from the development, Tesco were under a duty of care to the Church, and, Mr. Justice Walton pointed out, it is a principle in law "One cannot hire an independent contractor to carry out one's own duty of care to one's neighbour." The claim of the Church was eminently reasonable, seeking from Tesco only what Tesco should have done in the first place.

Mr Justice Walton went on, "The First Defendants [Tesco] seek to answer it by saying: 'Oh please, Sir, it's not me, Sir; it's that nasty Second Defendants' fault and I have nothing to do with it.'" As his sarcasm indicates, he found otherwise. "If one employs an independent contractor to do something which, of its own nature, is likely to – not necessarily, not bound to, but likely to – cause injury to other persons,

---

[338] Transcript of Judgement, P. 2

one cannot get out of responsibility for it oneself."[339] Tesco and Trenthams were dealt with forcefully by Mr. Justice Walton. "The First Defendants had the impudence to point to the fact that the Plaintiffs are now meeting elsewhere as a point which somehow entitled the work to be carried on, because that meant that there was no danger to life and limb. Having driven the Plaintiffs and their congregation out of their premises, that is now turned into a virtue. I must say that I find that a bit hard to stomach."[340] On the evidence it was "impossible to deny" that the excavations for Tesco's new store had caused the subsidence of the church building. "But very persuasive counsel [For G.P. Trentham] said I should not grant the relief which the Plaintiffs seek in their own best interest, because their own best interest requires that the work be pressed on with as quickly as possible so that a suitable retaining wall is built. Of course, while this is being done, doubtless there will be certain further settlement and damage to the building, but that will minimise that damage, and at the end of the day the Defendants' works will have been consolidated so that the Plaintiffs' building can settle down, and we will all know where we are. That seems to me a most ingenious way of describing 'riding roughshod' over the Plaintiffs' rights completely."[341] Finally, he remarked that, "If the terms of the injunction make it difficult for the Defendants to complete their building, I am afraid I cannot help that; they should have thought of the likely consequences of their construction before they ever commenced upon the building."[342]

With Tesco found legally responsible, it was hoped that they would be more reasonable and discussions out of court could bring about a speedy settlement. This did not happen; for a while it looked like there would have to be a full court hearing. This did not concern the Church much; it was now clear on whose side the law was. Thankfully in the autumn of 1975 an agreement was finally reached with which all parties were satisfied; the old Church would be demolished, and the store completed to ground level so a new church building could be put up.[343]

---

[339] Transcript of Judgement, P. 3
[340] Transcript of Judgement, Pp. 3-4
[341] Transcript of Judgement, Pp. 4-5
[342] Transcript of Judgement, Pp. 5-6
[343] Undated *Report of Bethel Evangelical Free Church* in the Church archives. Date probably early 1976 as it states that, "at the moment the present building is being stripped internally."

Plans for the new building were to be drawn up by Andre Clowes, architect and one-time Deacon, now based in Leicester. On 20th October 1975 a letter was sent from the Church to Mr. Clowes at the offices of Gordon, White and Hood, Architects, in Leicester. Certain requirements were laid down; the building would be single storey, covering a total area of about 3,600 square foot. Internally it would have a main sanctuary seating 150, with a further area partitioned from it (preferably at the rear) seating another 150. There would have to be a smaller hall, a vestry, a kitchen, a bookshop open to the public, and of course toilet facilities.[344] The cost would be around £120,000, covered by Tesco.

Fig. 21: Tesco-facing elevation of a rejected design for the new church

On November 15th 1975 a meeting was held in Twyford Hall to discuss the plans and specifications for the new building.[345] Several different plans and two models had been prepared for the meeting. These were examined and discussed by the 31 Church members, including the Pastor and Deacons, who were present. At the end of the meeting those present agreed unanimously on "a plan which seemed to incorporate the best features from all the others." That plan was largely the one of the present building.

Several of the plans drawn up survive in the Church archives, ranging from early sketches to full architects' plans. These show that a great deal of thought was put into designing a building that would be suitable for the Church's use. The earliest plan that we have is a sketch that is perhaps the most radical of the designs; the orientation of the building is completely changed, the pulpit against the wall that faces Hope Street. The hall is then at the end where the pulpit was, with other

---
[344] Letter in Church archives.
[345] Minutes of Church Meeting 15th November 1975

231

rooms on the remaining three sides, including a foyer and entrance on Newhall Street. This design makes for a sanctuary that is wider than it is long, which would have created a more intimate space. Very quickly, however, this was rejected, and instead a space more like that of the old building envisaged.

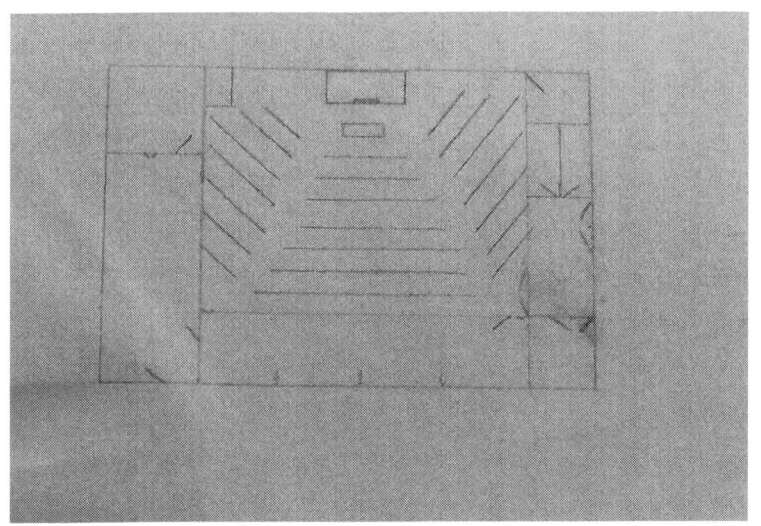

Fig. 22: The earliest known existing concept for a new church

By the 1970s Church architecture was firmly in the Modernist camp; the philosophy behind this being that, "Churches are secular buildings in the same way as schools and post-offices. Their design elements should be drawn from the vocabulary of general practice, and the architecture be modern in the fundamental sense of meeting functional and psychological requirements with contemporary efficiency and elegance."[346] Modernism also has the advantage of being fairly cheap, and keeping costs down was an important part of the plan. It could be argued, of course, that the 1812 chapel was also 'modernist' in the sense that its style was that of the age rather than imitating antiquity.

Though all the submitted designs were Modernist, some were more strikingly modernist than others. One would have presented a bold series of changing roof-lines when viewed from Hope Street, a series of

---
[346] Peter F. Smith, *Third Millennium Churches* (New York, 1972) Pp 74-5

inclined planes, rising to their highest point over the pulpit (Figure 23). This was rejected, almost certainly on the grounds that it would have created the need for a pair of gutters running over the Church building, gutters which would have caused major problems if they became blocked; the design chosen had a more traditional and practical pitched roof.

Fig. 23: Hope Street elevation of rejected design for the new church

Another aspect of 1970s Modernist Churches was the desire to create flexible spaces rather than the formal pewed sanctuaries that characterised older churches. One of the main drawbacks that had been felt in the old building was that it was inflexible; it was a space largely filled with pews for formal worship services. The new building was to be more flexible, capable of a number of uses. While in some other new buildings of the era pews were transferred from the old sanctuary, it was decided to replace pews with stackable chairs. A folding screen, supported by a beam at roof-height, enabling the sanctuary to be divided in two, was included in the design. The fact that the building was now all on one level meant that a Bible class room had to be included to replace the old Upper Room, and Paul Brown insisted that there should also be a bookshop, open to the public, on the premises. The placing of these elements, along with vestries, kitchen and toilets, were considered, the bookshop being the least flexible, as it would have to be located on Hope Street. At last the present design was fixed upon.

The building has the strengths and weaknesses of 1970s Modernist architecture. On the strength side is its flexibility and the varied spaces it contains, in contrast to the old building. Its weaknesses are also very much of its age. First of all, the relatively dark bricks used for the interior walls contribute to a rather gloomy sanctuary, not helped by the fact that 1970s Modernism was not in favour of a large number of windows, and the fact that the large clerestory window in the front wall had to be partially filled in because it leaked; some spaces have to be lit with artificial light even on the brightest summer days. Though most of the roofs have a pitch to them, there is a flat roof over the foyer that has caused trouble with water leaking through. Externally the paucity of windows can make the building look rather forbidding, but all of this is of its time, as the 1812 chapel was of its. In the final analysis, it is not fair to expect a Modernist building of the 1970s to look any different.

In terms of the specifications of the building, it was agreed that the main sanctuary would be of "facing brick relieved by plaster" internally, while all other rooms would be plastered. The Church roof would be open and of wood. "The seating was to be attractive and comfortable (i.e. Washington cathedral chairs[347]). Moulded chairs in the small hall." The chairs would allow for more flexibility than the pews, and would be hopefully attractive and modern. There was no agreement on whether the floor should be tiled, parquet, or carpeted, but eventually carpet won the day.

Before work could begin on rebuilding the Church had to obtain planning permission. Given that it was on a site that had been occupied by the Church since 1812, there was no difficulty in getting it. In a report, the city's Director of Environmental Services stated, "A Church is a suitable central area use, and the development of this strategic site could be a positive element in the townscape of the City Centre."[348] Permission was granted subject to certain conditions including access to the car park only from Hope Street, the approval of the plans by the local Planning Authority, and a satisfactory landscaping a tree planting scheme.

The old chapel was demolished in March 1976, having stood empty and unsafe since May of 1975; rebuilding did not begin until the

---

[347] This is a reference to a catalogue from Design Furnishing Contracts Ltd where a number of chair designs are shown in a variety of settings. The technical code for the chairs was DCHW. The catalogue is in the Church archives

[348] *Report of the Director of Environmental Services*

store had been completed to ground level, to ensure that there was no damage to the new building due to Tesco's construction work. When the underground work at Tesco was complete, the old galleried chapel went down, and the new, single-storey modern structure took its place. An article in the Evening Sentinel of March 13th 1976 recorded its passing with a picture of the forlorn chapel awaiting demolition.

While the new building was going up, the Church met in the temporary building on the old graveyard for services and for the Sunday school in the afternoon. The fact that the one space was used for both worship services and the Sunday school led to one particularly notable incident; on one occasion a boy let off a fire extinguisher in the hall. The extinguisher was of the powder type, and the sight of the hall coated with powder amused the children and no doubt horrified the Sunday school teachers. Despite the best efforts of the membership to clean up, traces of powder remained, sometimes causing rather humorous results. Summer heat required the installation of a fan to extract stale air from the rather low-ceilinged hut, which was provided by Richard Rowland. The fan meant that during cold weather more heating was needed, and the heating was not at first very satisfactory anyhow. This was rectified by the installation of more heaters.

Though by now the hut on the former graveyard housed most of the Church's meetings, there were still occasions when other buildings were used; three times the Mitchell Memorial Theatre hosted evening services of the Church, Hanley Baptist Church hosted a baptismal service, and a wedding was held in Wesley Hall Methodist Church.

Meanwhile rebuilding continued apace, overseen by various committees of Church members who threw themselves enthusiastically into the work. Although plans had been agreed, there were still minor interior issues such as the pulpit and flooring to be worked out as well as such technical issues as the lighting. Rising prices caused some anxiety; Mr. Clowes of course had his own views as to what would work best in the building that he was designing. The Church and Mr. Clowes actually disagreed over the chairs and carpet, but in the end the Church won, and so the seating and carpet are the choice of the congregation. Kitchen and bookshop were fitted out, and electrical wiring put in. Meanwhile

Church life went on with the usual concerns, such as repairs to Pastor Brown's car and the supervision of children during the Communion at the end of the morning service.

Fig. 24: The new building almost completed. The temporary hut is just visible on the car park

The question of the opening loomed large; it would be a major event, an opportunity to reach out to the wider community if handled properly. There would be advertising, of course, and special services to celebrate. The question of a speaker was raised at the Deacons' Meeting on 30th December 1976, and the name of Sir Fred Catherwood was suggested as a possible speaker. "Dr. Martyn Lloyd-Jones was also suggested as a possible speaker... in the event of Mr. Catherwood not being available." What the pre-eminent Evangelical Nonconformist leader of the era would have thought of being second choice to his son-in-law can only be imagined; he would probably have found it quite amusing. Both proved unavailable, and the Rev. William H. Davies of the Baptist Tabernacle, Blackpool was approached. It was felt that representatives of Tesco and Trenthams should be invited to the opening service as well as the Church's solicitors, Mr. Timothy Warren and Mr. John Mitchell.

By the autumn of 1977 the building was completed, and it was opened with great ceremony on Saturday 1st October, with services at 3PM and 6:30 PM, and a light lunch in the Small Hall between. The speaker was Rev. W.H. Davies. At the opening a statement from the Church was read which gave a brief version of the events that led to the building of the new church, in which it was noted that "What has happened to bring about this new building is rather unique." Going on, the statement reads, "The agreement which was eventually reached has resulted in this fine new building. We cannot pretend that we are not thrilled with it, for we are."[349]

---

[349] *Statement* in Church archives.

Chapter 19: Paul Brown: Later Years

With a new building, the Bethel was ready to move forward with the work in Hanley; the temporary hut had rather constrained some activities, and the freedom of the new Church was felt at once. Among the great gains was the bookshop. The Church had operated a bookstall for some years, but the new building incorporated a shop, open to the public, with a permanent stock. In the days before the internet and Amazon made book shopping something those who read usually do from their living-room, a shop was much busier than it is today, and in its first year of operation the shop took £3124 for books and cards and £208 for other items, giving a profit of £240.[350] The shop has never competed with other Christian bookshops in Hanley; it is meant to sell a selection of books that reflect the Church's teaching and would be helpful to Christians. It has always been run by volunteers, and in the 1970s and 80s in particular, while it was never busy, it did a reasonable trade and turned a small profit at the end of the year. Profits were used to support the work of the Church.

Evangelism and outreach became increasingly challenging as the years went on; the Church sought many ways to reach people. One approach was the display of posters and other materials, another door-to-door visiting, and a third open-air preaching.. Evangelistic services of various types were held; the Sunday evening service was primarily evangelistic. Special services were held as well; at the Deacons' Meeting on 18th January 1979, Pastor Brown informed the deacons of his intention to organise a series of lunchtime services on eight consecutive Wednesdays starting on the Wednesday before Good Friday. These would be evangelistic services with short addresses, intended to attract people on their lunch breaks or shopping. They were 25 minutes in length, and invitations were distributed. Films were still used on occasions; on 20th April 1979 the Church hosted a screening of an adaptation of *Pilgrim's Progress*. The screening was well attended, and it was felt that the event was a success.

---

[350] Minutes of Deacons Meeting 30th November 1978

Other evangelistic efforts included serving coffee to Christmas shoppers on the Saturdays in December and supplying evangelistic literature for them, and outdoor carol-singing the week-end before Christmas. An innovation that did not catch on was the distribution for Christmas 1979 of a 'flexi-disc' with an evangelistic address called *The Gift* on it.[351] These were made of plastic and, as the name suggests, were flexible. They could be played on record players. The Church obtained fifty to give away free, but does not seem to have repeated the experiment.

The Gift was not the only new audio venture of the Church in that year; Bethel took to the airwaves in 1979. Two programmes for broadcast were recorded in the church, and proved quite successful. There was also a broadcast on Radio Stoke, a special programme recorded at Bethel on 4th March 1987. Religious broadcasting has of course fallen out of favour since then; the suggestion that, in the interests of a spurious 'equality', the BBC's *Thought For the Day* programme, often woolly as it is, should feature atheist and secularist speakers is just a symptom of how much things have changed in the last thirty years.

Summer 1979 saw Mr. Goldstraw approached by the Milton Gospel Hall with a call to become their pastor; clearly the Assembly had departed from strict Brethren practice, as the Brethren are historically noted for not having a paid ministry. Mr. Goldstraw did not feel that he was called to such work, but did bring the matter to the attention of the Deacons' meeting at Bethel, explaining that the Milton Hall's minister was, presumably due to ill-health, only able to minister occasionally, and needed assistance. Though Bethel could not offer them a pastor, there were several men in the Church able to preach, and it was suggested that Bethel would give Milton all the help they could in that way. Help was also given to the small independent chapel at Fole, near Uttoxeter. Another sort of assistance was given to Capel Fron, Penrhyndeudraeth, in North Wales, a small evangelical Church started in 1975, which entered into a twinning relationship with Bethel in 1987.

---

[351] Minutes of Deacons Meeting 1st November 1979

The building was still in some demand by outside groups and Churches wanting to use the baptistery. Such requests were still usually answered in the affirmative, though on a few occasions it had to be refused, most often due to people not giving enough notice. The Church was asked to host the 1980 FIEC Youth Conference on 12th-13th September. Unlike conferences for adults, youth conferences are still fairly informal affairs, and they were even more so in 1980. Today it is almost seen as necessary for there to be beds and separate rooms for delegates; in 1980 they camped out in the building! The Church also provided food for the young people.

The proposed Papal visit in 1982, first announced as a possibility in 1980, of course attracted a great deal of media attention. Pope John Paul II was a popular figure; his opposition to Communism in his home country of Poland was well-known, and this helped to endear him to the British public. The difficulty that he presented to evangelicals was that, however nice he may have been as a human being, he represented a system that is still antithetical to everything that Protestantism stands for. It was once again, as Fairbairn had presented it, Sacerdotalism versus Puritanism. The Pope represented a system of priests who stood between God and the people, Bethel stood for the priesthood of all believers. Though under no delusions as to where the media would be, Paul Brown could not ignore the papal visit with all its pageantry, and proposed a series of meetings to inform people of the teachings of the Roman Catholic Church. It was hoped that these would be held in conjunction with Park Evangelical Church and Talke Parish Church. Given that the Pope's theme in his visit was the Seven Sacraments, it was quite proper to explain the real difference between Rome and Evangelicalism, whether in the Church of England or Nonconformity. The FIEC shared his concern; a meeting was arranged in London to discuss the appropriate response to the Pope's visit. Although an attempt to assassinate the Pope in May 1981 almost led to the visit being called off, in the event it took place, and so did the special meetings. Our disagreement with the Roman Catholic Church, it must be pointed out, is primarily doctrinal, not personal; it is not that the Pope is a bad man, but that what he teaches is in error.

Of course there is such a thing as unreasoning bigotry, but it must be distinguished from a principled stand. Where the vast majority of people hold very few principles themselves, there is always the risk of being misunderstood and principle taken for bigotry, but in a woolly-minded age, Bethel stands for definite truths. In this day and age in which truth and error are so seldom discussed, it is often hard to have to say that a nice man like John Paul II is wrong, but like Martin Luther, we are forced to say, "Here I stand, I cannot do otherwise." We cannot shy away from contending earnestly for the truth, no matter how unpopular it may make us.

There had been discussions about amalgamating the Monday evening Bible study and the Wednesday evening prayer meeting from some time, at least since 1968, when it was felt by some that there were too many meetings to allow for any breathing space, "With Deacons meetings, teenage meetings, missionary prayer meetings and Sunday School preparation, together with these two week night meetings there was no spare time for home life or for necessary work on the Church buildings."[352] At that time it was felt that an amalgamation was not a good idea, but the two meetings were finally amalgamated in 1989, following a general national trend in Evangelical Churches.

Among those sent out from Bethel into the ministry at this time was Barry Moult, who had served as a deacon in the Church. In 1985 he left to train for the ministry at Bible College, and on graduating he went out to Belgium as a minister to the British troops stationed there. On his return he applied to the Grace Baptists seeking a post and eventually went to minister in a Church in Felixstowe. He is now the minister at the Grace Baptist Church in the small Suffolk market town of Sudbury, a very different town from Hanley. That is not to say that Sudbury does not have its problems – in 2003 Pastor Moult had to contact the press when the town council failed to do anything to prevent turning lorries hitting the church building.[353] Another man who went out into the ministry from Bethel is James Hamilton, now pastor at Fole Chapel, who joined the Open Air Mission in 1987.

---

[352] Minutes of Extraordinary Church Meeting October 5th 1968
[353] *http://www.suffolkfreepress.co.uk/news/latest-news/church-in-firing-line-1-561993*

Among those who joined the Church in the 1980s was Mr. Tom Brennan. He was brought up Roman Catholic, but although he believed in God, he was not a devout man. In 1971 he was one of many people who were contacted by the Jehovah's Witnesses in their great outreach drive in anticipation of Armageddon in 1975. Like many others he was impressed by the zeal and apparent knowledge of the Witnesses, and joined them. He threw himself whole-heartedly into the life of the Witnesses, and persuaded his brothers and sisters to join the Society as well. The failure of the 1975 prediction stunned many of the Witnesses, and Tom Brennan was one of the huge numbers of disillusioned people who left the sect. He wrote, "I did not know what to do or where to go, but my faith in God's Word, the Bible, was strong. I realised that Jesus Christ was my Lord and Saviour and that he did have people on this earth who worship him in spirit and in truth and who let God speak through his Word without distortion."[354] Coming to Bethel he found a community quite different from the restrictive, controlling atmosphere among the Witnesses. In 1986 he asked to join the Church; the request was accepted, and Tom and his wife Irene remain with us to this day.

Vandalism has been a recurrent problem; there are just some people who seem to enjoy destroying things. Broken windows and graffiti have usually been the worst of it, but in spring 1987 there was a break-in at the Church. It was presumed that this had happened on Wednesday 1st April, and the motive was robbery. The box used for money from the sale of magazines was forced open. The thieves would not have got away with much, and as a rule valuable items are not left on the premises.

Though Paul Brown's connection with the FIEC had been one of the deciding factors in his being called to Bethel, by the mid-80s the attitude of Church and pastor towards the FIEC had cooled decidedly. In 1986 there was a question raised as to whether or not the Church should continue with the FIEC. Over the years there had been a number of changes in the FIEC, and a broadening of the FIEC on certain issues, most notably the Charismatic movement. The real question, of course, and one that has often been avoided, is the question of what the FIEC is, and what it is for. One proposal that Bethel opposed was that the FIEC

---

[354] 'God Speaks Through His Word' in *Faith For Today,* published by Bethel in 1992, P. 4

have a full-time three-year presidency. This was opposed, "On the grounds that it had episcopal overtones."[355] At a Deacons Meeting on 2nd April 1987 it was agreed that the Church remain in the FIEC, but also seek closer connections with other local Churches, a movement that was one of the things that resulted in the formation in 1990 of the North Staffordshire Fellowship of Evangelical Churches, also known as NoSFEC, with members including Park Evangelical Church, Blurton Free Baptist Church, Emmanuel Evangelical Church, and Milton Baptist Church.

The old *Pathfinder* had ceased publication some years before, and an attempt to revive it in 1970 seems to have been short-lived. It was revived as a *Church Bulletin,* but that too did not survive long.[356] A new series of publication ended in 1984. It seems that the prospect of twinning with Penrhyndeudraeth brought the idea of a monthly magazine back onto the agenda, as such a magazine could be exchanged with them. It was published, and christened *Still Believing*. Issue one appeared in June 1987. It then became bi-monthly, as the effort involved in producing a magazine with seven printed pages and cover every month became apparent, though issue 2 was slightly longer, at 11 pages plus cover.

The Pastor's letter on the first page of issue 1 began with an apology, "Unfortunately, this new magazine has not got off to a good start. It ought to have come out at the beginning of the month, and it hasn't. For that I take the main responsibility. In addition, it has come out in an experimental form. That is to say, it is not certain that it is going to remain at this size, and with this cover, or with this title." The title, Pastor Brown went on to explain, referred to the fact that the Church was "still believing" in "an age of doubt". "We are not afraid to tell it out, we are STILL BELIEVING." It contained both congregational notes and articles of a more general nature. By issue 2 the title remained the same, but the cover, initially just a picture of the front of the Church, had gained people going in to the open front doors. The increased number of pages allowed for more content, including a book review of the Puritan volume, *All Things for Good* by Thomas Watson.

---

[355] Minutes of Deacons' Meeting 25th March 1991
[356] The Church archives contain one copy of this, from October/November 1976

As well as the pastor's letter and book review, the second issue of *Still Believing* contained a report of the Church holiday at Kinmel Hall, the first held in over 16 years; it seems to have gone very well, balancing the holiday aspect with the spiritual. There is a large section on missionary news, marking among other things the twenty-fifth anniversary of David Mead's work in Europe. The 'Sermon Notes' are remarkably contemporary, dealing as they do with the question of marriage and the Biblical teaching regarding it, though the issue that is being dealt with is very much of the time; the question of *in vitro* fertilisation. It ends with a plea for all Christian debate to be carried out in a loving and gracious manner. This is followed by a report from Jim Hamilton on open-air preaching at Ascot races, the International Eisteddfod at Llangollen, and in Market Drayton, among other places. Finally there are notes on the Friday Club, a passage on revival from Jonathan Edwards, a letter about the Sisterhood and a piece on 'The Value of the Soul'. The magazine retained this format for some time, and continued in publication for some years, changing presentation to reflect the changing times. Paul Brown's own 'sequel' to *Pilgrim's Progress*, 'Little Pilgrim's Progress' was published in instalments in *Still Believing*.[357]

The question of Church government was raised once again; the proposal for elders in 1965 had been abandoned with Pastor Evans' departure, but by the 1980s the question of eldership and Biblical Church government was being raised more widely in Evangelical circles. Although the matter was discussed from 1991 onwards, no actual changes were made in the running of the Church until after the turn of the century.

A request in 1992 for the use of the baptistery from Life Changing Ministries Church, who were meeting in the Scout Hall at the time, led to the Church reconsidering its policy on the use of the building by other groups. In the case of Life Changing Ministries, the request was made too close to the proposed date on which they wanted to use the building, but the fact that Bethel knew nothing about the group led to a discussion that resulted in the production of a set of guidelines about

---

[357] The typescript of this book is in the Church library.

who should use the building.[358] There was already a Church policy on marriages limiting the use of the building for weddings to those from the Church family. The policy as agreed in April 1993 made it clear that no charge would be made on using the building, but that no activity could go on in the church building that the Church would not approve on in their own meetings.[359]

Paul Brown seemed to be practically a fixture by the early 1990s, and there was considerable surprise when he announced in May 1994 that he had received a call to the pastorate of Dunstable Baptist Church, Bedfordshire. By July he had come to the conclusion that he should accept the call, and would leave Bethel in October of that year. Appointed in 1966, he was the longest serving minister in the history of the Church, and in just a few years would have reached the thirty-year mark. But Pastor Brown knew that he would have to think about retirement soon, and a change of pace at Dunstable for the last eight years of his pastoral ministry was attractive.[360] He also felt that the Church might be better able to move forward if he made the move. There were ongoing discussions about the elder question, and pressure from some quarters to make major alterations in the Sunday services, "Beyond the bounds of what I would be able to take part in with a spirit of freedom, and perhaps an easy conscience."[361] It was still quite a wrench, but after prayer and consideration, Pastor Brown felt it was the right thing to do. The Church were sad to see Paul and Mary Brown leave, but it was agreed that this was the will of God.

Paul Brown spent the last eight years of his pastoral ministry before his retirement at Dunstable; he had in total served 42 years in the ministry. He now lives near Lancaster with his wife Mary. He is still a fixture at the annual Banner of Truth Ministers' Conference, and the author of a number of books including a popular commentary on Deuteronomy in the 'Exploring the Bible' series from Day One Publications; he has edited a volume on Homosexuality for the same publisher. His most recent book, a biography of Ernest Kevan, was published this year by the Banner of Truth Trust.

---

[358] Minutes of Deacons Meeting 30th November 1992
[359] Appendix to Minutes of Deacons Meeting 22nd April 1993
[360] Minutes of Church Meeting 27th July 1994
[361] Letter from Paul Brown dated 25th July 1994

Chapter 20: The Sunday School

There has been a Sunday school at the Hope Street Church since the early days, probably since the church began, and at least since the 1820s. Sunday schools have changed considerably during that time; as originally established they were schools which met on a Sunday because that was the only day off workers had. Although they were Christian in ethos, and taught Christianity, their main emphasis was basic literacy and numeracy. Most of the scholars were children who worked full time in factories in the week and who would otherwise have been without any formal education at all. As public education increased during the 19th century, and child labour became more strictly controlled, Sunday schools came to be more explicitly religious institutions where children were primarily taught the Bible.

The first record we have of a Sunday school at Hope is in 1824, when the *Evangelical Magazine* recorded that the boys of the school gave 7 shillings towards the work of the London Missionary Society. This school would have been a relatively small affair conducted in the body of the chapel on Sunday afternoon between services. In 1834, during the pastorate of John Edmonds, a dedicated Sunday school building was constructed. This was a substantial brick structure that stood to the rear of the chapel on what is now the overflow car-park. It had accommodation for some 300 students, who were divided into classes. An old map from 1879 indicates that the school at Hope was also used as a day-school, part of a patchwork of educational provision in Hanley at the time. The day school closed following the opening of the board school in Sampson Street nearby.

Many Churches built dedicated facilities for Sunday schools in the 1830s as the schools expanded. As the 19th century went on these buildings became increasingly elaborate, in some cases they were larger than the chapel itself. Compared to the buildings erected at George S. Barrett's Princes' Street chapel in Norwich, the Hope Street buildings were decidedly modest.

The Victorian era was the golden age of Sunday schools. In 1899, the first time that the Congregational Yearbook was able to get statistics for Church and Sunday school membership, the Hope School had 230 scholars taught by 25 teachers.[362] The numbers fluctuated year by year, with the highest recorded number of scholars being 392 in 1913, which must have been quite uncomfortable for some of the children if they were all being taught in the building at the same time. Of course, in fact not all would be coming every week. Numbers remained high even when the Church was experiencing falling membership in the 1920s. This was not an isolated phenomenon, but part of a national trend; parents who did not go to Church themselves still liked the idea of their children getting moral instruction – not to mention the idea of getting their children out of the house on Sundays!

By the latter part of the 19th century the Sunday school was where the majority of members of the church would come from; it was the single largest activity of the Church, and the core of its outreach. Children would have been taught the Bible and some basic Church history, and rewarded for their learning with prizes. Sunday school prizes provided a major part of the market for books in the era, and practically every publisher had an eye to them. There were inter-denominational organisations such as the Religious Tract Society and the Sunday School Union, as well as denominational publishing houses and private publishers producing thousands of attractively-bound books with colourful pictorial covers and perhaps even illustrations inside. The actual prizes were usually chosen by the staff of the Sunday School, and varied enormously. First of all there were popular religious biographies telling the stories of noted missionaries and evangelists. Then there were religious novels by such Victorian religious stalwarts as the Hocking brothers, Silas and Joseph, their sister Salome, and various lesser novelists, including Mark Bairstow and his *The Village Blacksmith and the Squire's Daughter*. Some would be not even religiously themed; in 1905 the Sunday School at Zion Methodist New Connexion Chapel, Longton, gave Nellie Booth a copy of Alexander Dumas' *Twenty Years After*, the sequel to *The Three Musketeers*.

---

[362] CYB 1899

Since the majority of people in Victorian Hanley had very little disposable income, Sunday School prizes were a major source of reading material, and books that were given were likely to be treasured possessions, even if they were not read by the children who received them. Those books that were more decidedly Christian in content also qualified as Sunday afternoon reading.

A lot depended on those choosing the prize books; if a lot of thought was put into it, then the children would go home with books that they would treasure and read. There were adventure books for boys, such as R.M. Ballantyne's *The Coral Island,* or the more excitingly-titled, *The Gorilla Hunters*, and for girls there were schoolgirl stories and uplifting stories of everyday life such as Silas Hocking's *Her Benny,* the first British million-selling novel. If very little effort was put in it was not unknown for little boys to be given such books as *Little Women* as prizes. In such cases the book would be likely to remain unread, at least by the child to whom it had been given. Sometimes a lack of care in selecting prizes could result in books being given that, had their contents been known, one could hardly imagine would have been even allowed in the Church. Among the more wildly inappropriate Sunday School prizes known to have been given is Mrs. Wood's novel *East Lynne*, which features a plot revolving around marital infidelity; this was given as a prize at the Hanley Baptist Sunday School in 1928. The Primitive Methodist Sunday school in Victoria Road, Fenton, gave one scholar a copy of George Eliot's *Romola* in 1908; given that Eliot was a decided Humanist in her religious views, it is also somewhat inappropriate. His daughter, Mrs. Mary Saltwell, is probably quite right to reflect that the recipient of the prize is unlikely to have been overly thrilled by it. Regrettably a search of local bookshops has failed to produce any books given as prizes in the Hope Sunday school.

The Bethel Movement had its own youth branches, and the old Hope Sunday school was fitted into these. The younger children were 'Sunbeams', and the older 'Bethel Crusaders'. The martial imagery is of course of the Christian soldier whose fight is not against flesh and blood, and the organisation of the Bethel Crusaders was based loosely on the inter-denominational uniformed Boys Brigade movement, though the Crusaders were made up of boys and girls together. The Crusaders worse a simple uniform consisting of a sash and a cap, and each wore a colourful enamel badge in the form of a sunburst with the name 'Bethel Crusaders' in gold on red, and the motto 'Shining for Jesus always everywhere' in gold on a blue background. While the Boys' Brigade emphasised physical training, and the Girls' Life Brigade, another uniformed organisation, taught basic medical techniques, the Bethel Crusaders were all about evangelism, teaching boys and girls to share their faith. They organised rallies and engaged in open air preaching. In 1935 Pastor Anderson Brown, then in Bootle, led a Bethel Crusader 'invasion' of Hanley with 700 Bootle Bethel Crusaders. This was a mass rally that emphasised singing the Gospel. A younger branch of the Crusaders was called the Sunbeams.

The winding-up of the Bethel Society meant an end to the Bethel Crusaders. The dark shadows of World War I affected the Church in every department, including the Sunday school; by Pastor Vernon's death in 1953 the work was apparently defunct. Pastor Mead worked to bring the Sunday school back, though the sale of the hall in 1949 imposed various restrictions on what could be done. In the minutes of the trustees' meeting on 27th April 1957, "a little thought was given to the possibility of a Sunday School in the distant future." By 1961 a new Sunday School had been started, returning by necessity to the situation that had prevailed before 1834, when teaching had to be done in the chapel itself between services. The Sunday School was at first held at 2:45, between the morning and evening services, but this was later changed to 12 noon. Mr. E. Bannister was the Superintendent of the school until 1964, when Andre Clowes took over the role.

By March 1962 the Sunday school was thriving once again, so much so that the class-rooms at the back of the chapel were insufficient. It was agreed to turn the corners of the church by the pulpit into classrooms by hanging up curtains on runners so they could be closed off.[363] The work was done by Church members to save expense. It was apparently done very well, as we find a minute in the next month saying it was "an excellent job." Then as now, the children could be boisterous, and there were some complaints about them playing in and around the pews in the chapel.

---

[363] Minutes of Deacons Meeting 31st March 1961

A Sunday School Carol Service has long been a part of the annual programme of the Church. This has been combined with a public prize-giving, and is an opportunity for the parents of children who attend the School to attend a service at the chapel, and for children to take a full part in the worship of the Church.

In 1965 The Sunday school was one of many things that was re-organised by Pastor Evans; the cover of the *Pathfinder* announced that, "Our new Sunday School is graded on day school lines and is modern in both method and materials." Its rationale was explained, "Christian teaching is the right of every British child and is more necessary in today's unstable, insecure world than ever before. A substantial amount of time and money have been invested in this fresh approach to Sunday School." Although pastor Evans wanted to change the time of meeting to 1 PM, this does not seem to have been done, and the time remained at noon. The school was regarded as a means of outreach, and many of the children who attended came from non-Christian homes.

By this time, owing in part to the depopulation of the central area of Hanley connected with urban regeneration, some children were travelling a distance to the Sunday School, leading to some concern among the membership about safety. At the AGM on October 30th 1965 it was suggested that the Church should either hire or buy a minibus to transport these children. An examination of the issues involved led to the conclusion that the hiring of a minibus was indeed the best way to deal with the transport issue. Over the years there have been various arrangements adopted for the transport of children both to the Sunday School and to week-night meetings. In 1985 the Church purchased its own coach, which was used for some years for a variety of Church activities. Eventually, however, the costs of running and maintaining it proved to be uneconomical, and the Church coach was sold in 1991 and replaced with a Minibus. This too was later sold, and the Church reverted to relying on hired transport.

In the Secretary's Report for the year 1969-70, it is recorded that, "The Sunday School has had much blessing although some children have been discouraged by the unreliability of the coach. Membership has risen to an average of 50 children a week – catered for in 10 classes. The Summer Mission during August proved a great success with about 70 children each day."[364] This Summer Mission was an annual event for many years. It took place over three days and centred on a Biblical theme, for example the life of the Apostle Paul. The sessions were on three consecutive afternoons, and were structured around a 25-minute illustrated talk with activities including modelling things connected with the theme; in the case of the Paul mission these included a first-century Synagogue, a Roman house and a Roman soldier.[365]

Andre Clowes remained superintendent until his move to Leicester in 1972, when Clive Shenton, son-in-law to Pastor Mead, was appointed in his place. Ill health forced Mr. Shenton to give up most of his commitments only a few months later, when David Saltwell took over the work temporarily. Though initially appointed only as a temporary measure due to Clive Shenton's illness, David Saltwell remained superintendent of the Sunday School and young people's work for many years. David and Mary Saltwell are from a Methodist background, and came to Bethel in the early 1970s with years of experience teaching Sunday school in a number of Churches in the Potteries. Like many, they left Methodism because of increasing liberalism in the denomination and found a home in Evangelicalism. Methodism's loss has definitely been our gain in this case; they were certainly a godsend when Mr. Shenton was forced to give up his work with the Sunday School.

By February 1975 the Sunday School had an average attendance of 55 children a week, divided into various age groups. The numbers were a little higher than the teachers at the time could cope with, since two of the teachers had recently retired. Mr. Saltwell asked for volunteers to help.[366]

The events surrounding the closure and eventual demolition of the old building initially affected the Sunday School. The uncertainty surrounding the first few months after the forced closure led to a drop in

---
[364] Report in Church archives
[365] Outline in Church archives
[366] Minutes of Quarterly Church Meeting 1st February 1975

251

numbers and the school, like the rest of the church's activities, had to be carried on in exile, meeting in the temporary building on the site. The August Mission was however a source of encouragement, described by some of the teachers as the "best yet."[367] Despite this, there were concerns that the level of attendance at these summer events did not translate into an increase in numbers at the weekly Sunday School.

The greater flexibility of the new building, constructed with the Sunday School partly in mind, gave even greater opportunities for the work. At the first Annual General Meeting of the Church after its opening it was reported, "That the number of children had increased since the new church had been opened and there was now a need to reconsider the arrangement of classes and also the recruitment of more teachers." This would be due partly to the better facilities, and partly to the publicity that had been given to the opening of the new building, which would have made more people aware that the church existed. Its being featured positively in the *Sentinel* would also have helped to allay fears about what might be taught there.

In addition to the annual Bible Mission, there were occasional 'Saturday Specials'; these were in effect Bible Missions in miniature. They were intended to increase the profile of the School, and provide occasional Saturday activities for children. Like the Bible Missions, these were a combination of teaching and activities. Some were quite successful, attracting over 100 children, and leading to youngsters asking questions about the things they had heard. In 1981 a Scripture Examination was introduced to the Sunday School.

By their very nature, children's activities tend to generate a certain amount of noise and disorder. Children will be children; even at their best-behaved they can be a handful at times. The fact that there have been so few complaints about the state in which rooms have been left following children's activities in the past is a testament to how efficiently leaders have cleaned up after the children. Twice, once in the 1980s and once more recently, lights at the back of the sanctuary have been knocked down by foam balls, which has led to a recent reluctance to use such things in the children's Thursday Club for fear of a repetition.

---

[367] Secretary's Report 1974-5 in Church archives.

The first issue of *Still Believing* recorded concern over falling numbers at Sunday School in 1987. The fluctuation of numbers has often been a cause for concern. In 1990 the opening of a new church led to children from the area where it was locating going to the nearer church rather than Bethel, where they had been attending before.

The passing of the Sunday Trading Act in 1994 meant a considerable relaxation of the restrictions of the Shops Act 1950. Now it was not just a few Jewish people who opened their store on a Sunday; the new Act allowed stores to open for a maximum of six hours between 10AM and 6PM. This meant that the lunchtime period, when the Sunday School operated, was now at the same time as the opening hours of many shops that chose to take advantage of the change in the law. "Since Sunday trading has started numbers have been erratic" reads the Sunday School report from the AGM in 1995.

Although the work is now quite small, there is still a Sunday school at Bethel; it meets during the morning service. We are indebted to the dedicated teachers who prepare their lessons for the children and who continue this long tradition of teaching the Gospel to the young.

For many years now the Church has used the 'Go Teach' and 'Come Learn' materials, produced by a joint board from the FIEC, the Evangelical Movement of Wales and the Grace Baptist Churches. Pastor Mead's daughter, Valerie Shenton, was involved with these until quite recently.

In addition to the Sunday School, there have been a number of other activities for children and young people over the years, including week-night meetings on Thursdays and Fridays. These meetings have always been a mix of teaching and games, but always with the greater emphasis on teaching the children the Bible.

Chapter 21: Public Worship

As has been mentioned, when the chapel first opened in 1812 the worship would have been very simple; singing would have been unaccompanied and led by a Precentor with a tuning-fork to set the opening note. The hymn book used would have been *Hymns and Psalms* by Isaac Watts, perhaps with another supplemental book. The minister would have prayed extemporaneously, and the central part of the service was the sermon, often an hour long or more, from a Biblical text. The administration of Communion would have been about once a month, and infants would have been baptised by sprinkling with water, either from a silver or ceramic bowl, or later, probably a ceramic fontlet made by one of the local factories and placed on the communion table for the occasion.

Both the first and second pastors of Hope had major Methodist influences in their lives and ministries; John Greeves had been converted in Methodism and later returned to it, while William Farmer had also been converted through Methodism and had been a minister with the Methodist New Connexion for a few years. Methodist worship emphasised evangelical preaching and joyful congregational singing; Methodists learned their theology at least as much from John Wesley's hymn-book as they did from his sermons. The famous preface to the 1933 *Methodist Hymn Book* proclaims, "Methodism was born in song. Charles Wesley wrote the first hymns of the Evangelical Revival during the great Whitsuntide of 1738 when his brother and he were 'filled with the Spirit,' and from that time onwards the Methodists have never ceased to sing."[368] In his "Directions for Congregational Singing", John Wesley urged Methodists to, "Sing *lustily*, and with a good courage. Beware of singing as if you were half dead, or half asleep; but lift up your voice with strength. Be no more afraid of your voice now, nor ashamed of it being heard, than when you sung the songs of Satan."[369]

---

[368] *The Methodist Hymn-Book* (London, 1933), P. v.
[369] John Wesley, 'Directions For Congregational Singing', *The Works of John Wesley* (London, 1872), Vol. 14, P. 346

Until 1836 hymnals, usually as supplements to Watts, were local and the work of individual compilers. The one exception was Philip Doddridge's book, *Hymns Founded on Various Texts in the Holy Scriptures;* this was, like Watts, one man's hymns. Supplements were quite diverse, each bearing the stamp of the man who prepared it. Some included hymns of their own, others did not. Among the many supplements to Watts was one by George Burder, published in 1787 during his ministry in Coventry and entitled *A Collection of Hymns from Various Authors, Intended as a Supplement to Dr. Watts*. It remained in print until the middle of the 19th century. John Greeves would have been familiar with Thomas Wilson's 1804 *Hymns for Hoxton Academy Chapel* during his student days. John Reynolds of Chester's *Supplement* of 1814 may well have been known in Staffordshire. Perhaps William Farmer used Edward Parsons' Leeds *Selection* of 1822. These are only a few of the extraordinary variety of hymnals in use in Congregational Churches in the first decades of the 19th century.[370]

In 1836 the Congregational Union issued a *Congregational Hymn Book*. Containing 620 hymns and edited by Josiah Conder, author of many hymns including "Tis Not That I Did Choose Thee' and 'Bread of Heaven, On Thee We Feed'; it was not intended to replace Watts, but to be a supplement to his book and replace the various supplements in use among the Congregational Churches. A completely new book, *The New Congregational Hymn Book,* was published in 1859 to replace the sometimes awkward combination of Watts and a variety of supplements, and a supplement containing additional hymns added to it in 1874. During this period many new hymns were being written by such writers as Horatius Bonar and Frances Ridley Havergal, and as these were being used in Churches it was felt necessary that they should be available in an authorised supplement. A replacement book, *The Congregational Church Hymnal*, edited by Lansdell's mentor George Slayter Barrett, was issued in 1887, and reflects the changes in the Churches since 1859. In addition to many new hymns, this book also contained litanies and chants and anthems for the choir, an indication that the services of Congregational Churches were becoming more elaborate. Barrett himself

---

[370] This list is taken from A.J. Grieve, 'Congregational Praise, Some Back-Numbers' in K.L. Parry and Erik Routley, *Companion to Congregational Praise* (London, 1953), Pp. xxxi-xxxiii

favoured a discretionary liturgy with responses from the congregation for worship. In leading worship, organs were fast replacing the old precentors. Almost certainly Hope would have first acquired a harmonium, probably during Smith's pastorate, and the 1891 alterations to the chapel included the placing of a pipe organ in the rear gallery, along with choir seating.

G.S. Barrett's *Congregational Church Hymnal* was warmly spoken of. Bernard L. Manning, whose father George Manning was pastor of Copeland Street Congregational Church in Stoke from 1916 until 1919, wrote of it, "Dr. Barrett's book is eminent as an exposition of what is best in Congregationalism. It reflects purely and clearly that mind which we should like to think is the Congregational mind: in taste, catholic; in feeling, evangelical; in expression, scholarly; in doctrine, orthodox... Dr. Barrett achieved this result because he allowed no variety of religious experience known in 1887 to escape his notice. He laid under contribution every age, every nation, every communion."[371] Though he certainly drew from a wide variety of authors, it must be said that Barrett drew most heavily on the hymns of the Evangelical Revival. Wesley, Newton, Cowper and James Montgomery figure largely in his pages. The older Congregational writers Watts and Doddridge also contributed many valuable hymns. Though he perhaps included too many mediocre hymns be his contemporaries, the book was as a whole excellent, and Barrett's *Hymnal* formed the congregational worship of a generation. The writers who figure most prominently in his book are those who still figure prominently in modern evangelical hymnals.

Though a new *Congregational Hymnary* was published in 1916, it is probable that Hope, in serious financial trouble at the time, retained the old *Congregational Church Hymnal* in its worship. The expense of replacing the older book would not have been the only reason why Hope is likely to have been less than enthusiastic about the *Hymnary*. The committee appointed to prepare the new book was decidedly varied, including both liberals evangelicals, and this was reflected in the volume that they produced. Although the *Hymnary* was similar to the *Hymnal*, yet it was different in its tone; It contained fewer hymns by Isaac Watts, a mere 24 as compared to 62 in the *Hymnal*, and was markedly less

---

[371] *The Hymns of Wesley and Watts* (London, 1942) P. 110

evangelical. John W. Grant writes, "There is considerable heresy in the book. More prominent, however, is the desire not to commit the Union too far in any direction, orthodox or heterodox."[372]

Victorian Evangelicalism as represented by men such as Mark Bairstow is best known for its rousing hymns, often sung to music-hall type tunes, with refrains, such as *Blessed assurance, Jesus is Mine* and *Count Your Blessings*. These were regarded by the more cultured as rather vulgar, and did not feature in books such as Barrett's, but were found in such books as *Sacred Songs and Solos*, edited by Ira D. Sankey, who had been the song-leader for D.L. Moody's missions in the United Kingdom. If the upper middle classes regarded them as vulgar, those less concerned about such things loved them. The Congregationalist Sir John D. McClure pilloried the sort of tunes that Sankey made popular from the Chair of the Union in 1920, and attacked Victorian music that was "content to achieve the merely pretty, or even the merely tawdry."[373] Evangelical congregations did not care.

Locally, the Potteries already had a tradition of loud and lively songs, thanks to the Primitive Methodists. C.H. Spurgeon notes that it was reported the Primitive Methodists, "sang so loudly that they made people's heads ache."[374] The Salvation Army, led into Hanley by Gipsy Smith in 1881, fitted into the same mould as the early 'Prims'. Primitive Methodist hymns were robust, fitting the manual labourers who sang them. They were full of the imagery of battle, and shouts of 'Glory!'[375] Their most characteristic hymn, 'Hark the Gospel News is Sounding' was a marching-song that would be sung as the people marched through the streets. Ian Sellers characterises the strength of Primitive Methodist hymnody as the fact that, "It proclaims the authentic Gospel with passion and sincerity."[376] Begun in the early hymn books of the denomination, this emphasis continued in the 1853 book edited by John Flesher, with such rousing verses as:

---
[372] John W. Grant, *Free Churchmanship in England, 1870-1940* (London, no date) P. 259. The *Hymnary* was replaced in 1951 by *Congregational Praise*, which contained 48 hymns by Watts and was considerably more evangelical.
[373] Quoted in Tudur Jones P. 370
[374] C.H. Spurgeon: *C.H. Spurgeon's Autobiography* (London, 1899) Vol. 1, P. 105
[375] See Ian Sellers, *The Hymnody of Primitive Methodism* (Englsea Brook, 1993)
[376] Sellers, P. 6

Arise, ye men of God
Go boldly to the field
Fight the good fight through Jesus' blood
Till your opponents yield.[377]

    Pastor Edward Jeffreys was a Welshman from the Valleys, and he had begun working as a soloist for his father. A great singer himself, he often sang at his own meetings as well as preaching, and recognised the importance of the 'service of song'. The Churches he founded were marked by their excellence in singing, and had singing groups even if they could not muster a choir, and there would often be solos sung in services, especially evangelistic meetings. Special services such as Harvest Festivals and Christmas Carol services gave further occasions for singing, and sometimes there were even special festivals of song. Young and old formed choirs and smaller groups, brotherhoods and sisterhoods, Crusaders and Sunbeams had their choirs and their opportunities to show their choral abilities. When the Bootle Crusaders 'invaded' Hanley in 1935, there was a great deal of singing; congregational, choir, duet and soloists. At the end of the meeting, "The Bootle Crusaders were heartily thanked for their ministry of song, which has never been equalled in Hanley."[378]

    Things declined during world War II and after, as the Church numbers fell off. With the arrival of Pastor Mead in 1953 the singing picked up again. Pastor Mead, having spent some years among the Brethren, had come to value the weekly communion or 'Breaking of Bread' service, and it seems that he is responsible for our current weekly communion. A document describing the worship in the 1970s states, "The Lord's Supper is celebrated every Sunday (or Lord's Day) as appears to have been the case in the early Church."[379] This is why the Brethren have a weekly Communion, and why we do.

    Pastor Mead introduced *The Believers Hymn Book,* a Brethren hymnal, into the worship of the Church. Its contents are probably close to what was being sung already, though we know there were three books

---

[377] By Edward Foizey, in John Flesher (ed.) *The Primitive Methodist Hymn Book* (London, 1876) No. 414
[378] *Bethel Messenger 1935* P. 207
[379] *Typed* document in Church archives

used at the Church at the time, this was the most popular. As numbers recovered in the 1950s, a new choir was formed, as was the quartette that caused some trouble. Hymn-singing before the evening service became common. The choir from Bethel sang at Pastor Mead's induction at Feltham.

Like Edward Jeffreys, Pastor Evans had a Welshman's love of song, and he was the leader of a choir at the Bethel in Leicester. He introduced the *Redemption Hymnal* to the worship of the Church. Other changes were cut short by his departure. Produced by the Elim Publishing House, *Redemption Hymnal* reflects a Pentecostal style of worship, with many hymns having refrains and an emphasis on the joyful and rousing. The preface to *Redemption Hymnal* reflects the Pentecostal theology of the compilers, and as Bethel is not Pentecostal, in 1972 one of the members, "Asked if the preface in the hymn books could be detached as the sentiments therein do not agree with our doctrinal basis."[380] It was decided not to do this, in part no doubt because the contents page of the book is on the other side of the leaf containing the preface. The book was quite popular among some members of the Church, and even after it was superseded by *Christian Hymns* there were requests for it to be used occasionally.

In 1970 it was agreed to introduce a children's talk into the morning service. Ernest Kevan, the man who had been Paul Brown's mentor in many ways, was known for his children's talks, and this probably played a part in getting the item introduced. The suggestion is first mentioned in the minutes in October 1970, and it has no doubt led to some of the more unusual, if not bizarre, occurrences in morning worship, such as the occasion when a member of the Church (not the pastor) addressed the children while wearing the upper portion of a Superman costume, and the various occasions when the speaker has produced a sword of some kind from behind the pulpit to illustrate Paul's description of the Bible as "The Sword of the Spirit, which is the Word of God." Such object lessons have been very popular, though coming up with them can tax the ingenuity of the speaker at times.

---

[380] Minutes of Deacons Meeting 9th November 1972

The choice of hymns by a minister can be a source of disagreement, as people often have very decided preferences in terms of the type of hymns they think suitable for worship. This happened at least once during Paul Brown's ministry. At the time the church was still using *Redemption Hymnal*, and Paul Brown was of the opinion that some of these were "inappropriate either in words or tone."[381] Pastor Brown therefore tended to choose certain types of hymns, and Mr. Frost expressed concern that "he thought the hymns were not bright enough", while Mr. Thorley "Thought there was a danger of losing the 'joy' of the Christian life if a service was too stereotyped." In reply, "The Pastor said that every meeting should not necessarily leave everyone rejoicing in the Lord." There is a place for the contemplative and the penitential in the Christian life as well, but variety is important. Perhaps the balance achieved by G.S. Barrett in his *Congregational Church Hymnal* is a lesson we all need to learn.

Fig. 25: The interior of the church today

---

[381] Minute-book 27th August 1970

When the new building was under construction, there were discussions about updating the book from which the praises of the Church were sung. While *Christian Hymns* was under consideration from the first, *Hymns of Faith* and *Grace Hymns* were also considered, but the vote of the Church was for *Christian Hymns,* and so the now-familiar books were purchased. Published by the Evangelical Movement of Wales, this was a conservative book of very high quality, a product of the Reformed resurgence led by Dr. Martyn Lloyd-Jones. Among the committee that edited it were Rev. Graham Harrison of Newport and Rev. Paul E.G. Cook, both very close to Dr. Lloyd-Jones. The book drew heavily from the hymns of the 18th century revival, and introduced into English for the first time a number of well-loved Welsh hymns, some translated for the first time into English. Copies of *Christian Hymns* were ordered for the opening of the new building, but had not yet arrived – indeed the first report that they had arrived is in the minutes for the Deacons' meeting on 15th December 1977!

Because of increasing need, the smaller book *Hymns of Faith,* published by Scripture Union in 1964 in collaboration with the CSSM was adopted as the Sunday school hymnal in 1981. It was later supplemented with *Jesus Loves Me*, edited by David Saltwell and Lynn Webber, both members of the Church.

While *Hymns of Faith* reflects a broad British Evangelicalism, *Christian Hymns* reflects a certain constituency, mostly Welsh, and mostly the circle of Dr. Martyn Lloyd-Jones, known for his love of the 18th century. This means that it is biased towards hymns of the more serious and sober type, with fewer of the chorus-type songs found in *Sacred Songs and Solos*. The membership of the Church includes those from the more Moody and Sankey, Keswick and Methodist traditions where such songs were popular. This led in 1992 to the consideration of a supplement to the book containing those older hymns which were not in *Christian Hymns* and newer hymns that might also be used.[382] to the production of a supplement, *Bethel Hymns,* which was published in 1994. It includes a number of hymns by David Saltwell.

---

[382] Minutes of Members Meeting 29th April 1992

Recently the Church was offered a number of copies of the 2005 revision of *Christian Hymns*, which is now used in the morning service and the Wednesday evening prayer meeting. The old book continues to be used on Sunday evenings. Though the new book contains a number of good hymns that were not included in the original, it also omits several that were, often in favour of modern compositions that are rather inferior.

The building is intended to reflect the Church's worship. A document introducing the Church from the 1970s explains, "It will be seen that there is an absence of excessive decoration or symbols such as crosses.[383] There is a simplicity about worship in the New Testament, which is to be in spirit and in truth and not in terms of ceremonial and ritual. The buildings is designed to be a place where the family of God meet together for praise, prayer and the reverent hearing of God's Word. The central pulpit shows the importance of the Word of God and preaching, while the fact that the baptistery and communion table are both just in front of the pulpit show that they belong together with the preaching of the Word."[384]

The period following the construction of the new building saw major changes in British Evangelicalism which were the continuation of existing trends. While the original Pentecostals had not been welcome in the historic denominations, later developments brought Pentecostal beliefs into the historic Churches. The Charismatic Movement in the UK was initially centred around the Fountain Trust, established by Michael Harper in 1964. Harper had been a curate under John Stott at All Souls' Langham Place when he had embraced Charismaticism. This led to conflict between him and Stott, and he resigned from Langham Place in June 1964, establishing the Fountain Trust some four months later. The Fountain Trust dissolved in 1978, but that was more because the Charismatic movement had spread so widely than because it was declining. Charismatic emphasis on glossolalia (mistakenly identified with the Biblical gift of tongues) and freedom in worship led to a distinctive style in which there were long periods of singing, simple chorus-type songs lacking anything in the way of substantive theology

---

[383] To a certain extent the lack of excessive decoration is simply a function of Modernist architecture, which eschews decoration.
[384] *Bethel Evangelical Free Church*, typed sheet in Church archives.

and physical expressions of emotion were encouraged. The physical and emotional effect of this prolonged singing and repetitive choruses is often mistaken for the work of the Holy Spirit, and the whole must be characterised as mystical. Rather than letting "The Word of Christ dwell in you richly, in all wisdom, teaching and admonishing one another in psalms and hymns and spiritual songs,"[385] the Charismatic movement seeks a direct and non-intellectual encounter with God through music, and commonly mistakes mere excitement for this. Bethel did not follow this direction and remained in the older traditions of evangelical Nonconformity, where emotion is shown most often in heart-felt singing of richly theological hymns.

In our Free Church tradition, the Bible is central. This means that it is important for the Church to have a policy on which version is used from the pulpit, since most of the congregation do not know the languages in which the Bible was originally written. In 1812 there was, for all practical purposes, only one English Bible; the King James or Authorised Version of 1611 (in the 1769 Cambridge revision, which was chiefly concerned with how words were spelled). This did not change until 1881, when the Revised Version of the New Testament was published. It was a discussion of this which kept Rev. Thomas Cocker and Rev. David Horne so late on the night of the 'Hanley Tragedy' of 1881. The RV, while technically very accomplished, never caught on for a variety of reasons, including its attempt to sound like the King James, and it was not until the publication of the *New International Version* in 1973 that the primacy of the King James Version among Evangelicals was seriously challenged. Since that date there has been a positive flood of new English translations of the Bible, some worthwhile, many not. Much of it has been driven by the desire among American Christian publishing companies to have their own 'in-house' translation. For the lucrative study Bible market.

Despite criticism of its 'dynamic equivalence' philosophy of translation in some quarters,[386] the NIV proved extremely popular among Evangelicals, to the extent that it almost became the *de facto* 'authorised

---

[385] Colossians 3:16

[386] e.g. Robert Martin, *Accuracy of Translation and the New International Version* (Edinburgh, 1989)

version' of Evangelicalism; Bethel adopted the NIV in the 1980s. In 1988 20 new NIVs were purchased for use in the Church to replace existing copies that were almost worn out.[387] By 1990, however, Paul Brown seems to have been feeling the limitations of the NIV, and was considering adopting the Revised Authorised Version, title under which the New King James Bible was published in Britain for a time.[388] Commissioned in 1975, the NKJV is translated from the same Hebrew and Greek texts as the 1611 King James, but is in modern English. The New Testament was published in 1979, and the whole Bible in 1982.

The change to the New King James Version was discussed for some years, and in 1993 the NKJV was adopted as the 'official' version that was read from the pulpit in worship. A straw poll taken at the members meeting on 3rd March 1993 found thirteen members in favour of returning to the old King James Version, twelve in favour of the NIV, and fourteen in favour of the New King James. It has proved a good standard translation, being decidedly conservative in its philosophy. Unlike the NIV, the NKJV translators have generally refrained from putting too much of themselves into the text; where the original is ambiguous, they have left the ambiguity.

Despite concerns that Paul Brown had at the time he left, Bethel has retained its conservative, traditional Nonconformist worship. Worship is still led by an organist, the structure of the service is still as it has been for decades, with free prayer and a simple liturgy leading up to a sermon of between 30 and 40 minutes. The pinnacle of the service is the Communion, which is simple and reverent, observed weekly, alternating between morning and evening. It is not, as some might think, an extra tacked on to the service, but the legitimate climax of the service, to which the sermon naturally leads.

---

[387] Minutes of Deacons Meeting 21st January 1988
[388] Minutes of Deacons Meeting 29th March 1990

Chapter 22: The Church Since 1994

The period since 1994 is too recent to be able to provide an objective and balanced history at the present time; the materials for it, including minute books and correspondence, exist in the Church archives. All that can be done now is to provide a brief sketch of events since Paul Brown left the post-industrial landscape of Hanley for Dunstable's rolling countryside.

Phil Roberts (1996-2000)

After the departure of Paul Brown, the pulpit was supplied by visiting speakers and those men in the Church able to preach, with the emphasis of course being on men who were under consideration for the pastorate. Among these men was Rev. Phil Roberts, who was working in Southern Ireland at the time. By the end of 1995 the Church was looking at Mr. Roberts as the most probable candidate for the pastorate. By February 1996 it had been agreed to invite him as the next pastor, and he accepted the call.

Phil Roberts was converted at the age of 16.[389] He had been drawn to the mission field along with his wife Joy, and both had signed on with Operation Mobilisation to join the crew of the MV Doulos. As Phil was an engineer by training, this seemed the logical move to make, but in fact neither ever sailed on the Doulos; not because of anything on their part, but because the crew was over-subscribed. Instead they became involved in work in the Republic of Ireland, first going out in 1978 with O.M. In the autumn of 1980 they settled in Clonmel, pioneering a new Church in the town. Clonmel became a centre of Church planting. The issue of support for the ministry of Irish pastors and evangelists arose, and Phil's answer was Tentmaker Publications, a Christian publishing operation that produces mainly high quality hardcover reprints of Christian books of lasting value.

---

[389] Typescript, *Introducing Phil and Joy Roberts* in the Church archives

Rev. Phil Roberts was an energetic man with all sorts of ideas for Bethel. He saw the future as being the transformation of Bethel into something like a central mission, still a Church, but also making use of its strategic site at the heart of the city, with outreach to the marginalised, those living on the street, and those in great need, as well as serving the local community in other ways. Congregationalists in the late 19th century would have recognised the scheme, which was a relatively common approach taken with city-centre churches. In 1884 Basil Martin was sent to London's Wardour Street, in Soho, to an old Congregational chapel that had, by replacing the pews with chairs and the pulpit with a platform, been turned into a mission hall; in this case the idea did not work; he found himself more or less alone, and with little support.[390] The greatest problem with such a plan is that it is usually extremely costly, and in our day and age requires a fair number of trained staff, such as the various City Missions employ. Such projects have been most successful as projects with a broad base, backed by a denomination or run by a committee. Unless a congregation is extremely wealthy, such schemes are very difficult. To transform a city centre church into a central mission may be attractive, but it requires more than enthusiasm; it requires specialists and serious backing, both of which Bethel lacked. In hindsight (and hindsight is always a wonderful thing), the plan was over-ambitious, but at the time this was not apparent to any.

The effort put a great deal of strain on all those involved, not least Mr. Roberts. In 2000 he resigned from the pastorate, and a large minority of the Church membership withdrew to form a new Church at Hartshill, inviting Mr. Roberts to be their pastor. Those who remained rallied round, refusing to allow the split to close the Church, and began the search for a new pastor. In the meantime the pulpit was supplied by visiting preachers and those remaining members of the Church who were able to preach.

The shock was considerable for all involved, leaving those on both sides wondering what had gone wrong. The effects of the split are still felt to this day, though there has thankfully been much healing of wounds over the last decade.

---

[390] *An Impossible Parson* Pp. 52-7

Hezron Muwowo (2003-2008)

The next minister, Hezron Muwowo from Zambia, came to Bethel fresh from training at the London Theological Seminary in Finchley, North London. It was hoped that the young minister would mean a fresh start for the Church after the split and the departure of Phil Roberts. Sadly there were some difficulties, and then the Home Office refused to extend Mr. Muwowo's visa and grant him permission to work in the UK. The Church sought advice from the FIEC on what to do next, and the FIEC legal department advised that Mr. Muwowo could no longer be the pastor of the Church. While the FIEC advised that he should return to Zambia and re-apply from there, Mr. Muwowo instead chose to remain in the UK and continue to seek leave to remain. Having obtained it, he is now (2012) the minister of Providence Chapel, Hookgate, on the border between Staffordshire and Shropshire.

Gervase N. Charmley (2009-)

Which brings us to the author of this book, the present minister, Mr. Gervase N. Charmley. I was born in Norwich, Norfolk, in 1980 and converted while a student at Chester College in 1998. After spending some years as a member at Hethersett Baptist Church, Norfolk, trained for the ministry at the London Theological Seminary in Finchley in 2004-6. Following a number of years of itinerant preaching, I came to Bethel after six months as an assistant pastor in Tabor Baptist Church at Llantrisant in the South Wales Valleys. I was ordained at Bethel in August 2010, with the preachers being Rev. Oliver Gross from New Street Evangelical Church in Welshpool, a friend from Seminary, and Pastor Martin Grubb of Charlesworth Baptist Church, who was the pastor at Upton Baptist Church, Chester, under whose ministry I was converted.

Epilogue

Though the history has been brought up to the present day, the story of our Church is far from over. For 200 years; since before there was a Hope Street, the Church has stood here on what is now the corner of Hope Street and New Hall Street; by the grace of God we hope to remain here for many years to come. What does the future hold for us? We cannot know, but we know that our God has not changed.

Our Bookshop is still open three days a week, though since Tesco closed in 2010 it has been very quiet. Through the wonders of modern technology and the website SermonAudio.com, our sermons are now listened to around the globe. Chris Roseborough, owner of the internet radio station Pirate Christian Radio and host of the programme *Fighting For the Faith* regularly plays sermons from Bethel on his programme, which has tens of thousands of listeners. For the first time there are more people outside Stoke hearing some of our sermons than there are people in the city.

Our services continue as they have for 200 years; though the congregation are different, and though we sit on chairs rather than pews, we have not changed fundamentally; we are as we have always been, by the grace of God an independent and evangelical Church with the same good news to proclaim; that Jesus Christ was crucified as the saviour of sinners, and that he lives today to save all who come to him.

In addition to the regular Sunday services, the Ladies' Meeting on Monday afternoons and the Wednesday night Bible study and prayer meeting, a Sunday School and Children's Thursday Club continue to be run on the premises, and recently a monthly fellowship breakfast for the men of the Church has been begun, with great success. We are not a large Church, and well aware of the fact. But we continue to look for God, and take courage from the remarkable facts of our long history. Our prayer is expressed in a hymn that has often been sung at the Church in the 200 years of our history, a hymn written by the Congregational pastor Philip Doddridge:

O God of Bethel, by Whose hand
Thy people still are fed,
Who through this weary pilgrimage
Hast all our fathers led.

Our vows, our prayers, we now present
Before Thy throne of grace;
God of our fathers, be the God
Of their succeeding race.

Through each perplexing path of life
Our wandering footsteps guide:
Give us each day our daily bread,
And raiment fit provide.

O spread Thy covering wings around,
Till all our wanderings cease,
And at our Father's loved abode
Our souls arrive in peace.

Illustrative Bibliography

E.C.W. Boulton, *George Jeffreys* (edited by Chris Cartwright, Tonbridge, 1999, originally published 1928)

Paul E. Brown, *Ernest Kevan* (Edinburgh, 2012)

Desmond Cartwright, *The Great Evangelists* (Basingstoke, 1986)

D.R. Davies, *In Search of Myself* (London, 1961)

John W. Grant, *Free Churchmanship in England 1870-1940* (London, no date)

Walter J. Hollenweger, *The Pentecostals* (London, 1972)

Edward Jeffreys, *Stephen Jeffreys* (London, 1946)

Mark D. Johnson, *The Dissolution of Dissent, 1850-1918* (New York and London, 1987)

R. Tudur Jones: *Congregationalism in England 1662-1962 (London, 1962)*

William K. Kay, *Pentecostals in Britain* (Carlisle 2000)

Elaine Kaye, *For the Work of Ministry: A History of Northern College and its Predecessors* (Edinburgh, 1999)

A.G. Matthews: *The Congregational Churches of Staffordshire* (London, 1924)

E.J. Poole-Connor, *Evangelicalism in England* (London, 1951)

Irene Turner: *Tomkin in the Staffordshire Moorlands* (Leek, 2006)

Henry Woodhouse: *The Story of a Leek Church* (Leek, 1988)

Made in the USA
Charleston, SC
19 October 2012